# Competitive Job-Finding Guide
## for
## Persons with Handicaps

# Competitive Job-Finding Guide
# for
# Persons with Handicaps

by

## Chet Muklewicz, Ed.D.
Career and Employment
Counselor, Private Practice

and

## Michael Bender, Ed.D.
Professor of Education
The Johns Hopkins University

**A College-Hill Publication**
Little, Brown and Company
Boston / Toronto / San Diego

College-Hill Press
A Division of
Little, Brown and Company (Inc.)
34 Beacon Street
Boston, Massachusetts 02108

**Library of Congress Cataloging in Publication Data**
Main entry under title:

Muklewicz, Chet, 1950–
   Competitive job-finding guide for persons with handicaps /
by Chet Muklewicz, Michael Bender.
     p.    cm.
   "A College-Hill publication."
   Bibliography.
   Includes index.
     1. Vocational guidance for the handicapped — United States.
2. Handicapped — Employment — United States.
3. Job hunting — United States. I. Bender, Michael, 1943–      . II. Title.
HV1568.5.M85 1988
650.1'4'0240816 — dc19
                                           CIP 88-584

**ISBN 0-316-58923-3**


Printed in the United States of America

# Contents

# Appendices

## ABOUT THE AUTHORS

# Chet Muklewicz, Ed.D.

In addition to serving as a counseling program director at Lackawanna Junior College, Scranton, Pennsylvania, Dr. Muklewicz maintains a private practice providing career and employment counseling to persons with handicaps. He is also a lecturer in counselor education for the graduate department of counseling and psychology at Marywood College, Scranton, Pennsylvania.

# Michael Bender, Ed.D.

Trained as a special and vocational educator, Dr. Bender is currently Vice President of Educational Programs at The Kennedy Institute in Baltimore, Maryland. A prolific author and national consultant in special and vocational education, Dr. Bender is a Professor of Education at The Johns Hopkins University with a joint appointment in Pediatrics at The Johns Hopkins School of Medicine.

# ACKNOWLEDGMENTS

Thanks are due to some very special people: to my wife Ann, for loving me and enduring through my career aspirations and writing adventures; to my children Maggie and Daniel, for the time I spent away from them; to my coauthor and writing mentor Mike Bender, for having faith in my ideas; to Pat Trozzolillo, for his help in clarifying my ideas; to Karen Legge, for cheerfully sacrificing countless hours of her time to help type and edit the manuscript; to Ann Marie Stelma, for proofreading the manuscript; and to Cathy McGinley and Keri Chofey for their clerical assistance. I dedicate my efforts in writing this book to my mother, Julia Muklewicz.

*Chet Muklewicz*

I am grateful to many individuals who have helped in the development of this resource. First, I would like to acknowledge the tireless efforts of my right and left hands, Jane Headings and Gloria Keep, who helped type parts of the manuscript and provided ongoing guidance. I would also like to thank Madelyn, Stephen, Andrew, and Sydney Amanda, who comprise the Bender family and whose support and encouragement made the project an enjoyable one.

Finally, I am grateful and indebted to all those clients and students I have worked with over the years who helped me formulate ideas that were both practical and relevant. Without their comments, critiques, and reactions, this book would not have been possible.

*Michael Bender*

# Preface

Throughout the United States and other industrialized societies, millions of people with handicaps live disadvantaged lives because they cannot obtain the economic and social benefits of employment. Although it is true that some of these individuals may not be able to hold a job, the majority of them can and do want to work. However, in spite of their ability to work and the availability of habilitation and rehabilitation services, most of them remain unemployed. This book provides realistic strategies to help persons with handicaps successfully compete for employment.

Because competitive job-finding is the way most workers, including those with handicaps, obtain employment, this text explains how to teach and counsel clients to find their own jobs. In an economy and culture that value competition, persons with handicaps can use the competitive spirit to displace employer perceptions of being disabled. The formula for helping clients find jobs is simple and straightforward: identify what they can do well, target employers who need their talents, and clearly communicate to those employers that they have the ability and desire to work. The channels of communication include direct-to-employer applications, networking, responding to help-wanted ads, and third party agencies.

By addressing such issues as work readiness and employment barriers, this book will help the reader confront the individual and life-situation problems that can interfere with a successful job-search. The authors, by combining their experiences from counseling, vocational rehabilitation, and special education, utilize numerous learning and counseling strategies to facilitate employment transitions. To insure that the counseling procedures can be replicated by others, the book includes model forms to structure the counseling process. Case studies are used to demonstrate the counseling forms. A separate publication entitled *Job-Finder's Workbook* includes instructions for clients and a complete set of blank counseling forms.

The information contained in this book and the *Job-Finder's Workbook* has evolved from ten years of the authors' experiences in helping students and clients obtain employment. Additionally, these resources have been field-tested with persons with mild to moderate mental retardation, learning disabilities, orthopedic handicaps, emotional disabilities, health impairments, and multiple handicaps.

# Introduction

Two studies recently conducted by Louis Harris and Associates (1986; 1987), the census data for 1980 and a (U.S. Dept. of Commerce, 1985), and a report by the President's Committee on Employment of the Handicapped (*Out of the Job Market,* 1987) collectively provide a definitive description of the employment status of individuals with handicaps. The Harris studies, conducted for the International Center for the Disabled, are the first national surveys assessing the employment of individuals with disabilities to be conducted among employers and persons with handicaps, (Louis Harris and Associates, 1987).

As advocates have long believed, the surveys confirmed that most persons with disabilities are quite employable. In fact, the surveys indicated that managers almost always rated their disabled workers as performing their jobs as well as or better than other employees in similar jobs, and virtually none of the managers said their disabled employees were poor workers. The Harris studies reported that only 35% of these individuals were provided with job accommodations, and the Job Accommodation Network (1987) indicated that half of all job accommodations cost less than $50. The Harris studies reported that approximately 80% of the managers indicated that the average cost of employing disabled persons was no greater than the cost of employing nondisabled persons.

Although it is encouraging to confirm that many individuals with handicaps are employable, it is discouraging to find that many of them remain unemployed. The President's Committee on Employment of the Handicapped reported that "disabled people today are less likely to be at work than they were in 1980 — and even less than in 1970" (Out of the Job Market, 1987, p. 1). Harris (1986) concluded that being unemployed is the truest definition of what it means to be disabled, when he reported that only one in four disabled persons works full time, with another 10% working part time. Those who were working were found to be better educated, to have more money, to be more satisfied with life, and to be less likely to consider themselves disabled. It is not surprising, therefore, that 66% of those not working reported that they wanted to work. The magnitude of the problem is staggering when one considers that there are 18.4 million people with orthopedic impairments or deformities, 17 million people with hearing impairments, 8.2 million with visual impairments, 2.1 million with speech impairments, and 5.7 million individuals who are mentally retarded (National Council on the Handicapped, 1986, p. 6).

Why are these people finding so few employment opportunities? The authors believe that the most revealing answer to this question was provided in the description of how workers with handicaps obtained their jobs. The Harris studies found that *68% of these workers obtained employment through their own initiative.* A study on the use and effectiveness of job-search methods, drawn from census data on 10 million people, verifies that most people find employment through their own efforts (*Job Search*, 1976). It is not surprising to learn that most individuals find their own jobs; however, it is astonishing to learn that many persons with handicaps believe they can, through noncompetitive means, obtain jobs that are competitively pursued by others.

These findings and conclusions have significant implications for individuals with handicaps, for vocational rehabilitation and habilitation professionals, and for the systems of vocational rehabilitation and habilitation. "These findings send a clear message to disabled people: the best way to find a job is through personal initiative and perseverance" (Louis Harris and Associates, 1987, p. 40). Perhaps the greatest barrier to employment occurs when persons with handicaps obtain the implicit, and often explicit, message from schools or rehabilitation agencies that someone will find a job for them, or when they assume that employers will provide them with good jobs without their having to compete for them.

The implication for vocational rehabilitation and habilitation professionals is that client-centered placement should be the rule and that counselor-centered placement should be the exception. Although a small number of people will always need placement assistance, the greater percentage should find their own jobs. Rather than conducting the job search *for* their clients, professionals should teach *them* to search competitively for employment opportunities. Thus, professionals must become well versed in competitive employment-seeking strategies. To habilitate or rehabilitate persons with handicaps without training them to compete for employment simply solves one problem by replacing it with another: now employable, they find themselves unemployed. The ideal was never to achieve equal unemployment opportunities.

These findings also suggest that the systems of vocational rehabilitation and habilitation should provide employment-seeking training both to staff members and to individuals receiving their services. Zandy (1979, p. 73) conceptualized the problem well when he stated, "In developing rehabilitation plans, counselors often concentrate on increasing a person's potential for productive work to the extent of ignoring the ultimate problem of finding a job . . . Building competence does not ensure employment. The skills required to hold a job differ from those necessary to find one." It is therefore ironic that rehabilitation and educational institutions offer little guidance and training in seeking employment when placement statistics are used so frequently to evaluate the effectiveness of their services.

Agencies offering placement services are often viewed by vocational rehabilitation clients as offering desirable invitations to relinquish job-finding responsibilities. Without intending to do so, some agencies imply that they possess significant influence among employers, when in fact they actually have very little influence. Providing employment-seeking training might better serve the immediate and future vocational needs of persons using these services because the dynamic nature of our labor market has made the ability to find a job an important life skill.

Individuals with handicaps must enter the world of work in the same manner as other workers: through a competitive job search. One of the reasons employment-seeking and training has received so little attention in schools and agencies is that the process of finding a job is often perceived as a chaotic, unknown, and unmanageable experience in which luck and fate are considered to be the job hunter's only valid resource. Lathrop (1977, p. 3) captured this perception when he portrayed the job search "as a castabout system . . . [that is] a tortuous, hit-or-miss, trial-and-error approach . . . which exposes you to numerous traps and hazards along the way that can bring you to the brink of despair . . ." The authors, drawing from their own experiences in career and vocational planning, employment counseling, and special education, present a systematic procedure of seeking employment that is both understandable and manageable.

In this text, readers are introduced to employment perspectives of individuals with handicaps, of their families, of employers, and of society; they receive suggestions about addressing the uniqueness of persons with selected handicaps; and they are provided instructions for organizing employment-seeking activities. Counseling strategies for facilitating employment transitions are provided as a resource, and procedures for assessing work readiness, removing employment barriers, and selecting employment objectives are presented. Readers are offered instructions for conducting job analyses, selecting job accommodations, and characterizing clients as qualified applicants. They are also presented with detailed descriptions of a comprehensive job-search strategy that employs the most effective methods of locating advertised and unadvertised job vacancies. Advice for post-employment work adjustments is provided, as well as a chapter on locating community resources and services. The text is filled with case studies demonstrating the use of forms that can be used to facilitate the employment-seeking process in a structured and consistent manner. The appendices include a listing of studies and reports on the employment status of persons with handicaps, other textbooks and resources, as well as a complete list of State Vocational Agencies and Governor's Committees on Employment of the Handicapped.

Throughout this resource, individuals with handicaps are predominantly referred to as clients, rather than as students, because this term more appropriately describes their status in the habilitation or rehabilitation process. The term *client* is also more widely acceptable, especially when working with community agencies and those organizations and industries associated with employment opportunities. The term *professional* refers to those special education teachers, counselors, rehabilitation specialists, diagnosticians, social workers, and other placement personnel who interact regularly with individuals who are handicapped. People who have the potential to influence the lives of clients are referred to as *significant others* and include parents, guardians, grandparents, personal friends, spouses, children, and other valued acquaintances.

The information contained in this book may not be applicable to all individuals who are handicapped. Some of our more severely and profoundly handicapped citizens may be able to benefit from certain suggestions, but other suggestions may prove to be impractical or inappropriate. These determinations are best left to professionals and their clients. However, this text may be helpful to other groups, such as persons who are elderly, individuals with learning disorders, and persons who are economically disadvantaged.

In conclusion, the ideal of equal employment opportunities for persons with handicaps can only be achieved through equal job competition. The search for employment, in many respects, serves as a preemployment test for measuring abilities, attitudes, and perseverance. For adult persons with handicaps, the ability to find a job serves as a rite of passage into the mainstream of society. This book provides the information necessary for vocational rehabilitation and habilitation professionals to instruct and guide clients through successful transitions into the world of work.

# Understanding Employment Perspectives

**T**his text is for professionals who are interested in helping people with handicaps obtain competitive employment. Therefore, the relationship between professionals and their clients is of primary concern; it will serve as the medium for facilitating the achievement of the client's employment goals. In most successful client–professional relationships, professionals teach, guide, and coach their clients. Consequently, it is important that professionals project a positive attitude about the employability of people with handicaps. Professionals must appreciate, however, that the behavior of clients is significantly affected by other people and groups. Figure 1-1 indicates that in addition to professionals, clients are also affected by the real or perceived beliefs of society, of significant others (i.e., parents, guardians, spouses, and dependents), and of potential employers.

This chapter includes an examination of the employment perspectives of society as well as those of significant others, employers, and clients. It is hoped that by examining these different viewpoints, professionals will develop greater insights into clients and their life situations, thereby increasing the effectiveness of client–professional relationships.

## SOCIAL PERSPECTIVE

A society's economy defines the way in which that society distributes goods and services to its members. In traditional agricultural societies, for example, most consumer goods and services were self-provided through hunting, fishing, farming, and various forms of handcrafting. In such societies, the roles of both producer and consumer remained in the control of individuals and small groups. At the turn of the nineteenth century, the economy of the United States was largely agricultural with approximately 42% of the population working on farms. In contrast, during 1980 only about 3% of the population earned a living on farms (Goode, 1984). Obviously, industrialism changed the way people live. It particularly changed the way they work and the way they obtain their consumer goods and services.

The industrial era forced a wedge between the roles of consumer and producer (Toffler, 1980). People were forced to assume specialized work roles, such as chef, sewing machine operator, butcher, farmer, and carpenter. These specialized work roles are now called jobs. In return for working at their jobs, individuals receive pay, which they use to purchase a wide range of consumer goods and services.

The effective functioning of industrialized economies requires individuals within the society to participate in the complementary roles of both worker and consumer. Since most people in industrialized societies purchase their goods and services with money earned in their jobs, the role of worker is highly valued.

Drawing from U.S. Census Data, the President's Committee on Employment of the Handicapped (Out of the Job Market, 1987) indicated that 78% of the 151 million Americans of working age (i.e., between the ages of 16 and 64) work at full- or part-time jobs. This percentage contrasts strikingly with the employment picture of peo-

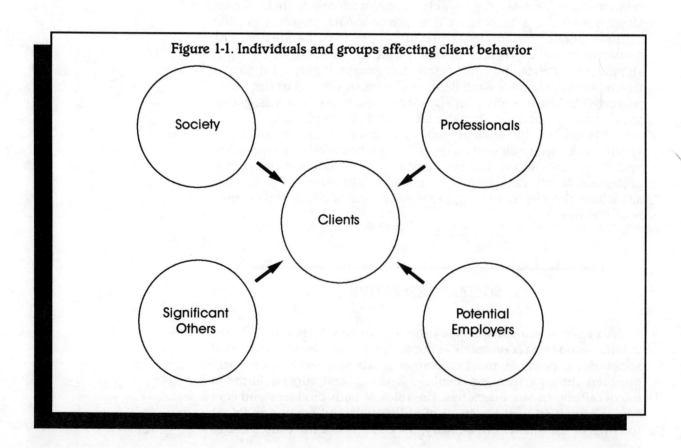

Figure 1-1. Individuals and groups affecting client behavior

ple with handicaps. Among working-age Americans with disabilities, only 31.3% are in the labor force, 41.2% receive Social Security Income (SSI) or Disability Insurance, and 25% are not working and receive no subsidies (Bowe, 1986). The 1980 Census Data (U.S. Department of Commerce, 1985), indicated that of the 12 million noninstitutionalized people with self-reported disabilities, 6.2 million reported that their disabilities prevented them from working.

The high unemployment among people with handicaps truly represents a significant social problem. Due to their inability to obtain employment, they are often segregated from their peers and consequently feel rejected by society. They often live on poverty-level subsidies and carry the negative social stigma often associated with being unemployed. This unemployment also creates economic problems. The President's Committee on Employment of the Handicapped reported that "in 1985, the Federal Government spent $62 billion on subsidies, medical care, and other programs for disabled persons, of which more than 93% was to support out-of-work individuals with disabilities" (Out of the Job Market, 1987, p. 1).

## PERSPECTIVE OF SIGNIFICANT OTHERS

Significant others are people who, out of desire or necessity, significantly influence the lives of clients. Usually they are parents, guardians, spouses, and dependents. However, they might also be siblings, relatives, clergy, and friends. Because the lives of clients and those of their significant others are not mutually exclusive, each significant other represents a potential resource or constraint. Clients may rely on or be dependent on significant others for such essentials as physical assistance in self-care, housing, transportation, and money. Conversely, some significant others may rely on clients for some of the same essentials.

Over time, the meshing of roles between clients and significant others results in a mutual interdependence that can cause resistance to role changes. It is important for professionals to appreciate, respect, and delicately handle the activities that may, as a result of clients finding jobs, change the relationships between clients and their significant others. For example, parents who dedicate their lives to the needs of handicapped children may be reluctant to make the changes in their own lives that must occur when those "children" become employed. Similar interdependence problems can occur between aging parents and middle-aged clients or between husbands and wives as well as between children and parents.

Professionals should be aware of how easily significant others can influence and control the lives of clients. Sometimes mere disapproval from a parent or a spouse will be enough to cause a client to abandon the search for employment. Significant others whose approval and consent are needed must be included when developing employment strategies for clients. They should also be encouraged, either directly or indirectly through clients, to examine how their own lives will change when clients obtain employment.

## INDIVIDUAL PERSPECTIVE

After completing formal education programs, competitive employment provides the means by which most people stay in the mainstream of society. Without the opportunity to work, individuals with handicaps can become segregated from the rest of the community. Additionally, this unemployment can result in diminished opportunities for personal development, for leisure activities, and for other life-enriching experiences. In a national survey of individuals with disabilities, Louis Harris and Associates (1986) found major differences in the lives of individuals with handicaps who did work and the lives of those who did not work. "Key comparisons between working and non-working disabled persons, aged 16 to 64, show that work makes a vast qualitative difference in the lives of disabled persons. Those who work are better educated, and have much more money. They are also more satisfied with life, much less likely to consider themselves disabled, and much less likely to say that their disability has prevented them from reaching their full abilities as a person" (p. 5).

Wehman (1981) also identified several positive personal outcomes for workers with handicaps in a survey conducted among the parents and guardians of clients involved in a competitive employment project. He found that clients, who were people with mental retardation ranging from moderate to severe, were assessed as ". . . living more independently . . . were more concerned about their appearance, and . . . spoke and communicated to people at home more often" (p. 147).

It is clear that work is an important avenue for fulfilling social needs. Belonging to a work group, socializing with co-workers during work hours, becoming close friends with co-workers, and attending employment functions are all common work-related social experiences. Many companies sponsor recreational and sports activities such as softball games, bowling teams, and picnics. Unfortunately, unemployed handicapped people have limited social opportunities because they cannot participate in these work-related activities. They often become isolated from other people because they are not members of any formal or informal social groups. This isolation, coupled with their awareness of their handicaps, often serves to convince them that they do not have any place in society's mainstream. As they become more isolated and withdrawn, they begin to regress in their development and often become less concerned with their appearance and social behavior.

Brolin (1976) indicates that work can offer a feeling of fulfillment and an improved self-concept. People who work have opportunities to increase self-esteem by participating in a socially valued activity that is verified by a paycheck, by becoming proficient in their jobs, by receiving positive work evaluations from their supervisors, and by being sought after by co-workers to solve difficult problems. Conversely, individuals with handicaps who are not working often assume household chores and errands that other family members are either too busy to do or simply do not want to do.

Upward social mobility and improved life-styles are achieved by most individuals through their roles as workers. As people become more proficient in their jobs, their value to employers increases, as does their ability to earn more money. Earning more money brings opportunities for better food, better housing, enriched cultural experiences, and in general, a greater chance for continued success. Living on fixed incomes and government subsidies, on the other hand, limits opportunities and, perhaps worst of all, increases dependence on other people, agencies, and institutions.

## EMPLOYER PERSPECTIVE

When assessing the attitudes of employers toward individuals with handicaps, it is important to separate the people from their positions. As a group of people, there is no reason to assume that employers do not have compassion or concern for the welfare of individuals with handicaps. In fact, the business leaders of any given community are typically the people who compose the memberships of civic organizations and the boards of social service agencies. In their work roles, however, employers are not functionally responsible for the vocational habilitation or rehabilitation of people with handicaps; they are held accountable for producing goods or providing services. Therefore, it should be expected that they will make personnel selections that are in the best interests of their organizations' productivity. It should not be assumed that employers, whose own jobs may depend on the output of the people they hire, will put a higher priority on the development of individuals with handicaps than on the productivity of their companies.

When employers evaluate potential employees, they primarily judge them according to who is best suited for the job. They usually have a preconceived profile of qualifications they are hoping to find in their applicants. The profiles often include various combinations of education, training, work experience, skills, attitudes, and personality traits. Applicants who most closely match the desired qualification profiles will have the greatest chance of being hired for the positions. Applicants who are presented as "handicapped" or as "disabled people deserving chances" will not come close to approximating the qualification profiles desired by employers.

Clients will have a greater chance of finding a job in a competitive labor market if they search for employment based on their abilities rather than on their disabilities. Supporting this notion, Hart (1962) observed that it is "not uncommon for an employer to state with sincerity that he does not have any handicapped employees, and to reveal later . . . that he does have a man with one eye, another with a leg brace, and another who is illiterate" (p. 35).

# EMPLOYABILITY OF PEOPLE WITH HANDICAPS

Employing people with handicaps is clearly in the best interest of society as well as the best interest of the individuals with handicaps. Is it, however, in the best interest of employers? In short, do people with handicaps want to work? Are they employable? Answers to these and other questions can be obtained from two sources: (1) people with handicaps who work, and (2) people with handicaps who do not work.

## People with Handicaps Who Work

While there are large percentages of people with handicaps who are not working, there are in fact many people with handicaps who do work. United States Census Data indicates that of America's 12 million working-age people with disabilities, 4,366,000 of them do work in full- or part-time jobs (U.S. Department of Commerce, 1985). In a national survey, the U.S. Department of Health and Human Services (1986) reported that 87,000 developmentally disabled persons have obtained jobs since 1983. The term *developmentally disabled* was used to include people with mental retardation, cerebral palsy, epilepsy, autism, and other conditions that limit normal activity.

Since 1967, the Association for Retarded Citizens (ARC) has trained and placed over 36,000 individuals with mental retardation through its On-The-Job Training Project (ARC Facts, OJT Project, 1987). Through this project, now called the National Employment and Training Project, employers are reimbursed one-half the entry wage for the first four weeks of employment and one-fourth for the second four weeks. ARC reports an 82% retention rate at the conclusion of the two-month training period and a 72% retention rate 90 days later.

Nathanson (1977) reported that Du Pont, one of America's leading chemical companies, studied the job performance, safety, and attendance of 1,452 company employees with handicaps. The study included employees with nine classifications of handicaps: nonparalytic orthopedic, 415; heart disease, 380; vision impairment, 277; amputations, 163; paralyses, 106; epilepsy, 56; hearing impairments, 43; total deafness, 14; and total blindness, 5. Highlights of the study revealed that 96% of Du Pont's employees with disabilities were rated as average or better for safety; 91% were rated as average or better for job performance; 91% were rated as average or better for job stability; and 79% were rated as average or better for attendance (Nathanson, 1977, p. 2–3). Du Pont repeated the survey in 1981 and found that their 2,745 employees with handicaps had received evaluations in all categories that equalled or surpassed ratings achieved in the 1973 study (Du Ponte de Nemours and Company, 1982).

A more recent Louis Harris and Associates (1987) survey indicated that 91% of employers rated the job performance of their workers with disabilities as good or excellent. In that survey, employers compared disabled and nondisabled employees on key criteria for job performance. The overwhelming majority of disabled employees was rated as good as, and often better than, their nondisabled peers. Line managers, who closely supervise workers, compared disabled and nondisabled workers in six key areas (Louis Harris and Associates, 1987, p. 47):

☐ Willingness to work hard — 46% rated disabled employees better than nondisabled employees, and 33% rated the two groups about the same.

☐ Reliability — 39% rated disabled employees better than nondisabled employees, and 42% rated the two groups about the same.

☐ Attendance and punctuality — 39% rated disabled employees better than nondisabled employees, and 40% rated the two groups about the same.

☐ Productivity — 20% rated disabled employees better than nondisabled employees, and 57% rated the two groups about the same.

☐ Desire for promotion — 23% rated disabled employees better than nondisabled employees, and 55% rated the two groups about the same.

☐ Leadership ability — 10% rated disabled employees better than nondisabled employees, and 62% rated the two groups about the same.

## People with Handicaps Who Do Not Work

Louis Harris and Associates (1986) conducted the first nationwide poll of a random sample of disabled Americans. The poll, conducted in December 1985, included 1,000 randomly selected adults who had disabilities. They found that two-thirds of Americans with disabilities do not work. Among these nonworking people with handicaps, the Harris poll discovered that 66% of them wanted to work. They were asked whether they would take a job if one were available, and two-thirds answered in the affirmative. When asked why they were not working, 78% cited their disabilities, and over half noted their need for medical treatment. Many of the other reasons cited for not working are conditions that professionals can address:

- ☐ 47% cited employer bias
- ☐ 40% said they could not find or did not know how to find full-time jobs
- ☐ 38% indicated lack of education or training
- ☐ 28% reported the lack of accessible transportation
- ☐ 23% indicated they need special devices or equipment
- ☐ 18% cited the loss of benefits

(Louis Harris and Associates, 1986, p. 70–71).

The President's Committee on the Employment of the Handicapped (1987) suggested that the job-finding conditions for people with handicaps have improved because of three factors: (1) there is an increased number of service jobs in the labor market, (2) the technology of job accommodation products has been greatly improved, and (3) the surplus of entry-level workers is diminishing as the baby-boom children are growing older and being absorbed into the labor market.

# 2

# Addressing the Uniqueness of Handicaps

**D**iversity and uniqueness among individuals with handicaps is the rule rather than the exception. Because handicaps are relative in both the degree of impairment and the adaptiveness of the individuals who have them, clients with similar handicaps may not be qualified for the same occupations.

An often-overlooked fact is that some handicapping conditions are multiple in nature and may affect several areas of functioning. For example, cerebral palsy may be accompanied by communication disorders as well as by motor impairments. Other clients with a primary impairment of mental retardation may have emotional problems as well as orthopedic impairments. Unless the emotional and orthopedic impairments are taken into consideration, these clients may find jobs that they will be unable to keep, resulting in frustrating and defeating experiences. Professionals who are aware of the diversified conditions and needs of clients can help to insure that they are seeking appropriate types of employment.

The life situations of people with handicaps are also unique. Health concerns such as heart conditions may require clients to have restricted diets and may limit their work availability to day shifts. Some clients may have therapeutic schedules that will interrupt their ability to complete a normal eight-hour workshift. Out of necessity or habit, clients may be dependent on significant others to assist them in such areas as self-care or transportation. Other clients may find it difficult to free themselves from nonworking roles that have developed in their homes, such as cooking, cleaning, running errands, or caring for elderly parents.

The uniqueness and complexity of the lives of individuals with handicaps should not be underestimated or overlooked when planning employment transitions. In an attempt to identify some of the important issues that might affect people with various handicaps, this chapter includes a brief review of selected handicapping conditions commonly encountered by professionals. It is not meant to be an exhaustive list, nor is it intended to be a thorough analysis of the handicaps discussed. It is, at best, a place to start. Each section includes a brief description and several key concerns that should be considered in planning employment strategies.

## MENTAL RETARDATION

The American Association on Mental Deficiency defines mental retardation as a "significantly sub-average general intellectual functioning existing concurrently with deficits in adaptive behavior and manifested during the developmental period" (Grossman, 1983). In addition to measuring intelligence, it is important to consider the adaptiveness of behavior. Intelligence-testing results often cannot present information concerning how clients cope with everyday stress, how they take care of themselves, or how they relate to other people. This information, in many instances, can make the difference between success and failure during the job-seeking process.

Included among the causes of mental retardation are infections, traumas, metabolic disorders, toxic agents, environmental deprivation, and chromosomal abnormalities. There are four classifications of mental retardation: mild, moderate, severe, and profound. Mild and moderate categories of mental retardation are reviewed below because they are most often encountered in competitive employment situations. For further information on the vocational habilitation or rehabilitation of individuals with severe and profound mental retardation, see Bellamy, Rhodes, Mank, and Albin (1987); Bellamy, Horner, and Inman (1979); Rusch (1986); and Wehman (1981).

### Mild Mental Retardation

(IQ range of 50–55 to 70). Approximately 89% of individuals classified as retarded are classified as mildly mentally retarded. These individuals usually do not stand out from their nonretarded peers because their differences affect primarily the rate and degree of intellectual development. Their intellectual differences often do not become obvious until they enter school. Impairments associated with this group sometimes include attention deficits, memory deficits, learning and motivational difficulties, and social adjustments. As a group, mildly mentally retarded people adjust well to competitive employment. The following are suggestions for helping clients with mild mental retardation.

- ☐ Select job targets based on an assessment of their abilities, interests, and training.
- ☐ Conduct a job analysis of clients' employment objectives to identify work requirements that clients may have difficulty performing. Further training or accommodations

in some work requirements may be necessary to achieve adequate work adjustments.

☐ Assist clients in their job searches by structuring their daily activities and by helping them write résumés and letters, and complete applications.

☐ Seek support from parents or guardians. They may wish to participate in the employment planning.

## Moderate Mental Retardation

(IQ range of 35–40 to 50–55). Approximately 6% of the individuals classified as mentally retarded are classified in the moderate category. As adults they usually function at learning and intellectual levels that are between one-half and one-third of their chronological age. With the appropriate use of job-learning strategies and supportive services, many moderately retarded people can work in competitive employment environments. Impairments associated with this group include limited levels of conceptualization, limited ability to read or write, and a slow rate of learning. Physically, they may appear clumsy, may have communication problems, and may exhibit poor motor coordination. The following are suggestions for helping clients with moderate mental retardation.

☐ Limit employment alternatives to light manufacturing and service jobs.

☐ Conduct a thorough job analysis to establish a baseline of work performance to be used in subsequent on-the-job training experiences.

☐ Make sure clients receive structured on-the-job training with the assistance of a job coach.

☐ Make sure the job coach helps build a social support system at the worksite.

☐ Make sure that coordination and implementation of the employment plan includes parents, guardians, work supervisors, job coaches, and rehabilitation counselors.

## LEARNING DISABILITIES

Public Law 94-142, the Education for All Handicapped Children Act, provides a definition of learning disabilities:

The term *children with specific learning disabilities* means those children who have a disorder in one or more of the basic psychological processes involved in understanding or in using language, spoken or written, which disorder may manifest itself in imperfect ability to listen, think, speak, read, write, spell or do mathematical calculations. Such disorders include such conditions as perceptual handicaps, brain injury, minimal brain dysfunction, dyslexia and developmental aphasia. The term does not include children who have learning problems which are primarily the result of visual, hearing or motor handicaps, of mental retardation, of emotional disturbance, or environmental, cultural or economic disadvantage (Federal Register, 1975).

Among work impairments experienced by people with learning disabilities are job inefficiency, errors, accident proneness, difficulty with academic skills, problems in learning a sequence of tasks, difficulty meeting time commitments, and social-skills problems (Brown, 1980). The following are suggestions for helping clients with learning disabilities.

☐ Identify those skill areas in which clients function best, and target jobs in which they will be able to rely on their strengths.

☐ Help clients organize those daily activities associated with their job searches. Encourage them to use calendars, checklists, and personal journals.

☐ Help clients learn job requirements and organize their daily activities once employment is secured.

☐ Assist clients in developing a social support system at their place of employment.

☐ Develop a plan of action to obtain help or guidance should problems occur.

## ORTHOPEDICALLY HANDICAPPED

Impairments of individuals with orthopedic handicaps are usually motor in nature. In the case of individuals with cerebral palsy, this is a result of brain damage to the motor areas of the brain. Three common classifications of cerebral palsy are spacticity, athetosis, and ataxia. In spacticity, contracted muscles result in stiff, rigid, and jerky motor activity. Athetosis is characterized by uncontrollable and involuntary motor movement. Ataxia is a disturbance of equilibrium that impairs posture and gait. Cerebral palsy is also classified according to degree of impairment: mild, moderate, and severe. In mild cases, individuals will be limited in their ability to perform precision motor movements. In moderate cases, the general motor functions of walking and the gross as well as the precision motor functions are impaired, but not to an incapacitating degree. In severe cases, individuals may be unable to perform the usual activities of daily living.

For some people with cerebral palsy, orthopedic handicaps may be accompanied by mild mental retardation, seizures, speech difficulties, and sensory deficiencies. Severe intellectual deficits are not necessarily present, nor are they related to the degree of an individual's motor problems. For example, individuals with moderate motor and speech problems may be highly intelligent, whereas others with only mild motor difficulties may be mentally retarded. The following are suggestions for helping clients with orthopedic handicaps.

□ Make no assumptions about clients' abilities or disabilities. Conduct a careful assessment of their range of motion and level of intelligence. This data should be available from agencies or schools in which they have received habilitation or rehabilitation services.

□ After conducting a client assessment, select job targets in which clients will have the abilities to perform. A thorough job analysis should be conducted to identify areas in which accommodations may be required.

□ Review available augmentative or accommodation products and evaluate the feasibility of altering the job requirements or the work environment to accommodate the abilities of the clients.

□ Advocacy assistance may be necessary because employers may underestimate the ability and intellectual functioning of clients with severe orthopedic handicaps.

□ Postemployment services should include educating co-workers about orthopedic handicaps.

## OTHER MOBILITY IMPAIRMENTS

Other motor impairments are those that limit or restrict the use of the head, arms, legs, or trunk. Mobility impairments are those that cause affected individuals to have difficulty moving themselves within their environment, usually requiring the use of wheelchairs, crutches, braces, or artificial limbs. Obviously, some motor impairments such as quadraplegia result in mobility impairments as well. However, there are some motor impairments that do not affect mobility. Paralysis of an arm or hand are motor impairments, but not mobility impairments.

There are a variety of motor and mobility problems that act as handicaps. Among them are arthritis, pain, paraplegia, and quadraplegia. Arthritis causes an inflammation of the joints that may limit both motor functions and mobility. The degree of impairment will vary from those who move with some pain and stiffness to those who find movement difficult or impossible. Pain may become a handicap when it causes individuals to limit their motor or mobility activities. Common causes of chronic pain are back or neck injuries. Paraplegia refers to a condition in which individuals experience varying degrees of paralysis from the waist down. This condition is often caused by an injury to the spinal cord. Like paraplegia, quadraplegia is often the result of an injury to the spinal cord. Individuals with quadraplegia, however, experience varying degrees of paralysis from the neck down.

The following are suggestions for helping clients with motor and mobility impairments.

☐ Make no assumptions about clients' abilities or disabilities. Assess both the range and the degree of any limitations in motion, and target jobs that best suit their abilities.

☐ Assess clients' unique adaptations to their impairments. They will often develop some unique solutions to circumvent their limitations.

☐ Conduct a careful job analysis to identify areas needing job accommodations.

☐ If clients are unable to drive a car, insure that reliable transportation is available, either publicly or privately, before conducting a search for employment.

☐ Be sure to include clients when discussing potential augmentative and accommodation products, job alterations, or changes in the work environment.

## VISUAL IMPAIRMENTS

Individuals are legally blind if their visual acuity, with glasses or lenses supplied, is 20/200 or less. This means they will be able to see at twenty feet, with glasses or lenses supplied, what others are able to see at two hundred feet. This legal definition also includes people whose visual field is restricted to 20 degrees or less. A normal visual field is 180 degrees. This legal definition, sometimes called *industrial blindness* is used to determine eligibility for various public benefits (Mainstream, 1985). The following are suggestions for helping clients with visual impairments.

☐ Review available accommodation products to identify those that might expand the range of employment alternatives.

☐ Insure that clients have reliable transportation available to them.

☐ Because job accommodations may be necessary, provide advocacy or placement assistance when required.

☐ Seek to obtain the approval and support of significant others. Be sure to include them as well as supervisors, and vocational rehabilitation counselors when developing employment strategies.

☐ Include clients in the development of job-accommodation strategies.

☐ When appropriate, encourage clients to discuss their handicaps with supervisors and co-workers.

## HEARING IMPAIRMENTS

*Hearing impaired* is a term referring to individuals who are either deaf or hard of hearing. Deafness refers to the "inability to hear, even with a hearing aid, well enough for the ordinary purposes of life" (English & English, 1958, p. 8). "The hard of hearing are those whose hearing is defective but functional and useful in daily life even though, in many instances, an auditory aid is necessary" (Cleland & Swartz, 1982). Hearing impairments are classified as congenital, present at birth, or aventitious (i.e., acquired as a result of illness or injury). Depending on when hearing impairments begin, individuals may also have speech impairments. When hearing impairments develop before individuals learn to speak, they will usually not be able to speak. These individuals will usually rely on sign language, or alternate forms of communication. Individuals whose hearing impairment developed after they learned to speak will be able to use some spoken language as well as alternate forms of communication; however, their verbalizations may be somewhat difficult to understand. The following are suggestions for helping clients with hearing impairments.

☐ Review available augmentative or accommodation products that may diminish the functional limitations of clients' handicaps.

☐ Because job accommodations may be necessary, provide advocacy or placement assistance when required.

☐ Seek to obtain the approval of significant others (parents, guardians, spouses). Include significant others, vocational rehabilitation counselors, and supervisors in developing employment strategies.

☐ When appropriate, recruit the assistance of an interpreter for hearing-impaired clients who have underdeveloped speech. Interpreters can be located geographically by writing or calling The National Registry of Interpreters for the Deaf, Inc.; 814 Thayer Avenue; Silver Spring, Maryland 20910.

☐ Conduct a careful job analysis to identify those job-performance areas needing job accommodations. Always include the individual in planning job accommodations.

☐ Assist and encourage clients to inform their supervisors and co-workers of their hearing impairments, and discuss how clients can effectively communicate with them.

# 3

# Organizing Client Activities

It is not uncommon to observe clients who are anxious to find employment applying for jobs without assessing the strengths and skills they have to offer potential employers. Nor is it uncommon to find that the same clients were unsuccessful in their efforts and have concluded that "there are just no jobs out there." One such client reported that she traveled up and down the East Coast distributing over 500 resumes to potential employers, as she searched for a job doing "anything." Ultimately, she came to believe that there was no place for her in the world of work. This example brings into question the very real problems faced by individuals with handicaps. Some clients may accept jobs for which they are ill suited, only to quit or to get fired. Others may obtain desirable employment, only to leave the job later because members of their family did not support their working.

Clients, as well as many education and counseling professionals, tend to view obtaining employment as an event (i.e., getting hired). The influences of the economy, the complexity of the labor market, the uniqueness of individuals and of their life situations, and the interpersonal dynamics of a job search cause many people to believe that the process of finding a job is not even known, much less manageable. It is therefore not surprising to find that many people tend to focus on employment-seeking outcomes rather than on the process, concluding that luck is the employment seeker's only valid resource.

However, if employment seeking is approached as a process, care is taken to select the most desirable employment alternatives, plans are developed for the life adjustments that will need to be made when employment is found, strategies are prepared to remove potential barriers, and plans are developed for postemployment adjustments and continued career development. By approaching the search in this manner, the process becomes more manageable, and the results become more predictable and positive. Table 3-1 outlines a model for obtaining competitive employment. It can be used to obtain an overview of the process and as a procedural outline for providing services to clients.

This chapter includes sections on productive professional–client

**Table 3-1. Model for Helping Clients to Obtain Competitive Employment**

I. ESTABLISH PRODUCTIVE PROFESSIONAL–CLIENT RELATIONSHIPS
  A. Express commitment to client
  B. Request commitment from client
  C. Clarify roles of counselor and client
  D. Both parties sign employment-seeking contract[a]
II. GATHER INFORMATION
  A. Complete client data form[a]
  B. Complete sociogram[a]
  C. Estimate role changes[a]
  D. Complete work-readiness assessment[a]
  E. Survey employment barriers[a]
  F. Select an employment objective[a]
  G. Complete job analysis and job accommodation[a]
  H. Get educational and rehabilitation records
III. DEVELOP INDIVIDUALIZED PLAN FOR EMPLOYMENT[a]
  A. Identify work-readiness concerns
  B. Identify barriers to employment
  C. Develop strategy for diminishing limitations of handicap
  D. Develop strategy for discussing handicap[b]
  E. Identify jobs and industries for search[a]
  F. Identify search strategies and monitoring procedures[a]
IV. PREPARE FOR SEARCH
  A. Develop and implement strategies for resolving work-readiness concerns
  B. Develop and implement strategies for removing employment barriers
  C. Develop and implement strategies for job accommodations[b]
  D. Write résumé[b]
  E. Provide job-interview training
  F. Review employment-seeking information and guidelines[a]
V. MONITOR SEARCH ACTIVITIES
  A. Complete "Weekly Job-Search Plan of Action" form[a]
  B. Gather necessary information for weekly search activities
  C. Facilitate and provide support for clients
  D. Prepare for scheduled job interviews[a]
  E. Solve problems
VI. PROVIDE POSTEMPLOYMENT SUPPORT
  A. Arrange for on-the-job training[b]
  B. Guide client in learning job tasks
  C. Facilitate social adjustment at the job site[a]
  D. Develop career-development strategy
  E. Assist with problem solving and role-change adjustments
  F. Provide periodic follow-up

[a]Ready-to-use forms are available in the supporting publication "Job-Finder's Workbook."
[b]If applicable

relationships, employment-seeking information and guidelines, and organizing information. It concludes with a case study using an "Individualized Plan for Employment" form.

## PRODUCTIVE PROFESSIONAL–CLIENT RELATIONSHIPS

If obtaining competitive employment is the desired end of employment counseling, establishing a productive relationship between professionals and clients is the desired beginning. When attempting to enter or reenter the world of work, clients bring with them a variety of mixed and ever-changing attitudes, feelings, and conditions. They may have hope and still feel despair; they may feel confident and still have self doubts; they may feel ready for work but still want to wait for some undefined condition; they may know what they want and still feel uncertain; and, they may have support from significant others at one moment and lose it the next. Clients must rely on professionals to help them address their concerns as they plan and implement strategies for obtaining employment. Desirable characteristics of productive relationships include: (1) showing respect for clients, (2) understanding client viewpoints, (3) listening to client concerns, (4) being positive and honest, (5) sharing important related self-information, (6) helping clients explore new ways of looking at themselves, (7) focusing on present concerns, and (8) confronting clients about counterproductive attitudes and behaviors. Professionals should facilitate support from the individual's friends and significant others.

### Role Clarification

The roles of professionals and clients should be mutually understood and agreed upon at the very beginning of the counseling relationship. Only after these roles have been clarified should professionals and clients sign an Employment-Seeking Contract. Some professionals may wish to develop their own forms, which may include material or information they feel is necessary, or the model contract can be used in its present form or can be modified to suit the needs of the situation.

### Clients

Clients should understand that they are expected to participate in the search for employment. In doing so, they can gain confidence and self-esteem by solving their own problems and helping others with their job-searches. The following suggestions are recommended as client responsibilities.

**ASSUME RESPONSIBILITY.** Depending on their handicaps, clients will need varying degrees of support in obtaining employment. Some clients, such as those who are moderately mentally retarded, will need to receive placement services, on-the-job training, and postemployment supportive counseling. Most clients, however, should assume the basic responsibility of obtaining employment.

**COMMITMENT OF TIME AND ENERGY.** Clients should not be led to believe that they can obtain employment without investing significant amounts of time and energy in the job search. Sometimes clients may take the offer of help with the covert hope that someone will find a job for them. In essence, they take a wait-and-see approach. The duration of help or services provided to clients should not continue for indefinite periods of time, but should have a beginning and an ending date.

**ATTENDANCE.** Clients should attend all scheduled classes, meetings, interviews, or other systems of appointments developed for information sharing. They should be taught or reminded to telephone appropriate personnel in the event that they are unable to attend a scheduled appointment. Absenteeism is usually a symptom of a problem, and it must be investigated immediately.

**HOMEWORK.** Many clients will be required to complete forms, complete job applications, gather information, participate in developing résumés and other correspondence, and keep records of their search activities. Those with minimum reading and writing skills should use alternate methods of completing forms (i.e., have friends or significant others help them).

**LEARN EFFECTIVE SEARCH ACTIVITIES.** Clients should commit themselves to learning about the labor market and to exploring effective ways of communicating with employers.

**CONDUCT SEARCH ACTIVITIES.** Except for clients whose handicaps prevent them from conducting employment-search activities, they should be required to telephone employers, telephone or correspond with people on their networking lists, conduct information interviews, and attend job interviews.

**HELP OTHER CLIENTS.** When the employment-seeking services are provided in group settings, clients should be encouraged to share ideas, feedback, and job leads with other members of the group. They should also be reminded to maintain confidentiality regarding the information learned about the other participants.

**TALK OUT PROBLEMS.** Clients should be encouraged to talk with professionals when problems arise throughout the employment-seeking assistance phase.

### Professionals

Professionals must not overstate the services they can realistically offer their clients. Most clients will appreciate any help, especially guidance, that is given to them. The following suggestions are recommended as responsibilities for professionals. Of course, the availability of time and other resources will affect the amount of assistance that can be provided by professionals.

**CLIENT DEVELOPMENT.** Professionals should communicate verbally, as well as through their deeds, that they are working in the best interest of their clients. Clients should feel safe with the guidance provided by professionals.

**CAREER DIRECTION.** Professionals should provide guidance for making career decisions. They should assist clients in selecting jobs in which they are likely to be productive and which they are likely to find satisfying.

**JOB SEARCH GUIDANCE.** Professionals should help develop individualized employment-seeking strategies and assist clients in learning the skills necessary to obtain a job in a competitive labor market. Skills should be taught through teaching, modeling, rehearsing, and role-playing.

**WRITING ASSISTANCE.** Professionals should assist clients in filling out job applications and writing résumés, cover letters, and thank-you notes.

**CLERICAL HELP.** When appropriate and if resources allow, professionals should provide typing assistance, photocopying, forms, and paper supplies.

**ON-THE-JOB TRAINING AND SUPPORT.** Some clients, especially those who are mentally retarded, may require extensive on-the-job training and supportive assistance. A job coach should help them learn the job tasks, adjust to the social environment, and solve problems at the worksite.

**POSTEMPLOYMENT SUPPORT.** Once employed, professionals should be available to assist clients in learning their job tasks, adjusting socially in the work place, and solving problems that may affect their overall work adjustment.

# EMPLOYMENT-SEEKING INFORMATION AND GUIDELINES

The job search is filled with confusion and uncertainty. This section provides important employment-seeking information and guidelines that will help to make the difficult process of seeking employment easier to understand and manage. Included are a brief discussion of the labor market, suggested job-search strategies, and a look at how job security can be sustained through self-development.

## The Labor Market

The labor market is composed of jobs, or occupations, located within various industries that make up our economy. Occupations can be classified by level of training and type of function. Levels of training might include such categories as unskilled, semiskilled, skilled, and professional. There are a variety of occupational classification systems. For example, one practical classification system organizes occupations into three simple groups, jobs that require people to work with data, with people, or with things. (Chapter 7 includes occupations classified by both level and function.)

The Standard Industrial Classification (SIC) Manual (U.S. Office of Management and Budget, 1972) lists 11 major industrial categories: (1) agriculture, forestry, and fishing; (2) mining; (3) construction; (4) manufacturing; (5) transportation, communications, electric, and sanitary services; (6) wholesale trade; (7) retail trade; (8) finance, insurance, and real estate; (9) services; (10) public administration; and (11) nonclassifiable establishments. Some jobs such as janitors can be found in virtually all industries, whereas jobs such as nurse aides can be found only in service industries. Once employment seekers have selected the jobs they want to pursue, they can easily identify the types of industries they should target for their search. Information regarding the names of employers within each industry is readily available in community industrial guides and in the yellow pages of telephone books.

### The Nature of a Competitive Labor Market

When people with handicaps attempt to make the transition from the somewhat secure world of education or rehabilitation into the world of work, they may have to alter their life roles, self-perceptions, and interpersonal behaviors before employers consider them to be truly employable. Rather than playing the role of helpee, clients must play the role of helpers; rather than clients being the center of attention, employers must become the center of attention; rather than focusing on the productivity of others, clients must focus on their own productivity; rather than focusing on disabilities, clients must focus on abilities; rather than having others concerned with their problems, clients must be concerned with the problems of others; and, rather than communicating a need for help, clients must communicate the ability to be of help. The hiring criteria used by most employers is, "hire the worker who is best suited for the job." In essence, the labor market is a very competitive environment, and applicants should not expect to find competitive employment by non-competitive means.

### How Job Vacancies Occur

Job vacancies result either from expansion or from replacement needs within given industries. When a company expands or increases the volume of its production or services, additional workers are needed to meet the increased workload. Generally speaking, except for highly technical industries, most new jobs are currently developing in the service industries rather than in the manufacturing industries. Service industries, such as hotels, fast-food restaurants, computer services, financial institutions, and nursing homes are among those that are expanding in our economy. Other job vacancies are created by the need for employers to replace employees who transfer, get promoted, find new jobs, quit, get fired, retire, or die. Job vacancies may still exist in an industry even when there is a zero or negative growth rate. Therefore, even during periods of high unemployment, job vacancies may be available because of the need to replace workers.

### Most Employers Do Not Advertise

Employment seekers who use want ads as their main strategy for searching for employment may be limiting themselves to as little as 15% of the available jobs. In a study of the use of want ads Olympus Research Corporation (1973) reported that 85% of the employers in San Francisco and 75% of the employers in Salt Lake City did not hire people through such advertising. Informal and formal conversations with employers currently indicate similar results. Although want ads are still a good source of job leads, other methods of seeking a job should be included in the employment-seeking strategy.

### Search Strategies

Most employers hire people through means other than want ads. In fact, when there is an abundance of workers, employers do very little recruiting. Therefore, seeking a good job in a competitive labor market requires individuals, first, to locate job vacancies that are not likely to be advertised (most of them) and, second, to persuade employers that they are the persons best suited for the position. There are at least five strategies that should be considered by employment seekers: (1) applying directly to employers; (2) networking — calling friends, acquaintances, family members, schoolmates, and former co-workers; (3) applying for jobs found in want ads; (4) contacting third-party agencies — Offices of Employment Security, temporary employment services, and employment agencies; and (5) locating advocacy and placement assistance — individuals or groups who will assist the employment seeker.

### Emphasize Abilities

Disabilities can become central to the self-perceptions of some individuals with handicaps. Disabilities of clients can overshadow their abilities to such a degree that they may identify more with their disabilities than with their abilities. The wide variety of occupations available in our labor market, however, provides most disabled people with job alternatives that will not require them to function in areas affected by their impairments or disabilities. In effect, they are unimpaired workers who have unrelated handicaps. Therefore, the importance of carefully selecting employment objectives and conducting job analyses cannot be overstated.

### Search for a Good Job

There are both desirable and undesirable jobs in the labor market. The good ones offer job satisfaction, adequate pay, and an avenue for personal and career development. Common sense would suggest that obtaining a desirable job will take more effort than obtaining an undesirable one. Since most individuals quickly quit undesirable jobs, it is recommended that employment seekers be encouraged to search for a good job. Hope for a desirable job and career is a powerful force for most employment seekers. It often creates a feeling of enthusiasm, which in itself, is a desirable trait that will increase the chances of finding a job in a competitive labor market.

### Focus on Problems of Employers

In the hiring process, both employment seekers and employers are trying to solve problems. The employment seekers are trying to solve whatever problems are associated with their unemployment, their underemployment, or their need to change jobs. Employers, on the other hand, are attempting to solve whatever problems are associated with needing another employee. There is a natural tendency for both groups to focus their attention on their own problems.

Although both groups have problems, only the employers have decision-making powers. Therefore, employment seeking should always be approached as an attempt to solve the problems of the employers. In doing so, employment seekers will indirectly solve their own problems. There is a subtle but profound difference in communications between employment seekers and employers when the applicants use an employer-centered approach, instead of a seeker-centered approach. In the seeker-centered approach, the applicant's communications are, "I have a problem. Can you solve it for me?" In the employer-centered approach, the applicant's communications are, "Do you have a problem? If so, may I solve it for you?" People with handicaps will have a far greater chance of obtaining competitive employment when they present themselves as "people with solutions" rather than as "people with problems."

### Communicate Employability

When trying to determine who is best suited for the job, employers usually consider certain categories of information. Four of the most common categories include, but would not be limited to, education, experience, competencies, and personality traits. The categories eminate from simple, common-sense questions. The education category evolves from the question, "Do you have formal training for this work?" The experience category results from the question, "Have you ever done this work or work similar to it?" The competencies category relates to the question, "Do you have the skills and abilities to perform the tasks for this work?" Finally, the personality traits category results from the question, "Do you have the disposition for this work?" Employers usually have preconceived notions of the qualifications they are hoping to find in their applicants. By using these categories to communicate their qualifications, clients will be presenting themselves in the decision-making formats used by employers.

### Independent Job Searching

People with handicaps should assume as much responsibility for obtaining employment as their disabilities will permit. Because employers are seeking to hire the best-suited people for their positions, they will often look for motivation, eagerness, determination, and communication skills in their applicants. Qualified applicants whose rehabilitation or placement counselor applies for jobs on their behalf are sending mixed messages to employers. Their absence in the search process raises doubts in the minds of employers, who become suspicious of applicants supposedly able to work but unable to participate in their own search for employment. In a competitive labor market, employers may choose from other applicants who do not raise these suspicions.

### Time, Place, and Luck

It has often been said that finding a job is a matter of being lucky enough to be in the right place at the right time. In many respects, this statement is true; however, it involves more than luck. Over time, job vacancies will occur throughout the labor market. Employment seekers have no control over when and where these job vacancies will appear. On the other hand, employment seekers can and do control whether or not they are among an employer's active applicants. In other words, they can put themselves in the right places, and with a little "luck," they will be there at the right time. If they are not among an employer's active applicants when the right time comes along, they will need more than luck to get the job.

## Job Security Through Self-Development

A generation ago, the strategy for job security was to find a good company and serve it well. Although that strategy is still sound, it can no longer guarantee job security. Technological progress, changing consumer needs, oil embargoes, union strikes, corporate takeovers, and cost-efficient foreign labor are just a few of the circumstances that can undermine the most secure companies. The most reliable approach to job security is through self-development. If workers continue to improve their efficiency and learn new skills, they will always be of value in the labor market.

## ORGANIZING INFORMATION

Understanding the labor market and the process used to seek and obtain employment is an excellent learning opportunity for clients. Maintaining their own information will give clients a greater understanding and more control over their lives. The authors recommend that clients be furnished with a three ring binder, a package of 8½x11-inch loose-leaf notebook paper, and notebook section dividers. Figure 3-1 lists the information that clients should maintain in their binders.

Professionals may wish to maintain records of counseling forms and other information on the progress of their clients. Figure 3-2 lists the information that should be maintained by professionals.

**Figure 3-1. Organizing Client's Information**

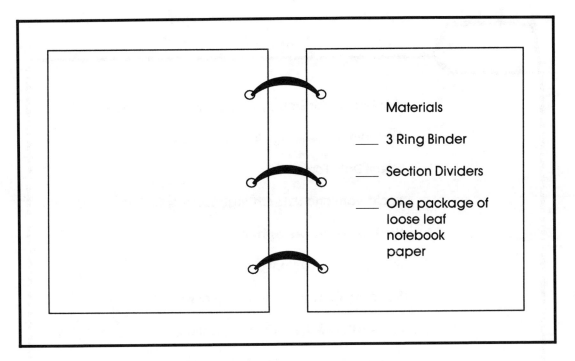

SECTION A: General Information

___ List of Contents

___ Calendar

___ Welcome

___ Employment Seeking Contract

___ Employment Seeking Information and Guidelines

___ Individualized Plan for Employment (Copy)

SECTION B: Notes from Classes, Meetings, and Interviews

SECTION C: Records of Search Strategy A — Direct-to-Employer Applications

SECTION D: Records of Search Strategy B — Networking

SECTION E: Records of Search Strategy C — Help Wanted Ads

SECTION F: Records of Search Strategy D — Third Parties

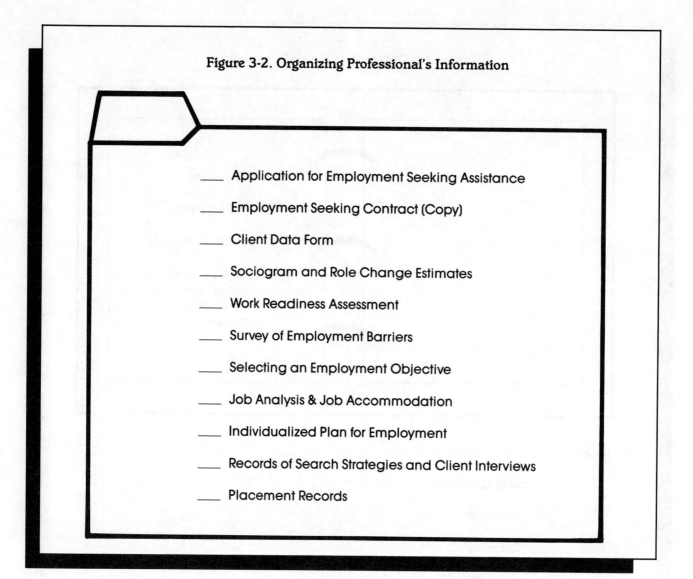

Figure 3-2. Organizing Professional's Information

___ Application for Employment Seeking Assistance

___ Employment Seeking Contract (Copy)

___ Client Data Form

___ Sociogram and Role Change Estimates

___ Work Readiness Assessment

___ Survey of Employment Barriers

___ Selecting an Employment Objective

___ Job Analysis & Job Accommodation

___ Individualized Plan for Employment

___ Records of Search Strategies and Client Interviews

___ Placement Records

## INDIVIDUALIZED PLAN FOR EMPLOYMENT

The model form "Individualized Plan for Employment" provides professionals with a comprehensive and completely structured format for providing employment counseling to clients. Even professionals with little or no experience should be able to provide adequate guidance by using this format for finding a job. Figure 3-3 presents a case study demonstrating the use of an "Individualized Plan for Employment" form. By completing and implementing this form, clients and professionals will anticipate and address problems before they occur, identify appropriate employment objectives, develop plans to improve client job competitiveness through self-development, define a weekly job-search strategy, facilitate support from other people and agencies, and establish a system for monitoring the frequency of their job-search inquiries.

**Figure 3-3. Case study: individualized plan for employment**

# INDIVIDUALIZED PLAN FOR EMPLOYMENT

Name _____ Mary Xxxxxxx _____ Date ___ 9/7/87 ___

Organization _____ Staff Member _____

1. Realistically describe the characteristics of desired employment

    Time: _X_ Full-time ___ Part-time

    Level: _X_ Unskilled/Semiskilled ___ Skilled ___ Professional

    Geographical location: _____ Hometown, USA _____

    Salary associated with level of employability: _____ $4.00 per hour _____

    Other: _____

2. List the work-readiness concerns that must be addressed before conducting a
   search for employment. _____ (from "Work-Readiness Assessment") _____

    1) Slow rate of learning

    2) Low level of reading comprehension

    3) Economic disincentive — receives $400 a month from Supplemental Security
       Income (SSI)

3. List the employment barriers that must be addressed before conducting a search
   for employment. _____ (from "Survey of Employment Barriers" form) _____

    1) Problem work history

    2) Low self-esteem

    3) Lacks reliable transportation

4. Describe job accommodation and other strategies for diminishing the functional
   limitations caused by the individual's impairment or disability.

    1) Mary should not seek positions requiring difficult levels of reading

    2) She may benefit from on-the-job training for at least four weeks.

    3) Apply for Association for Retarded Citizens (ARC) funding for employer salary
       reimbursement during initial training period.

            (from "Job Analysis and Job Accommodation" form)

**Continued**

**Figure 3-3 Continued**

5. Will it be necessary to inform potential employers of the individual's impairment or disability? If so, how will it be done?

If ARC funding is received, employers will have to be informed of her disability. If this occurs, her employment conselor will provide information to the employer. Otherwise, informing employers would not be necessary. However, Mary should clearly state the range of tasks she is able to perform with her current level of training.

6. List the first-choice job(s) that will be pursued in the search for employment. Identify second-choice alternatives.

1) Clerical aide, 2) General office clerk, and 3) Mailroom clerk

(from "Selecting and Employment Objective" form)

7. In the order of desirability to the individual seeking employment, list the general types of industries targeted for the employment search.

Mary should search for jobs in larger industries that are likely to have more specialized work roles such as: (1) Banks, (2) Insurance companies, and (3) Post Offices

(from "Selecting an Employment Objective" form)

8. List three to five qualification highlights for the jobs the individual will pursue.

(1) Competencies in basic clerical skills, (2) Clerical experience received through volunteer experience, (3) Punctuality and reliability, and (4) Desire to work in a clerical occupation

9. What can the individual do to improve competitiveness for the desired positions?

(1) Obtain clerical experience through volunteering

(2) Register for a personal typing course at the local community college

10. Describe the search strategies that will be used to obtain employment. Include weekly frequency of contacts and an estimate of time commitment.

(1) Direct-to-Employer Applications — 25 contacts per week

(2) Networking — 20 contacts per week

(3) Want Ads — read daily classified ads in two local newspapers

(4) Third Parties — Make weekly inquiries at the Office of Employment Security

(OES) and at four Temporary Employment Agencies

(from "Weekly Job Search Plan of Action" form)

11. Describe the plans for monitoring search activities, self-rewards, and duration of search.

Use the Weekly "Job-Search Plan of Action" form to set goals and monitor progress. Rewards will include going to movies, attending dances, and bowling. The search will be actively and consistently pursued for six weeks and will be followed by a one-week vacation from the job search. The search will be continued in these cycles until Mary finds a job.

12. List the names of people or community agencies that might be of help to the individual. Describe how they might be of assistance.

(1) Mary's mother — will help by reading the classified ads

(2) Susan (sister) — will help to complete applications and other written correspondence

13. List important commitments that must be maintained during the search for employment.

(1) Volunteer activities at the Local Hotel

(2) Household chores

Continued

**Figure 3-3 Continued**

14. What are the individual's early warning signs of frustration? Describe an intervention strategy that will be implemented when the individual becomes frustrated.

Feels anxious and tends to withdraw from activities. Absence from program services should be checked immediately. As an intervention, Mary should sign an "Agreement" form (Behavioral Contract) to obtain a commitment to call a counselor or friend when she feels anxious.

15. List recreational or other activities that would balance the frustration of searching for employment.

(1) Going to movies

(2) Spending time with friends

(3) Going on nature walks

(4) Visiting the zoo

# Strategies to Facilitate Employment Transitions

**H**elping people with handicaps obtain competitive employment requires professionals to function as teachers, counselors, psychotherapists, facilitators, advisors, coaches, mentors, and friends. There are a variety of counseling strategies and techniques that professionals can employ to function successfully in these roles. Proven effective in a wide range of counseling situations, the strategies and techniques presented in this chapter have been adapted or developed from a number of theoretical orientations and human service disciplines. These orientations and disciplines include trait and factor theory, cognitive theory, behavioral and learning theory, systems theory, job accommodation strategies, and selected counseling techniques. Table 4-1 provides an overview of the counseling strategies and techniques recommended for helping clients obtain employment.

## TRAIT AND FACTOR STRATEGIES

Effective career decision making, in this case selecting the jobs to pursue while searching for employment, is the foundation for a successful transition into the world of work. Effective decisions are made when clients target jobs in which they will be productive and find satisfying. The central aim of trait and factor counseling is to help clients make effective career decisions. The theory can be traced to the work of Parsons (1909) and was furthered by E. G. Williamson (1965) and his colleagues at the University of Minnesota. The principles of trait and factor decision making can be summarized as follows: (1) Each person has a unique profile of employable traits, (2) each occupation requires workers to use differing sets of those employable traits, (3) career decision making is a process of matching the individual's employable traits to the worker traits required for the job, and (4) worker productivity and job satisfaction are likely to

**Table 4-1.** Strategies and Techniques to Facilitate Employment Transitions

| Strategy and purpose | Techniques |
|---|---|
| *Trait and Factor:* to identify career and employment alternatives that are congruent with the abilities and personality traits of clients. | □ vocational–career assessments<br>□ matching persons with jobs<br>□ job analyses |
| *Cognitive:* to externalize intrapsychic conflicts and barriers that may cause ambivalence among clients. | □ empty chair<br>□ role reversal |
| *Behavioral:* to learn and perform behaviors that lead to obtaining and maintaining employment. | □ self-management<br>□ behavioral contracting<br>□ modeling<br>□ behavioral rehearsal<br>□ role rehearsal<br>□ assertiveness training<br>□ relaxation training |
| *Systems:* to obtain acceptance and support from the people important in the lives of clients for changes in employment status. | □ sociograms<br>□ estimating life-role changes |
| *Counseling:* to facilitate employment transitions by providing supportive assistance. | □ providing information<br>□ decision making<br>□ problem solving |
| *Job Accommodations:* to use accommodation products or changes in job requirements or worksite environment. | □ job accommodation products<br>□ job restructuring<br>□ worksite modification |

occur when individual traits and work-requirement traits are congruently matched. Techniques borrowed from trait and factor theory include vocational–career assessments, matching clients with jobs, and job analyses.

## Vocational–Career Assessments

Professionals should gather a wide range of client information from such areas as education, training, work experience, aptitudes, abilities, interests, and personality traits, and summarize that information in vocational profiles to be matched with career alternatives.

### Matching Clients with Jobs

After developing profiles of their clients' employable characteristics, professionals should match those profiles with congruent career alternatives.

### Job Analyses

Desirable career alternatives should be fully assessed in job analyses in order to identify any functional limitations that may require further client development or job accommodations.

## COGNITIVE STRATEGIES

Vocational rehabilitation counselors are often puzzled and frustrated by clients who demonstrate an ambivalence about working. It should be noted, however, that ambivalence about working is not limited to people with handicaps. Many individuals, ambivalent about working, apply for services and receive training and counseling only to fail to apply for and accept employment when it becomes available to them. Therefore, it is imperative that professionals recognize the cognitive barriers of their clients. Ignoring them may result in clients becoming frustrated, as they may not know why they are receiving negative feedback from their counselors. These frustrations may, in turn, further contribute to their problematic ways as they begin to ask themselves, "Is something wrong with me?" or "Do they dislike me?" It is also important to remember that being labeled handicapped or being raised as a person with special problems can leave clients with cognitive barriers that can undermine their willingness to risk change.

The objectives of the cognitive therapies are to help clients replace self-defeating thoughts and attitudes with self-enhancing thoughts and attitudes (Gilliland, James, Roberts, and Bowman, 1984). In the context of employment counseling, emphasis is placed on fostering positive perceptions of self, the work world, employers, and hiring practices; as well as on examining the private logic and self-talk of clients. Once the self-defeating perceptions have been identified, professionals can help clients reconstruct alternate views of themselves and of their situations that are more objective and congruent with competitive job-search behaviors. The cognitive restructuring process involves the following: (1) externalizing self-defeating perceptions, (2) establishing a relationship between the faulty perceptions and the self-defeating or nonproductive behavior, (3) exploring alternate ways for clients to view themselves or their situations, and

(4) examining how new positive perceptions might contribute to adaptive behavior. Two cognitive strategies are known as *empty chair* and *role reversal.*

## Empty Chair

This technique is an exercise rooted in psychodrama and used commonly in Gestalt Therapy (Hansen, Warner, & Smith, 1980). It is useful in helping clients to gain insight into conflicting thoughts that may be at the root of their ambivalence, low self-esteem, or incongruent vocational self-concepts. Once the conflicting or incongruent thoughts are externalized, they can be discussed in a more straightforward fashion.

The empty-chair technique requires clients to have a dialogue with two potentially incongruent sides of themselves. The opposing sides might include the *handicapped* self dialoguing with the *non-handicapped* self, the *old* self dialoguing with the *new* self, the *employable* self dialoguing with the *unemployable* self, or the *good* self dialoguing with the *bad* self. Clients should assume both sides of themselves, taking turns speaking from one side to the other. An empty chair is placed in front of the clients to represent the opposite side of themselves. They should be directed to switch chairs to make clear which side they are representing while speaking. For example, the *employable* self would make a statement to the *unemployable* self sitting in the empty chair. The client should switch seats and respond to the *employable* self from the position of the *unemployable* self.

Professionals should guide clients through the dialogue, instructing them to shift seats, clarifying statements, and identifying incongruencies for more direct discussion. Clients will often develop powerful insights into incongruent ideas that are making it impossible for them to succeed. For example, a 30-year-old man participating in a job-finding program after eight weeks had never applied for one job. The counselor had him speak from the *I-want-to-work* side of himself to the *I-don't-want-to-work* side of himself. During the dialogue, he identified incongruent attitudes that were preventing him from pursuing employment. On the one hand, he wanted only a job he would enjoy. On the other hand, he knew very little about the world of work and would not consider jobs he knew nothing about. Therefore, he negated all jobs because he could not determine whether they would be satisfying. The professional guided him in understanding how these incongruent attitudes were preventing him from applying for jobs. They then discussed ways of resolving the conflict.

## Role Reversal

This technique is utilized in psychodrama, in Gestalt, and in rational-emotive therapies (Hansen, Warner, & Smith, 1980). Role reversal has a variety of potential counseling uses. In employment counseling, it can be especially useful for helping clients obtain more objective views of themselves and of their situations by having clients assume the roles of other people. For example, they can play the roles of employment interviewers discussing their job qualifications, counselors discussing their readiness for work, or family members discussing how their being employed will affect significant others. Placed in the roles of other people, clients can gain new insights into the attitudes or beliefs of other people as well as of themselves. In these alternate roles, clients should respond as if they were, in fact, those other people. The attitudes and perceptions expressed in those alternate roles may be projections of attitudes that are either shared or held exclusively by clients.

An 18-year-old woman with a learning disability was asked to assume the roles of her mother, father, sister, and her favorite teacher. In each of these roles, she was asked to describe herself. As her mother, she described herself as lazy. As her father, she described herself as not very social. As her sister, she described herself as fun. As her favorite teacher, she described herself as amusing and clever. Once these perceptions were externalized through the role reversals, the professional and the client were able to discuss these mixed self-descriptions, whether she held the same views, and how these perceptions affected her ability to search competitively for a job.

## BEHAVIORAL AND LEARNING STRATEGIES

Seeking, finding, obtaining, and maintaining competitive employment typically requires clients to demonstrate overt behavior. Depending on their handicaps, some clients may not be able to participate fully in the employment-seeking process, and they may need placement assistance. However, clients should participate to the highest degree possible within the constraints of their handicaps. For example, they should at least participate in job interviews. When counseling individuals with handicaps, professionals often encounter clients who are unable to carry out their job-search tasks even though they are sufficiently motivated to work and have developed comprehensive job-search plans. Behavioral and learning strategies help these clients learn, produce, and sustain behaviors needed to conduct a competitive job search for employment. Theoretically, the behavioral and learning approach views clients as both producers and products of their environments (Kazdin, 1978). They are capable of imagining desirable behaviors (Meichenbaum, 1977) and of converting those images into behavioral realities (Watson & Tharp, 1981). Actual strategies can include self-management, behavioral contracting, modeling, behavior rehearsal, role-playing, assertiveness training, and relaxation techniques.

## Self-Management

Use of self-management strategies in the search for competitive employment shifts the responsibility for finding a job from the professionals to the clients. Regretfully, and too often, vocational rehabilitation clients expect professionals to assume all or most of the placement responsibilities. Self-management embodies the trend toward expecting clients to become active collaborators in the counseling relationship. The self-management model developed by William and Long (1979) includes the following: (1) selecting task goals, (2) creating conditions conducive to success, (3) monitoring task behaviors, and (4) establishing effective consequences. Many of the model counseling forms have been developed with these principles in mind.

## Behavioral Contracting

Behavioral contracts are agreements between clients and professionals in which clients sign a written contract to perform a specified task by a certain date. The contract usually includes positive reinforcements for contract compliance and may include some undesirable consequence when clients fail to comply with their agreements. Contracting is particularly helpful when clients are at an impasse and cannot seem to get started in their activities, or when they are demonstrating strong avoidance patterns of behavior. In such cases, the completion of a specific activity can help them break through the impasse or interrupt the pattern of avoidance behavior. For example, a client in an employment program participated in all program activities, but he simply could not apply for a job. A behavior contract was written requiring the client to complete an application for employment at a specified place of employment on a specified date. For completing the task the client rewarded himself by purchasing an article he wanted to buy. If he failed to comply with the contract he would have to wash the family dishes for one week. Figure 4-1 demonstrates the use of a behavioral contract in a case study.

## Modeling

"Modeling is the overt and explicit demonstration of appropriate behavioral choices available to the client" (Bandura, 1969). Modeling can be done by professionals, by other clients, or by video recordings. Modeling is especially useful in demonstrating methods of inquiring about job vacancies and conducting job interviews.

## Behavioral Rehearsal

Clients practice specific responses that have been learned through either didactic teaching or modeling. The technique of behavioral rehearsal is especially effective when it is preceded by

**Figure 4-1. Case study: (behavioral contract) agreement**

# AGREEMENT

I, _____ Mary Smith _____ , agree to conduct the

following activities that will lead, directly or indirectly, to securing a job.

Description of activities: _Telephone an employer about a job recently advertised in_

_the local newspaper. (Mary is attempting to interrupt an established pattern of_

_avoidance behavior)_

_____

These activities will be completed by ____ Friday, Oct. 16, 1987 ____

For completing these activities, I will reward myself by _going to see a movie_

_____

If I fail to comply with this agreement, I will _volunteer to wash the dinner dishes for_

_one week._

_____

Signatures:

_Mary Smith_                                    _John Doe_
Person Seeking Employment                        Witness

10/11/87
Date

modeling and followed by coaching from professionals. For example, after watching and listening to the professionals telephone employers about job vacancies, the clients can practice prepared scripts while the professionals listen and offer constructive feedback.

### Role-playing

Role-playing allows clients to practice behavioral responses in anticipated employment-seeking, working, or social situations. Role-playing is most effective when feedback is provided to the clients by the professionals through verbalizations or reviews of video recordings.

### Assertiveness Training

The objective of assertiveness training is to develop alternate response behaviors in clients whose shyness and passivity are limiting the effectiveness of their communication or behavior. Clients who are afraid to make job inquiries or who are intimidated in job interviews can benefit most from assertiveness training. Assertiveness may be achieved through a combination of instruction, modeling, and behavior rehearsal. Again, feedback from professionals is beneficial.

### Relaxation Training

Relaxation training involves learning how to relax muscles systematically and how to focus on mental images to produce psychic relief of body tension and stress (Wolpe, 1958). For some clients, anxiety associated with the job search becomes so intense that they may have no alternative but to avoid those behaviors. Avoidance behavior may cause them to miss appointments, cancel job interviews, or fail to show up on the first day of work. One client, who had a controlled seizure disorder, was afraid to go on job interviews because he was afraid that the anxiety associated with interviews would trigger a seizure. After learning to reduce his anxious feelings through relaxation techniques, he was able to resume an active search for employment.

## SYSTEMS STRATEGIES

Banathy (1973) defined a *system* as an interacting group of entities forming an organized whole. The systems approach regards individuals as parts of social networks made up of family members, friends and acquaintances, and members representing community organizations. What individuals do in their daily routines and the changes they make in their lives do not occur within a social vacuum. Consequently, their daily routines, the roles they play, and especially the changes they make affect the people who make up their social environments. All roles become integrated into a larger social picture.

Work-role changes occurring among clients will often necessitate role changes among their significant others. For example, parents of children with handicaps, often assume the roles of helpers as their children grow up. If the children change and become independent young adults, parents will have to adjust to this change. Although they may value the independence being developed in their children, some parents have difficulty accepting their children's independence, and they display a reluctance or a lack of support. Homebound individuals with handicaps often assume valued roles around the house, such as cleaning, running errands, and taking care of children. The abandonment of these roles for jobs leaves a lot of work that someone else must assume. Clients may find their new roles desirable, whereas their family members may find the subsequent changes in their own lives undesirable.

As professionals attempt to facilitate changes in the lives of their clients, they should be aware that they are facilitating role changes among the people in their clients' social network as well. Sometimes clients are dependent on the people in their social environments for such necessities as transportation, money, housing, food, and emotional support. Consequently, changes in the lives of clients may require the approval and support of parents, guardians, spouses, friends, teachers, or caseworkers. The systems strategies include using sociograms to identify the important others in the lives of clients and to estimate the role changes that may occur in their lives.

## Sociograms

Sociograms can be used to identify clients' significant others who will be affected by the changes facilitated by professionals.

## Estimating Life-Roles Changes

After completing sociograms or role reversals, professionals can assist clients in making the changes necessary to accommodate the life-role adjustments that will occur when they become employed. Providing information, contracting, writing letters requesting support, and clarifying roles between clients and important others are ways of facilitating smooth life-role transitions.

# COUNSELING

Previous sections of this chapter describe strategies and techniques developed from some of the major theories of counseling and psychotherapy. In addition to those specialized disciplines, several additional counseling skills can be used to help clients obtain employment. They include providing information, decision making, and of problem solving.

## Providing Information

Clients need information about themselves, about the world of work, about where they best fit into the world of work, about community resources, and about what they must do to obtain competitive employment.

## Decision Making

Professionals should assist clients and relevant support people in developing options, weighing alternatives, assessing risk, and planning strategies for desired changes.

## Problem Solving

The most thoughtful strategy for obtaining employment is usually interrupted by problems that can come from within the individual, from their social support systems, from their life situations, and from the labor market. Professionals should be prepared for and anticipate as many problems as possible as they work with their clients.

# JOB ACCOMMODATIONS

Job accommodations are reasonable adjustments made to jobs or work environments that enable individuals with handicaps to perform jobs at acceptable levels. Appropriate accommodations should be approached on a case by case basis. Factors determining the need for and the kind of accommodation include the nature and extent of the individual's handicap, the job requirements, the work environment, and the practicality of the proposed accommodation. Accommodations may involve the rearrangement of furniture, a specially adapted piece of technical equipment, or the reorganization of work requirements or schedules. Types of job accommodations can include accommodation products, job restructuring, and worksite modifications. Chapter 8 provides additional information on job accommodations.

## Accommodation Products

Job accommodation products include specialized equipment and assistive devices such as magnifiers, electronic visual aids, telephone amplifiers, speaker phones, talking calculators, braille devices, communication boards, electrified tools, and other simple equipment.

## Job Restructuring

Job restructuring involves a revision of job duties to accommodate the functional limitations of an individual's handicap. In job restructuring, tasks that individuals cannot perform are eliminated or transferred to other workers in exchange for responsibilities they can perform.

## Worksite Modification

Worksite modification involves the restructuring of machinery or the physical environment to accommodate the functional limitations of an individual's handicap.

# 5

# Assessing Work Readiness

**V**ocational habilitation and rehabilitation processes usually include the following steps: assessment of the disability, development of an individualized plan of treatment, and delivery of a vocational-training program. This process is then followed by placement. The primary emphasis of these processes, as measured by money spent and by the volume of professional–client contacts, is on the delivery of vocational-training programs. After clients have successfully completed their training programs, it is assumed that they are ready for employment. Unfortunately, this definition of work readiness focuses too narrowly on the development of job skills and excludes other important characteristics of work readiness.

The selection of an employment-seeking strategy, the ability to conduct a job search, the willingness to accept employment, and the ability to keep a job depends on a much broader concept of work readiness. In addition to having the ability to work, clients must be sufficiently free from ambivalence, be released from competing commitments, have means of reliable transportation, and possess the interpersonal skills required to adapt to work environments. Therefore, work readiness includes at least four important characteristics: (1) ability to work, (2) desire to work, (3) availability to work, and (4) adaptability to work. Figure 5-1 presents a model of work readiness using a formula to describe its essential elements.

Conceptually, complete readiness for work can be reduced by individual or life constraints that may, in some cases, be remedied through counseling or other interventions. For example, the ability to work can be diminished by client disabilities and can be enhanced through job accommodations. Similarly, desire to work can be decreased by such things as economic disincentives, availability to work can be limited by the lack of transportation, and adaptability to work can be blocked by poor appearance. Focusing on factors reducing work readiness will help professionals identify these constraints and develop intervention strategies to eliminate them.

The model "Work-Readiness Assessment" form, presented in Figure 5-3, measures client ability, desire, availability, and adaptability to work, and it concludes with a summary of work readiness. The primary objective of this book is to help clients obtain competitive

## Figure 5-1. Work readiness formula

$$\text{Work Readiness} = Ab + D + Av + Ad$$

Ab = **Ability** (Abilities Minus Disabilities plus Job Accommodations)

D = **Desire** (Incentives Minus Disincentives)

Av = **Availability** (Availability Minus Commitment Constraints Minus Transportation Constraints)

Ad = **Adaptability** (Adaptability Minus Inappropriate Appearance Minus Unacceptable Social Skills Minus Poor Work Attitudes)

employment; it is not a vocational training manual. Therefore, the model of work readiness does not rely on comprehensive diagnostic batteries. Taking a similar position, Azrin and Besalel (1980) stated that: "The Job Club program differs from many job finding assistance programs in that it emphasizes placement rather than vocational counseling or testing . . . If a behavior pattern is interfering with a member's being hired, the problem is dealt with as a specific behavior to be changed, not as a trauma requiring psychotherapy . . . This more extensive kind of change is neither necessary nor, at times, possible or even desirable . . ." (p. 94).

The authors have found through years of experience that employers are not interested in test scores. They are interested only in knowing whether applicants can satisfy the requirements of the job. A model "Work-Readiness Assessment" form developed for this text measures general, rather than specific, work abilities. Sufficient data will usually be available from educational records, work histories, test batteries used in previous assessments, reference assessments, and reports from clients. Figure 5-2 presents a procedural description of how to assess work readiness.

## ABILITY TO WORK

Ability to work includes cognitive abilities, motor–mobile abilities, communication abilities, sensory abilities, and general health. This model uses general areas of functioning to avoid stereotypical

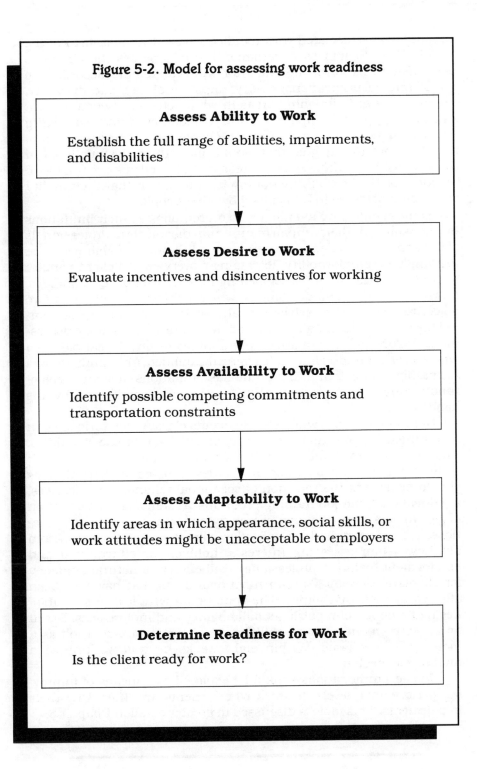

**Figure 5-2. Model for assessing work readiness**

**Assess Ability to Work**

Establish the full range of abilities, impairments, and disabilities

**Assess Desire to Work**

Evaluate incentives and disincentives for working

**Assess Availability to Work**

Identify possible competing commitments and transportation constraints

**Assess Adaptability to Work**

Identify areas in which appearance, social skills, or work attitudes might be unacceptable to employers

**Determine Readiness for Work**

Is the client ready for work?

thinking often associated with handicap classifications. Part I of the model "Work-Readiness Assessment" form assesses the ability to work. Using this form, the evaluator will rate abilities according to one of three classifications: ability, impaired ability, and disability. *Ability* refers to functioning areas in which clients have no demonstrated or apparent impairments or disabilities. *Impaired ability* refers to functioning areas in which clients have observable limitations, but not to a degree that would make them dysfunctional in those areas. *Disability* refers to areas in which clients are unable to function, or the level of functioning is so impaired that their ability would be considered to be disabled by other people.

Some clients have a tendency to overemphasize their limitations by focusing on their impairments and disabilities. Professionals should encourage clients to examine the full range of abilities when defining their employability. To obtain an overview of a client's ability to work, profiles can be developed by making lists of their abilities, impaired abilities, and disabilities, which help clients obtain a more objective view of themselves. Usually their list of abilities far outweighs their list of impairments and disabilities. The sample assessment (Figure 5-3) summarizes the abilities of an 18-year-old man who was diagnosed as having learning disabilities. An examination of his profile reveals that although he has limitations in some areas of functioning, he has many abilities that are unaffected by his handicap.

Summary profiles will also help clients classify the world of work according to the jobs that are congruent with their profile of abilities. They will learn to identify jobs that will require them to rely on their abilities rather than on their disabilities. Profiles of their abilities should be used in the selection of vocational rehabilitation services, in educational and job-training programs, as well as in the selection of jobs to pursue during their search for employment. In many situations, job accommodations will allow clients to use their impaired abilities. When assessing interests, hobbies, or educational and employment histories, professionals will observe a natural tendency for clients to develop skills in functional areas that have not been affected by their disabilities. The young man with learning disabilities had a hobby of repairing small engines and motorcycles. Based on an assessment of these abilities, he chose to pursue a job as a motorcycle mechanic. Within eight weeks he was working as a motorcycle mechanic.

Job accommodations should be explored as a means of improving performance levels in areas where clients are limited by their impairments. This topic is discussed in greater detail in Chapter 8.

## DESIRE TO WORK

Desire to work is an essential element of any work-readiness model. The objective of including an assessment of the desire to work is to identify work disincentives that may cause ambivalence in clients. After completing vocational-training programs, clients may express reservations that prevent them from searching for a job. This ambivalence results in procrastination, missed appointments, and negative thinking that can turn into self-fulfilling prophecies of failure. However, if clients' reservations are identified, they can be discussed and, perhaps, resolved through counseling interventions. Evaluating the desire to work involves the assessment of five categories of incentives and disincentives: (1) perceived self-development, (2) desire for work activities, (3) willingness to risk, (4) willingness to accept life change, and (5) economic disincentives.

## AVAILABILITY TO WORK

Accepting employment results in significant life changes for both the clients and the people whose daily activities are synchronized with them. Therefore, it is important to assess all constraints, those existing within clients and those in their life situations. Nonworking life roles can evolve for people who are unemployed. In these nonworking life roles, clients might assume responsibilities for child care, household responsibilities, or running errands, to name just a few. Some clients may want to postpone the search for employment pending outcomes of litigation on Workmen's Compensation rulings. Transportation problems are one of the most common employment constraints. The "Availability to Work" section of the "Work-Readiness Assessment" form allows professionals and clients to anticipate a variety of potential constraints. Once aware of these constraints, clients can plan appropriate adjustments to remove them. Each item in the "Availability to Work" section is classified as not a problem, somewhat of a problem, or definite problem.

## ADAPTABILITY TO WORK

Adaptability to work includes appearance, social skills, and work attitudes. As in the section on desire to work, each item is evaluated as a potential constraint. The objective for assessing adaptability to work is to identify client characteristics that employers might find undesirable and to alter them through teaching and counseling interventions. Undesirable characteristics might include poor hygiene, inappropriate dress, and unacceptable social behavior. Such undesirable characteristics attract attention, and those who possess them are quickly screened out from possible employment consideration.

Figure 5-3. Case study: work-readiness assessment form

# WORK-READINESS ASSESSMENT

Name _____ Mark Xxxxx _____ Date ____ 9/7/87 ____

Organization _____ Staff Member _____

## PART I. ABILITY TO WORK

*Instructions:* Rate each ability according to one of the following classifications:

A. *Ability* — No impairment or disability has been documented or demonstrated in behavior. The individual's abilities do not appear to be deficient when compared to average adults.

B. *Impaired Ability* — Ability impaired but not dysfunctional, as evidenced by evaluations and observations.

C. *Disability* — Significant dysfunction, as evidenced by evaluation and observation.

Describe ratings of B or C in the remarks sections.

COGNITIVE ABILITIES

__A__ 1. *Higher Levels of Thinking:* Ability to use abstract thinking, reasoning, evaluating, problem solving, and decision making.

__A__ 2. *Memory:* Ability to retain information.

__B__ 3. *Learning:* Ability to acquire new information and skills.

__C__ 4. *Reading:* Ability to acquire information from written sources with comprehension levels similar to newspapers (third- to fourth-grade reading level).

__A__ 5. *Vocabulary:* Ability to use a vocabulary that does not appear to be obviously deficient.

__A__ 6. *Computation:* Ability to perform simple math functions (addition and subtraction).

MOTOR-MOBILE ABILITIES

__A__ 7. *Hand-Finger Dexterity:* Ability to use hands and fingers to perform fine motor functions.

__A__ 8. *Use of Upper Extremeties:* Ability to move head, trunk, arms, and hands to use simple hand tools (e.g., a rake).

__A__ 9. *Use of Lower Extremeties:* Ability to use hips, legs, and feet for standing, walking, climbing, lifting, and stooping.

COMMUNICATION ABILITIES

__A__ 10. *Speaking:* Ability to use language to express oneself in normal conversation.

__A__ 11. *Understanding:* Ability to comprehend simple instructions.

SENSORY ABILITIES

_A_ 12. *Vision:* Ability to use vision, with the aid of corrective lenses, in day-to-day living.
_A_ 13. *Hearing:* Ability to hear, with a hearing aid, sounds in the frequency range of normal conversation.
_A_ 14. *Other Senses:* Ability to use touch, taste, smell, and vestibular senses.

GENERAL HEALTH

_A_ 15. *Physical Strength:* Ability to carry heavy objects and operate heavy equipment.
_A_ 16. *Stamina:* Ability to attend to tasks that are able to be performed for a period of eight hours (with breaks and a lunch period).
_A_ 17. *Freedom from Pain:* Free from acute and chronic pain in conducting day-to-day activities.
_A_ 18. *Emotional Stability:* Ability to tolerate routine stress.
_A_ 19. *Consciousness:* Full consciousness is not interrupted by seizures, insulin shock, or other medical problems.

OTHER CONCERNS

___ 20. _____

_____

Remarks  #3 and #4: Mark has a learning disability that limits his ability to read

 and learn from printed material _____

_____

_____

_____

_____

_____

_____

_____

_____

**PART II. DESIRE TO WORK**

*Instructions:* Rate each item according to the following classifications:
   A. Incentive
   B. Possible Disincentive
   C. Disincentive
Describe ratings of B or C in the remarks sections.

_A_ 1. *Perceived Self-Development:* Individual views work as an opportunity for self-development.
_A_ 2. *Desire for Work Activities:* Individual looks forward to spending a good part of the day working at jobs within his or her skill level and qualifications.

**Continued**

**Figure 5-3 Continued**

<u>A</u>  3.  *Willingness to Risk:* Individual is willing to risk the uncertain outcomes of change.

<u>A</u>  4.  *Willingness to Accept Life Change:* Individual is willing to give up present activities to accept a job.

<u>A</u>  5.  *Economic Disincentives:* Individual and significant others are willing to accept the economic changes that will occur if the client takes a job earning wages associated with his or her skill level.

Remarks _____

_____

_____

_____

_____

_____

_____

## PART III. AVAILABILITY TO WORK

*Instructions:* Rate each item according to the following classifications:
   A.  Not a problem
   B.  Somewhat of a problem
   C.  Definite problem
Describe ratings of B or C in the remarks section.

<u>A</u>  1.  *Work Commitments:* Accepting a job would conflict with existing part- or full-time employment

<u>A</u>  2.  *Rehabilitation Schedules:* Accepting a job would conflict with schedules of therapy, education, or training.

<u>A</u>  3.  *Civic and Social Responsibilities:* Accepting a job would conflict with civic and social responsibilities.

<u>A</u>  4.  *Household Responsibilities:* Accepting a job would limit ability to maintain present level of household responsibilities.

<u>C</u>  5.  *Willingness of Significant Others to Accommodate Change:* The significant others (parents, guardians, spouses, children) are willing to accept and support the role changes and the reduced availability of the individual in their lives.

<u>A</u>  6.  *Dependent Care:* Accepting a job would interfere with responsibilities of caring for dependents (e.g., children, parents).

<u>A</u>  7.  *Litigation, Workmen's Compensation, or Subsidy Claims:* Accepting a job would jeopardize pending claims for Workmen's Compensation, Social Security benefits, or other litigation.

<u>B</u>  8.  *Transportation:* Reliable transportation to and from work on a daily basis would be available to the individual.

Remarks ___#5: Mark lives with his mother and two brothers. His mother maintains___

___strong control over all of his decisions. Mark has stated that his mother is very___

___overprotective.___

___#8: Mark must rely on public transportation until he can afford a car.___

_____

_____

_____

## PART IV. ADAPTABILITY TO WORK

*Instructions:* Rate each item according to the following classifications:
   A. Not a Problem
   B. Somewhat of a Problem
   C. Definite Problem
Describe ratings of B or C in the remarks sections.

_A_ 1. *Hygiene:* Individual regularly bathes, brushes teeth, and has clean hands and nails.

_A_ 2. *Grooming:* Individual has hair trimmed and combed, and looks presentable.

_B_ 3. *Clothing:* Individual wears clothing that is clean, neat, and appropriate for the weather.

_A_ 4. *Meeting People:* Individual is capable of meeting new people and establishing friendships.

_A_ 5. *Working with Others:* Individual can work cooperatively with a small group of co-workers.

_A_ 6. *Free of Maladaptive Behavior:* Individual is free of serious maladaptive behaviors such as aggressiveness or inappropriate display of emotions.

## WORK ATTITUDES

_A_ 7. *Understands Employer's Viewpoint:* Individual can understand the needs and concerns of employers.

_A_ 8. *Follows Directions:* Individual will accept guidance and directions from supervisors.

_A_ 9. *Reliability and Punctuality:* Individual will attend work on assigned days, will be on time, and will demonstrate responsibility in completing work assignments.

Remarks ___#3: The clothing Mark has worn to the counseling appointments would be___

___somewhat inappropriate for wearing to job interviews___

_____

_____

_____

_____

_____

**Continued**

**Figure 5-3 Continued**

## PART V. DETERMINING WORK READINESS

*Instructions:* Answer each question with a YES, a NO, or a question mark ("?"). All YES answers indicate that the client is reasonably ready for work. A NO or "?" answer to any of the four questions indicates that either the individual is not ready for work or the individual's level of readiness may not be sufficient to search for employment or to accept a job. If the individual still wishes to pursue employment, intervention strategies should be developed and implemented for all circumstances that lead the evaluator to answer any of the readiness questions with a NO or "?."

_?_ 1. *Abilities:* Does the individual have functional abilities that are acceptable for employment?

_?_ 2. *Desire:* Does the individual desire work activities enough to tolerate the uncertainties and changes that accompany employment transitions?

_?_ 3. *Availability:* Is the individual sufficiently free from competing commitments to hold a job, and does the individual have access to reliable transportation?

_?_ 4. *Adaptability:* Are the individual's appearance, social skills, and work attitudes acceptable for competitive employment?

List the concerns that must be addressed in order to improve the individual's level of work readiness:

1. Search for jobs requiring minimal amounts of reading

2. Teach effective listening skills

3. Include Mark's mother in all planning meetings. Obtain her approval for all employment-seeking decisions.

4. Search for jobs that are accessible by public transportation.

5. Describe the appropriate clothing that should be worn to job interviews.

CONCLUSION: Should work be pursued at this time? _____ Yes _____

# 6

# Removing Employment Barriers

**C**lients are likely to encounter a number of employment barriers throughout the job-search process. These barriers have the potential to interrupt, delay, or prevent clients from achieving their vocational goals. Although it is impossible to predict all of the barriers that jeopardize the ability of clients to obtain a job, there are many employment barriers that can and should be anticipated by clients and professionals. Often, the mere awareness of employment barriers will be enough to avert their frustrating effects. Professionals should use this chapter as a troubleshooting guide to identify potential employment barriers and develop intervention strategies for removing them. Table 6-1 provides an overview of selected barriers to employment and suggested intervention strategies. Some barriers can be removed by applying a little common sense or creativity, whereas others may require the application of one or more of the counseling strategies discussed in Chapter 4. Subsequent sections of this chapter review selected employment barriers and offer advice on how to eliminate them. A case study using the model "Survey of Employment Barriers" form is presented in Figure 6-1, and a remedy using the model "Strategies for Removing Employment Barriers" form is presented in Figure 6-2.

## AMBIVALENCE ABOUT WORKING

There is no reason to assume that people with handicaps have any less ambivalence about wanting to work than people without handicaps. As any employed person can attest, work has both desirable and undesirable features. In addition to taking up most of the day's time, work can bring frustration, fatigue, and personality conflicts. The fact that clients may have health problems, transportation problems, economic disincentives, long periods of unemployment, or

**Table 6-1.** Employment Barriers and Suggested Intervention Strategies

| Employment barriers | Trait & Factor | Cognitive | Behavioral | Systems | Counseling | Job Accommodations |
|---|:---:|:---:|:---:|:---:|:---:|:---:|
| Ambivalence about working | X | X |  | X | X |  |
| Problem work histories | X | X | X |  | X |  |
| Vocational self-concepts | X | X |  |  | X | X |
| Low self-esteem |  | X | X | X | X |  |
| Work attitudes | X | X | X | X | X |  |
| Poor appearance |  | X | X | X | X |  |
| Social skills |  |  | X | X | X |  |
| Independent-living skills |  |  | X | X | X | X |
| Self-management skills |  |  | X | X | X |  |
| Basic academic skills | X |  | X |  | X | X |
| Avoidance behaviors |  | X | X |  | X |  |
| Transportation |  |  | X | X | X | X |
| Care of dependents |  |  |  | X | X |  |
| Economic disincentives | X |  |  | X | X |  |
| Social support |  | X |  | X | X |  |
| Visibility of handicap |  |  | X |  | X |  |
| Employer perceptions |  | X | X |  | X |  |

**Figure 6-1. Case study: survey of employment barriers**

# SURVEY OF EMPLOYMENT BARRIERS

Client _____ Bill Xxxxxxxx _____ Date ___ 9/7/87 ___

Organization _____ Staff Member _____

*Instructions:* Rate each employment barrier according to one of the following classifications:
  A.  Not a Barrier
  B.  Somewhat of a Barrier or a Potential Barrier
  C.  Definite Barrier

A strategy for removing employment barriers should be developed and implemented for ratings of B or C.

## INDIVIDUAL — ATTITUDE

  A  1.  *Ambivalence about Working:* Individual has mixed feelings about taking a job at this time.

  C  2.  *Problem Work Histories:* Individual has no work history, long periods of unemployment, or an unstable career pattern consisting of a variety of unrelated jobs.

  A  3.  *Vocational Self-Concept:* Individual has no sense of identification with any occupation or career field.

  A  4.  *Low Self-Esteem:* Individual seems to be affected by low self-esteem.

  A  5.  *Work Attitudes:* Individual has attitudes about work that would not be acceptable to most employers.

## INDIVIDUAL — BEHAVIOR

  A  6.  *Appearance:* Individual's hygiene, grooming, or manner of dress would be unacceptable to most employers.

  A  7.  *Social Skills:* Individual would have difficulty working harmoniously with other people, or individual displays behavior that would be unacceptable at most worksites.

  A  8.  *Independent-Living Skills:* Individual is unable to care for self (i.e., bathing, toileting, dressing) or has difficulty functioning in the community (food shopping, cooking, caring for clothes).

  A  9.  *Self Management Skills:* Individual has difficulty managing self by organizing tasks, by making decisions, by budgeting time, or by attending to tasks until they are completed.

  A  10.  *Basic Academic Skills:* Individual has difficulty with basic reading, writing, or computation skills.

  A  11.  *Avoidance Behavior:* Individual tends to avoid situations and behaviors that are likely to lead to positive changes.

**Continued**

**Figure 6-1 Continued**

EXTERNAL — SITUATIONAL

_B_ 12. *Transportation:* Individual does not have reliable transportation.

_B_ 13. *Care of Dependents:* Individual has primary responsibility of caring for children, aging parents, or other dependents.

_B_ 14. *Economic Disincentives:* Individual will lose some form of financial subsidy as a result of taking a job.

_A_ 15. *Social Support:* Individual is not likely to receive needed support (moral, emotional, financial, general help) from important others.

EXTERNAL — EMPLOYER

_A_ 16. *Visibility of Handicap:* Individual's handicap would be obvious to employment interviewers.

_A_ 17. *Negative Perceptions Among Employers:* Individual has experienced or anticipates negative perceptions among potential employers.

OTHER

___ 18. _____

_____

_____

Figure 6-2. Case study: strategies for removing employment barriers

# STRATEGIES FOR REMOVING EMPLOYMENT BARRIERS

Client _____Bill Xxxxxxxx_____ Date ____9/7/87____

Organization _____ Staff Member _____

*Instructions:* Complete this form for each barrier that was rated B or C on the Survey of Employment Barriers.

## PART I. DESCRIPTION

Description of Employment Barrier __Since Bill has been unemployed, he has__ __assumed child-care responsibilities while his wife worked. They will need someone__ __to care for their children when they return home from school.__

## PART II. STRATEGIES TO REMOVE BARRIER

*Instructions:* Check the strategies to be used in developing plans for removing the employment barrier: ( ) Trait and Factor, ( ) Cognitive, ( ) Behavioral, ( ) Systems, (x) Counseling, and ( ) Job Accommodations.

1) Bill will explore various latchkey programs that exist in the school district and community.

2) Bill's mother will watch the children until they obtain extended child-care alternatives.

3) Bill will ask neighbors with children in the same school if he can pay them to watch the children until he or is wife return home from work.

no employment histories would suggest that they are likely to have ambivalent feelings about working. To maximize their chances for success, professionals need to assist clients in examining their ambivalence and in planning strategies to remove it. In some cases, their ambivalence may cause clients to postpone their search for employment. For example, one client who was receiving employment counseling was in the middle of litigation over a work-related injury. After examining her fear that obtaining a job might jeopardize her settlement, she decided that she would not begin her search for employment until the litigation was settled. The following are suggested intervention strategies for addressing ambivalence about working.

☐ Help clients appreciate that their ambivalence is normal, and encourage them to explore their thoughts and the circumstances that may be causing it. They may have good reasons for feeling ambivalent (e.g., concerns about health, safety, finances, or effect on significant others).

☐ Have clients use a notebook as a journal to record thoughts and ideas that come to them as insights during times of reflection or frustration.

☐ Use the empty-chair technique (discussed in Chapter 4) to externalize private logic or conflicting thoughts that may be at the root of their mixed feelings. Encourage them to develop a dialogue between opposing sides of themselves, such as their *yes* sides dialoguing with their *no* sides or their *I-want-to* sides dialoguing with their *I-can't* sides.

☐ Use the model "Work-Readiness Assessment" form to identify potential constraints that may be contributing to their ambivalence.

☐ Have clients complete sociograms to identify the significant others in their lives, and have them use the role-reversal technique (discussed in Chapter 4) to obtain their perceptions of how other people feel about them working.

☐ Use a vocational–career assessment to help resolve doubts about clients' vocational–career choices.

☐ Once the sources of ambivalence are identified, assist clients with decision making, planning, and problem solving.

☐ Identify other employment barriers and review strategies for removing them.

## PROBLEM WORK HISTORIES

A common barrier occurs when clients have less-than-perfect work histories. They may have a pattern of job hopping, may have gotten fired from jobs, may have quit jobs, may have long periods of unemployment, or may have no work histories. There are a variety of ways to interpret these past experiences. Some are self-enhancing, others are self-defeating. For example, one client had been unemployed for eight years as a result of his epilepsy. He felt that this long absence from work would ruin any chance for future employment. Therefore, he began to accept this perception as an unfortunate life situation. Although he thought about working, he never actually applied for a job because he assumed employers would consider the long period of unemployment as an indication that he was unmotivated. When the counselor reviewed the history of his illness, it was found that he had been a dedicated worker for ten years prior to the time when his condition deteriorated. Two years before beginning the employment counseling program, a change in his medication resulted in his becoming seizure free.

The counselor suggested a more positive, as well as more accurate, interpretation of his work history (i.e., he was a good worker who was disabled for a period of time and who was now rehabilitated and thus ready to return to work). His unemployment was reinterpreted as a positive work characteristic because he now thought of himself as being "hungry" for work. By exchanging the self-defeating attitude for a self-enhancing attitude the client was able to see himself in a more positive light. He was then able to actively participate in a search for employment. It is important to note that regardless of how obvious the perceptual problems appear to professionals, clients will not have positive behavioral changes until they personally experience the cognitions as insights. This often occurs to clients as an "aha" experience. These new insights can generate enormous amounts of energy and new found enthusiasm. The following are suggested intervention strategies for addressing problem work histories.

- ☐ Point out how negative interpretations are self-defeating, and attempt to characterize clients' work histories from a self-enhancing point of view.
- ☐ Explain to clients that when faced with a variety of interpretations, realities are merely selected perceptions. In choosing perceptions, it would be to their advantage to choose self-enhancing or positive perceptions over self-defeating or negative perceptions. Choosing positive interpretations of their lives, in itself, demonstrates a positive outlook.
- ☐ Find some turning point that gives clients a new beginning in their vocational life (e.g., change in health, completion of training, change in life responsibilities).
- ☐ Administer a vocational–career assessment to clients who have a considerable amount of job hopping in their work histories. Use the vocational decisions resulting from the assessment as a turning point for further career direction and development.
- ☐ Inform clients that an absence of work experience is not always a disadvantage. Some employers prefer to train their own personnel.

☐ Inform clients that work attitudes are often more important than work experience. This is especially true for unskilled and semiskilled jobs. Work attitudes affecting attendance, punctuality, reliability, and honesty are often of greater concern to employers than experience in these types of jobs.

☐ Remind clients who are fearful of working without supervision that without experience, they are not likely to be hired for jobs that require them to work independently.

☐ Have clients rehearse verbal descriptions of their work histories until they are comfortable with its truthfulness and with the verbal presentation.

## VOCATIONAL SELF-CONCEPTS

A vocational self-concept is the perception of self in a work role that is learned through vocational socialization. These self-concepts are acquired through a complex process that involves being aware of occupations and learning to identify with selected work roles. Vocational self-concepts serve as barriers to employment when they are incongruent with clients' projected work roles. For example, clients who view themselves as being shy would have self-concepts that are incongruent with the work role of a salesperson. Such incongruencies have a tendency to neutralize job-search activities. Some individuals, especially those who are economically disadvantaged, will have difficulty identifying with some work roles because they have little firsthand knowledge of people working in those roles. Individuals with handicaps, especially those with severe handicaps, have relatively little opportunity to view successful role models who are similarly handicapped. Professionals assisting clients with poorly defined vocational self-concepts, or self-concepts that are incongruent with targeted work roles, should appreciate that changing self-concepts is more of a process than an event. Consequently, clients will need time and assistance in exploring new ways of looking at themselves. The following are suggested intervention strategies for addressing problems related to vocational self-concept.

☐ Inform clients that effective career choices involve selecting career options based on their unique profiles of employability.

☐ Introduce clients to a simple career-classification system. Have them review the want ads from a local newspaper and classify jobs into categories requiring people to work with data, people, or things. Have them identify their likes and dislikes for five or six types of jobs.

☐ Conduct a thorough vocational–career assessment, measuring such variables as interests, abilities, and personality traits. The summary profile should be matched with career alternatives that are congruent with client profiles. Try to identify career-related themes that have remained consistent within those profiles over time.

☐ Review job modification and accommodation products that may extend the range of client functioning, thereby increasing the number of career options.

## LOW SELF-ESTEEM

Low self-esteem is manifested in self-doubt and social withdrawal. Individuals with low self-esteem seem excessively self-conscious, seem critical of their own behavior, and believe that others think poorly of them. Low self-esteem becomes a barrier to employment when it prevents clients from initiating activities that lead to positive vocational adjustments. Clients often drop out of training programs because they assume no one will hire them. One such client gave an estimate of his low self-esteem by saying, "If I were an employer, I wouldn't hire me." Such low self-esteem may be deeply rooted within the self-perceptions of clients, and it may cause them to be resistant to intervention, especially short-term intervention. It is important to remember that a primary objective of vocational counseling is not to resolve self-esteem problems completely, but to limit the interfering effect they may have on clients' abilities to obtain and maintain employment. The following are suggested intervention strategies for addressing low self-esteem.

☐ It may be helpful to facilitate an emotional venting of feelings by encouraging clients to talk about how they feel about themselves.

☐ Use the empty-chair technique (discussed in Chapter 4) to explore the private logic and thinking patterns that may be contributing to the low self-esteem of clients. Using this technique, have them dialogue between their *employable* self and their *unemployable* self.

☐ Have clients identify the significant others in their lives, and have them use the role-reversal technique (discussed in Chapter 4) to describe themselves as well as the roles of their significant others. Develop plans to minimize the effect of others who may be contributing to clients' self-esteem problems.

☐ Point out how clients' negative self-evaluations are minimizing their successes and predisposing them to failure.

☐ Plan employment-related activities in very small steps. Use behavioral contracts discussed in Chapter 4 to obtain a commitment to completing specific tasks by specific dates. Offer positive feedback for successfully completing those tasks.

☐ Present clients with positive perceptions of themselves

and of their adaptive behaviors. Reinforce those perceptions frequently.

☐ Request that clients telephone specified professionals when they feel like giving up their search for employment. A behavior contract may be used to achieve these commitments.

☐ Remind clients that seeking employment is basically a negative experience for everyone. Encourage them to focus on the completion of activities that will ultimately lead to positive outcomes, rather than focusing on the outcomes themselves.

## WORK ATTITUDES

Positive work attitudes are a necessity in a competitive labor market. When an abundance of applicants have the necessary work skills, positive work attitudes often differentiate those who will get hired from those who will remain unemployed. Undesirable work attitudes are those that lead to absenteeism, tardiness, unreliability, indifference, lack of trust, and poor work performance. Again, the objective is not to provide counseling to change personalities, but to help clients understand how they are predisposing themselves to failure. In this way, clients can explore more adaptive ways of viewing employment. The following are suggested interventions for promoting positive work attitudes.

☐ Evaluate clients' vocational socialization experiences and work ethics by reviewing their attitudes about their educational and work experiences. If possible, examine the education and work histories of clients' significant others.

☐ Describe how clients' work attitudes can limit chances for success.

☐ Encourage clients to view work as a means of self-development in which they can pursue desired growth through selected work experiences.

☐ Help clients to obtain a sense of life and career direction through a vocational–career assessment, followed by a matching of client profiles with congruent career alternatives.

☐ Make video or audio recordings of role-played employment interviews or work situations. Use the role-reversal technique (discussed in Chapter 4), by having clients review the recordings as if they were employers evaluating potential employees.

☐ Use behavioral contracts (discussed in Chapter 4) to obtain commitments to control undesirable behaviors.

## POOR APPEARANCE

Individuals whose poor appearance causes them to stand out in a crowd will be screened out early in the employment selection process. Most may not even get an opportunity to discuss their qualifications. Often, individuals fail to care for themselves. They may not bathe regularly. They may fail to brush their teeth, or groom their hair. They may wear unclean and unkempt clothing, or dress inappropriately. The self-care of individuals who are not part of the mainstream of society can sometimes deteriorate over time due to the lack of feedback regarding their appearance. The following are suggested intervention strategies for addressing poor appearance.

- ☐ When appropriate, offer clients honest feedback about their poor appearance. Explain how poor appearance is likely to be unacceptable to employers and is therefore likely to eliminate their chances of obtaining employment.
- ☐ Rate clients' appearance in all relevant categories as either acceptable or unacceptable. Provide descriptions of acceptable levels of appearance in areas that are presently unacceptable.
- ☐ When appropriate, inform clients' significant others about their poor appearance, especially if those important others are partially responsible for maintaining the appearance of clients.
- ☐ Make video or audio recordings of role-played employment interviews. Have clients review the recordings as potential employers evaluating themselves for employment.
- ☐ Have clients sign behavioral contracts to obtain commitments to improve self-care as needed.
- ☐ Have clients participate in dress rehearsals for employment interviews. Provide the necessary feedback and instruction to improve their appearance.

## SOCIAL SKILLS

A primary concern in the area of client social skills is the self-control of destructive, disruptive, aggressive, or other forms of unacceptable behavior. Such behaviors will restrict or eliminate clients' chances in the competitive labor market. It is also important for individuals to be able to accept the authority of supervisors, receive directions or criticisms, ask for help or information, and work cooperatively with fellow workers. The following are suggested intervention strategies for promoting positive social skills.

☐ Make a list of the undesirable behaviors a client must eliminate and the adaptive social behaviors he or she must acquire before being considered employable.

☐ Model appropriate social skills for work situations that require clients to control undesirable behavior (such as feeling angry when disciplined) and situations that require adaptive social skills (such as saying good morning).

☐ Have clients rehearse modeled adaptive social skills. Provide instruction and positive feedback for acquiring appropriate behaviors.

☐ Encourage clients and their significant others to record their progress, and provide positive reinforcement for demonstrating desired behaviors.

☐ Use behavioral contracting to facilitate the acquisition and maintenance of designed behaviors.

## INDEPENDENT LIVING SKILLS

Individuals working in the competitive labor market must have the independent living skills of caring for themselves and functioning within their communities. Clients who are limited in these abilities will need to acquire new skills and develop support systems from important others or community services. In some cases, clients must seek out employers who are willing to provide accommodations for their special needs. The following are suggested intervention strategies for promoting independent living skills.

☐ Make a list of the self-care and community-living skills needed for clients to become employable. Identify those skills that serve as barriers to employment.

☐ Identify independent-living skills that clients can acquire through learning. Professionals can model desired behaviors and have clients rehearse these skills (such as preparing lunches or clothing for work). Provide reinforcement schedules where appropriate.

☐ Identify potential resources among clients' significant others and social service agencies within the community. Request help from significant others (such as help with self-care or money management) and social service agencies (such as transportation or interpreters for individuals with hearing impairments).

☐ Search for job openings among employers that already have the necessary physical accommodations for individuals with orthopedic handicaps (such as wide doorways and bathrooms with wide stalls and bars).

## SELF-MANAGEMENT SKILLS

Self-management skills refer to the skills of making decisions, gathering information, organizing tasks, budgeting time, and attending to tasks until they are completed. Some clients have had little opportunity to develop self-management skills because their parents or guardians have found it easier to take care of their business for them, rather than training them to do it themselves. These skills are needed by clients to manage the complexities of seeking, obtaining, and maintaining employment. Clients limited in these skills often become overwhelmed and confused by the complexities associated with situations of change. This confusion results in anxiety and uncertainty that, in turn, causes them to retreat to more familiar environments and routines. The following are suggested intervention strategies for promoting self-management skills.

☐ Encourage clients to take an active part in the decision making and planning that affects their lives. Give recommendations to clients as well as to their significant others.

☐ Teach clients self-management skills through daily activities. Select goals, plan activities, and set dates for the completion of activities.

☐ Have clients make notes on all interviews and meetings. They should write summaries that will be reviewed by professionals.

☐ Plan activities in small steps. Use behavioral contracts (discussed in Chapter 4) to encourage clients to complete specific activities by specific dates.

☐ Encourage clients to develop weekly and daily checklists of self-management activities. Have them reward themselves for completing activities as planned.

☐ Have clients request support from their significant others, and encourage them to conduct similar self-management activities with home responsibilities.

## BASIC ACADEMIC SKILLS

The abilities to read, write, and perform basic computations are required in many occupations. In addition to serving as a barrier to performing in some jobs, the lack of basic skills can impair the ability to search for employment. For example, completing job applications requires individuals to read and write, and using public transportation requires clients to count money and tell time. The following are suggested intervention strategies for addressing basic academic skills.

☐ Insure that clients apply for jobs that do not require considerable academic skills.

☐ Whenever possible, encourage client to use résumés or letters of application to apply for jobs. Where applications are required, clients should obtain and complete applications before visiting the employer to apply for the job. Professionals or significant others should assist clients in completing job applications.

☐ In some cases, restructure job requirements to accommodate clients' academic deficiencies.

☐ For clients who cannot read, use pictures or drawings to describe job tasks and the sequence in which they should be completed.

☐ Record job instructions on audio or video tapes.

☐ When appropriate, encourage clients to receive remedial instruction in areas of deficiency.

## AVOIDANCE BEHAVIOR

As an employment barrier, avoidance behavior refers to the tendency of individuals to consistently avoid circumstances or behaviors that are likely to lead to positive vocational adjustments. Such individuals may participate in the employment-seeking program until it is actually time to apply for a job, when clients find other responsibilities more important than the task at hand. It may not become apparent that individuals are avoiding these situations until a pattern begins to develop. For example, one client enrolled in a job search program participated in all aspects of the program except one: He never applied for a job. Whenever the counselor requested that he apply for specific jobs, he presented an excuse for not applying and would often absent himself from his next appointment. After confronting him about his avoidance behavior, counselors learned that he felt extremely insecure in job interviews. The counselor and the client role-played interviews until he felt more comfortable expressing himself. The following are suggested intervention strategies for addressing avoidance behavior.

☐ Explore the reasons motivating the avoidance behavior by using the strategies suggested in the previous section, "Ambivalence About Working."

☐ Attempt to break the cycle or pattern of avoidance behavior by selecting a single task that is relatively easy to complete, and write a behavioral contract (discussed in Chapter 4) with positive rewards for completion and negative rewards for failing to complete the task.

☐ Explain to clients how anxiety can be reduced by completing tasks rather than avoiding them.

☐ Have clients learn relaxation techniques to control anxiety that may be contributing to avoidance behavior.

☐ Provide assertiveness training if their avoidance behavior involves difficulty in expressing themselves.

## TRANSPORTATION

Not having reliable transportation to and from work is commonly encountered, and it is an often-overlooked employment barrier for individuals with handicaps. Clients will sometimes search for employment without exploring the transportation alternatives available to them. Transportation resources may limit the geographic area in which clients can search for employment. The following are suggested intervention strategies for addressing transportation problems.

☐ It is critically important to examine clients' transportation needs and resources before they begin the search for employment.

☐ Explore transportation resources among significant others, community agencies, and public transportation agencies, and explore car-pooling among selected employers. Public forms of transportation are required by law to make their services accessible to the handicapped.

☐ If transportation will be provided by significant others, explore the degree of commitment they are willing to make to clients. It is perhaps too large a commitment to provide daily transportation for an indefinite period of time. They may wish to provide transportation for a limited period of time until other more stable means can be established.

☐ Insure that clients relying on public transportation are familiar with pick-up locations, time schedules, procedures for paying for services, exit stops, and directions from drop-off locations to worksites. Some clients will need to transfer between buses or use several sources of transportation.

☐ In some cases, geographical location will be the deciding factor in determining which companies are approached for employment.

☐ Clients may have significant others who live close to places of employment or public transportation. In such cases, relocation may be desirable.

## CARE OF DEPENDENTS

It is not uncommon for unemployed individuals with handicaps to acquire the home responsibilities of caring for family dependents. They may care for children, parents, or other family members. These responsibilities may prevent clients from accepting employment. The central problem is that clients often find it difficult to shift these responsibilities to other family members. The problem can be further complicated because quality personal care may be expensive or difficult to find. The following are suggested intervention strategies for addressing problems related to care of dependents.

☐ Make plans for alternate care of dependents before conducting the search for employment.

☐ Explore the resources for care among significant others, neighbors, private sources, and community service agencies. Check the yellow pages under "Child Care," "Day Nurseries," and "Home Health Services."

☐ Examine the attitudes and willingness of significant others to accept the responsibility of caring for dependents when clients obtain employment. They may support the client's vocational aspirations, but they may remain reluctant to alter their own lives to accommodate these aspirations.

☐ Establish alternate resources for unexpected situations or emergencies. For example, someone will need to care for dependent children who are unable to attend their regular day-nursery because of illness.

## ECONOMIC DISINCENTIVES

Clients receiving income from such economic subsidies as Social Security Disability Insurance, unemployment compensation, or Workmen's Compensation often express serious concerns about the economic effect of accepting employment. Because they fear the loss of a primary source of income and health benefits, they may be reluctant even to let anyone know that they are considering employment. Significant others may be concerned that income received from subsidies will be lost when clients obtain employment. This is especially true for clients whose employability is questionable. Clients waiting for the outcome of litigation or of claims from Workmen's Compensation or Social Security often fear they may jeopardize potential awards. The following are suggested intervention strategies for addressing economic disincentives.

☐ Respect the need of clients and significant others to protect their income. This money is often an essential and reliable source of family income.

☐ Insure that clients and their family members are fully informed about the specific details of the economic effects of accepting employment (e.g., when probationary periods begin and end, procedures for refiling claims, and the time it will take before subsidies are reestablished).

☐ Decide whether this is the appropriate time to search for employment. Clients waiting for the outcomes of disability or other claims may wish to postpone the job search until their claims have been decided.

☐ Evaluate the level of earned income that will be needed to replace their economic subsidies. The Social Security Administration offers probationary periods of up to nine months for disabled people to try out employment without jeopardizing their income. Call the local Social Security office for details.

☐ Evaluate the nonmonetary value of accepting employment (e.g., sense of purpose, personal growth, social involvement) as well as the monetary effect of accepting employment.

## SOCIAL SUPPORT

The life roles of clients and those of their significant others are intricately synchronized because changes in the lives of clients result in corresponding changes in the lives of significant others. Although these people may support the vocational adjustments sought by clients, they may not have thought about how their own lives will be affected when clients obtain employment. A lack of support or an overt display of reluctance at the right time can undermine all efforts to obtain employment. Clients may rely on significant others for food, housing, clothing, transportation, money, and emotional support. Conversely, clients may be relied on for house cleaning, running errands, and caring for children or aging relatives. Therefore, consent, or at least approval and support, should be sought from the people who are important to clients. The following are suggested intervention strategies for gaining social support.

☐ Use a sociogram (discussed in Chapter 4) to identify the significant others in the lives of clients. Identify those who must consent or approve of changes sought by clients.

☐ Use the role-reversal technique (discussed in Chapter 4) to estimate how significant others will react to the changes that will occur when clients become employed. When playing the role of each important other, the client might be asked, "How will your life change when _____ (client's name) obtains a job?"

☐ Include significant others, who must approve of client life changes, in the job-search planning.

☐ Enlist the support of significant others by encouraging clients to ask for help.

☐ Mail letters to the significant others requesting support for clients. A form letter, "Someone Needs Your Support!" is modeled in Figure 6-3.

## VISIBILITY OF HANDICAP

Handicaps such as paraplegia are obvious to others and can impair the ability to search for a job more than they impair the ability to hold one. Clients with less visible impairments are usually uncertain about when to tell potential employers of their handicaps. They fear that they will be eliminated from consideration if they include information about their handicaps on résumés or applications. However, if they wait until they meet with prospective employers at the job interview, the employer may react with surprise that they were not told previously. The objective is to avoid surprising employers by providing information about clients' handicaps in a way that will not result in their being screened out of the interviewing process. The following are suggested intervention strategies for addressing this issue.

☐ Do not include information about clients' handicaps on their résumés unless they are applying for positions under a special handicap-hiring program.

☐ Present clients' profiles of employability as the primary rationale for employment consideration.

☐ Inform potential employers about a handicap just prior to the job interview. After employers arrange the job interview, have the client telephone employers the day before the interview to confirm the date, time, and location. After confirming the information, clients should tell employers of their handicap. For example, they might say, "I want to tell you that I have an orthopedic handicap. I walk with the aid of crutches and braces. However, I assure you that it will have no effect on my work or my attendance record. I'm telling you now to avoid surprising you at the interview. Please feel free to ask me any questions about how my handicap might affect my work performance."

**Figure 6-3. <u>Someone needs your support</u> form letter**

## SOMEONE NEEDS YOUR SUPPORT!

Person's Name: _____ Mary Xxxxxx _____

The person whose name appears above is participating in our employment seeking program. This person has indicated that you are a very important person (VIP) to them. As you probably know, searching for employment is not an easy task. It is a time filled with hopes, fears, and frustrations. People seeking employment need all the help and support they can get. As a VIP you can help to influence this person's outcome by providing help and support.

The help and support needed by this person include:

**1. Providing transportation:** This person may need a reliable source of transportation.

**2. Freeing them from commitments:** This person may need additional free time from existing responsibilities for searching for a job and holding a job once they find one.

**3. Financial support:** This person may need additional money for the expenses of searching for employment (i.e., postage, printing, materials, clothing).

**4. Writing assistance:** This person may help in completing applications and preparing correspondence.

**5. Clerical assistance:** This person may need help with typing, preparing mailings, and keeping records of employer contacts.

**6. Gathering information:** This person may need help in reading want ads, preparing lists of potential employers, or telephoning employers.

**7. Emotional support:** This person may need to talk-out his or her frustrations and feelings with a trusted friend.

You can take pride in the fact that this person considers you a very important person. On behalf of this person, I thank you for your help and support.

Sincerely,

Staff Member: _____ Mr. John Bxxxxx _____

Organization: _____ Career Services, Inc. _____

## NEGATIVE PERCEPTIONS AMONG EMPLOYERS

Clients should be prepared to encounter employers who believe that people with impairments or disabilities are unemployable. Such perceptions are often the result of a lack of information. In many instances, employers lack information about limitations associated with handicaps, work potentials of workers with handicaps, how hiring workers with handicaps may affect their insurance rates, and how they might cost-effectively accommodate clients at their worksites. Because some employers may assume that people with handicaps are very fragile, they may be unable to question clients in a direct and open manner, thereby limiting their access to appropriate information. The following are suggested intervention strategies for addressing negative perceptions among employers.

☐ Separate client assumptions from their actual experiences by evaluating the actual volume of job applications they have completed. If clients assume employers will reject them, they may not apply for jobs at all, or they may give up after making just a few applications.

☐ Remind clients that almost all applications for employment result in negative responses. It happens to all job seekers, not just disabled ones. Encourage clients to focus their attention on completing tasks that are likely to lead to obtaining employment, rather than focusing on the outcome of their activities.

☐ Approach employer attitudes with the assumption that negative attitudes toward people with handicaps are the result of limited information and fear. Approaching the problem from this viewpoint requires clients to communicate with employers to provide information and to comfort their fears. Approaching the problem from the viewpoint that people with handicaps are simply unwanted leads to inactivity and withdrawal.

☐ It is important for employers to get to know the people behind the handicaps. Clients must assume the primary responsibility of communicating with potential employers. They may need to learn to express themselves by sharing appropriate information in appropriate ways. Professionals may need to provide additional information as well as encouraging other people to support their clients.

☐ Identify and get to know the employers in selected segments of the labor market by networking. Clients should learn the networking strategies described in Chapter 10.

☐ Explain that some employers will not be open to hiring workers with handicaps, whereas others will. Bolles (1985) pointed out that there are just two types of employers: those who will hire you and those who will not hire you. To obtain employment, it is necessary to approach enough employers to find those who will hire disabled clients.

☐ Help clients anticipate the potential concerns employers are likely to have about their employability. Develop solutions to anticipated employer barriers before beginning job searches or placement activities.

☐ Prepare the client for job interviews by summarizing the profiles of their qualifications and the solutions to anticipated problems. Chapter 9 provides information on preparing for job interviews.

☐ Prepare clients to talk about their handicaps, especially if their handicaps are visible to job interviewers. Assume employers have questions. If employers do not ask questions about obvious handicaps, have clients raise the issue and discuss the effects their handicaps will have on their employability. They should address such employer concerns as job accommodations, attendance, stamina, work rate, work quality, and safety as these concerns relate to the position for which they are being considered.

# 7

# Selecting Employment Objectives

The Olympus Research Corporation's (1973) study of employer usage of want ads reported that as few as 15% of the employers studied hired people through help wanted advertisements. These results, which are widely accepted by job-search authorities, suggest that if employment seekers are using want ads as their only method of searching for a job, they may be overlooking as many as 85% of the jobs that are available at any given time. To further diminish clients' chances of obtaining a job, want ads attract very large numbers of applicants, hundreds in many cases.

In a competitive labor market, employers often have an adequate supply of qualified workers applying for their jobs without recruiting applicants through such paid advertisements. Although applying for advertised job vacancies is still a valid strategy for obtaining employment, searching among employers who do not advertise their vacancies will provide employment seekers the greatest number of opportunities for finding jobs. Job search authors Jackson and Mayleas (1981) referred to these unadvertised job vacancies in the title of their book, *The Hidden Job Market for the Eighties*.

The selection of an employment objective provides job seekers with the opportunity to develop directed strategies for locating jobs among employers who do not advertise their vacancies. An employment objective should include a job title, industrial classification, and geographical location. For example, a person might have the objective of finding a position as an automotive mechanic (job title) in a new car dealership (industrial classification) in northeast Pennsylvania (geographical location). This person will have a specific plan of action for finding unadvertised vacancies and will not have to rely on those few employers who recruit employees through want ads. In addition to providing direction for the employment seeker, there are other benefits to selecting an employment objective: careful assessment of client employability insures that clients are qualified for the jobs they are seeking, and applying for jobs that are not advertised implicitly suggests that clients are motivated to work.

Employment opportunities exist in occupational groups that can be found in a variety of industries. These job vacancies may exist because employers must replace employees who have vacated their jobs or because new positions have been created to accommodate growth in the industry. The U.S. Bureau of Labor Statistics (Personick, 1985; Silvestri & Lukasiewicz, 1985) reported on the current status and future projections of labor market needs. Table 7-1 lists total 1984 employment statistics by major occupational group and industrial classification.

The Bureau of Labor Statistics (Silvestri & Lukasiewicz, 1985) identified the 37 most-available occupations that are estimated to account for approximately one-half of all job growth between 1984 and 1995. About one-fourth of the occupations generally require a college degree, which is approximately the same proportion found among all jobs in the economy. Table 7-2 lists those 37 occupations and indicates the general industrial classifications in which they are likely to be found. This data can be used to help clients plan for

## Table 7-1. 1984 Employment

| Employment by Occupational Group | % |
| --- | --- |
| Executive, administrative, and managerial workers | 10.6 |
| Professional workers | 12.0 |
| Technical and related support | 3.0 |
| Salesworkers | 10.5 |
| Administrative support workers, including clerical | 17.5 |
| Private household workers | .9 |
| Service workers, except private household workers | 14.6 |
| Precision production, craft and repair workers | 11.4 |
| Operators, fabricators and laborers | 16.2 |
| Farming, forestry, and fishing workers | 3.3 |

| Employment by Industrial Classification | % |
| --- | --- |
| Agriculture | 3.1 |
| Government | 15.0 |
| Mining | .6 |
| Construction | 5.5 |
| Manufacturing | 18.5 |
| Transportation, communications, and public utilities | 5.1 |
| Wholesale and retail trade | 22.7 |
| Finance, insurance, and real estate | 5.9 |
| Services | 22.4 |
| Private households | 1.2 |

Data from Silvestri and Lukasiewicz (1985) and from Personick (1985).

# Table 7-2. Thirty-Seven Most-Available Jobs by Industry[a]

| Most-available jobs | A | B | C | D | E | F | G | H | I | J |
|---|---|---|---|---|---|---|---|---|---|---|
| Cashiers | — | — | — | — | — | F[b] | G | — | — | — |
| Registered nurses | — | — | — | — | — | — | — | — | I | — |
| Janitors and cleaners | — | — | — | D | E | F | G | H | I | J |
| Truckdrivers | a | b | c | D | E | f | g | — | i | — |
| Waiters and waitresses | — | — | — | — | — | — | G | — | I | — |
| Wholesale trade sales workers | — | — | — | — | — | F | — | — | — | — |
| Nursing aides, orderlies, attendants | — | — | — | — | — | — | — | — | I | — |
| Salesworkers, retail | — | — | — | — | — | — | G | — | — | — |
| Accountants and auditors | a | b | c | D | e | f | g | H | I | J |
| Kindergarten and elementary teachers | — | — | — | — | — | — | — | — | I | — |
| Secretaries | a | b | c | D | E | F | G | H | I | J |
| Computer programmers | a | b | c | D | e | F | G | H | I | J |
| General office clerks | a | b | c | D | E | F | G | H | I | J |
| Food-preparation workers, excluding fast food | — | — | — | D | — | — | G | — | — | — |
| Food preparation, fast food | — | — | — | — | — | — | G | — | — | — |
| Computer systems analysts, electronic data processing | a | b | c | D | e | F | G | H | I | J |
| Electrical and electronic engineers | — | — | — | D | e | — | — | — | i | — |
| Electrical and electronic technicians | — | — | — | D | e | — | g | — | I | — |
| Guards | — | — | — | D | e | F | G | h | I | j |
| Automotive and motorcycle mechanics | — | — | — | — | — | — | g | — | — | — |
| Lawyers | — | — | — | d | — | — | — | h | I | J |
| Cosmetologists and related workers | — | — | — | — | — | — | — | — | I | — |
| Cooks, restaurant | — | — | — | — | — | — | G | — | — | — |
| Maintenance repairers, general utility | — | — | — | D | — | — | — | — | — | — |
| Bookkeeping, accounting, and auditing clerks | a | b | c | D | E | F | G | H | I | J |
| Bartenders | — | — | — | — | — | — | G | — | I | — |
| Computer operators, excluding peripheral equipment | a | b | c | D | E | F | G | H | I | J |
| Physicians and surgeons | — | — | — | — | — | — | — | — | I | — |
| Licensed practical nurses | — | — | — | — | — | — | — | — | I | — |
| Carpenters | — | — | C | D | — | — | — | — | — | — |
| Switchboard operators | — | — | — | — | E | — | G | H | I | J |
| Food service and lodging managers | — | — | — | — | — | — | — | — | I | — |
| Electricians | — | — | C | D | E | — | — | — | I | — |
| Teacher aides and educational assistants | — | — | — | — | — | — | — | — | I | — |
| Blue-collar worker supervisors | — | — | c | D | e | — | — | — | — | — |
| Receptionists and information clerks | — | — | — | D | E | F | G | H | I | J |
| Mechanical engineers | — | — | — | D | — | — | — | — | i | j |

[a]Industry key:
A —Agriculture, forestry, and fishing
B —Mining
C—Construction
D—Manufacturing
E —Transportation, communications, electric, gas, and sanitary services
F —Wholesale trade
G—Retail trade
H —Finance, insurance, and real estate
I —Services
J —Public administration
[b]Upper case letters indicates higher concentrations of these employees
Data from Silvestri and Lukasiewicz (1985).

employment searches for the listed occupations as well as to demonstrate how to select employment objectives.

This chapter provides the necessary information for helping clients select employment objectives. It includes sections on developing profiles of employability, selecting specific jobs to pursue in the search, and targeting industries for the job search. It also provides information on jobs held by people with handicaps and lists possible occupations for selected handicapped groups.

## DEVELOPING A PROFILE OF EMPLOYABILITY

Individuals have a variety of reasons for choosing the jobs they pursue in their employment searches. Some clients choose jobs that are advertised, some choose jobs that pay well, some choose jobs they have heard about through friends, and some do not choose at all. The objective of developing a profile of employability is to highlight client information that will identify the employment alternatives to be pursued in the job search. Generally speaking, the most reliable vocational choices are made by matching the unique traits of clients with corresponding job requirements. Figure 7-1 presents a graphic

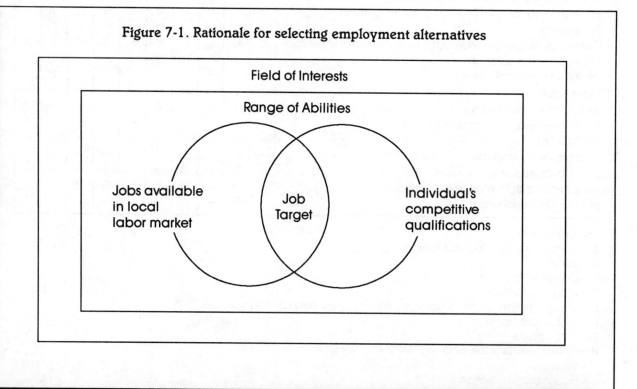

Figure 7-1. Rationale for selecting employment alternatives

Field of Interests

Range of Abilities

Jobs available in local labor market

Job Target

Individual's competitive qualifications

description of a practical rationale for selecting employment alternatives. As one can see from the figure, clients should be encouraged to examine a broad range of activities in which they have an interest (i.e., things they might like to do). Within that field of interest, they should identify work activities reflecting their strongest abilities (i.e., things they can do best). After identifying potential jobs within their areas of interest and ability, they should select their job-search targets based on a combination of job availability in the local labor market and the competitiveness of their qualifications.

Identifying employable traits and matching them to roles in the labor market contributes to improved self-esteem in clients and helps them crystalize a sense of vocational self-concept. Such crystalization of self-concept can be observed in clients when they say, "I can see myself doing that." These insights should be pursued by professionals because they often serve as verifications of good vocational choices. Self-differentiation, an important vocational decision-making skill, can be observed when clients begin to see how they might fit into some work roles and not others. Sometimes a vocational decision is made as a simple conclusion to the individual's vocational information. However, for many clients, vocational decision making is more a process of altering self-perceptions as they imagine themselves in different occupational roles. Because this process often takes time, professionals should not become impatient with their clients when they appear reluctant to make a vocational decision; they may, in fact, be engaged in the process of trying to see themselves in new ways.

The work-related information summarized in the model employability profile form "Selecting an Employment Objective" (Figure 7-2) includes highlights from seven categories: education, work experience, work skills and abilities, transferable non-employment skills, knowledge of industries, interests, and personality traits. There is also a category for other information. Only information having employment-related value should be included in the profile. The data for the employability profile can be drawn from references, educational records, vocational rehabilitation records, client reports, and observations by professionals. The following is information that might be listed in the profile:

- Education — degrees, training, certificates, licenses, favorite courses, homestudy courses
- Work experience — actual experience obtained through paid employment
- Work skills and abilities — a summary of employable skills and abilities
- Transferable non-employment skills — skills learned through hobbies, volunteer activities, and other life roles (e.g., child care)
- Knowledge of selected industries — information on industries learned through employment or other experiences
- Interests — self-assessed or inventoried interests

Figure 7-2. Case study: employability profile

# SELECTING AN EMPLOYMENT OBJECTIVE

Name _____ Cathy Xxxxx _____ Date ___ 9/7/87 ___

Organization _____ Staff Member _____

## PART I. EMPLOYABILITY PROFILE

Many factors can be used in estimating employability. Highlights of employment-related information in each of the following eight categories will help to match an individual's employability with employment alternatives. Each entry should be coded for factors that differentiate levels (Unskilled/Semiskilled, Skilled, Professional) or areas (Data, People, Things) of employability. At the end of this section, selected factors can be used to develop a profile for one or more employment alternatives.

| Code | |
|------|---|
| | *Education:* Degrees, training, certificates, licenses, favorite courses, homestudy courses, self-study. |
| Data | Associate's degree in business |
| Data | Major courses: typing, business communications, data processing |
| People | psychology |
| | |

| Code | |
|------|---|
| | *Work Experience:* Actual experience obtained through paid employment. |
| Data | Worked as a clerk in a part-time job |
| People | Worked as a substitute teacher's aide |
| | |

| Code | |
|------|---|
| | *Work Skills and Abilities:* Summary of the most employable skills and abilities. |
| Data | Clerical skills of typing, filing, and data entry |
| People | Teaching and helping skills |
| | |

| Code | |
|------|---|
| | *Transferable Nonemployment Skills:* Skills learned through hobbies, volunteer activities, and other life roles (e.g., child care). |
| People | Taught Sunday school |
| | |

| | |
|---|---|
| *Code* | *Knowledge of Selected Industries:* Information on industries learned through employment or other experiences. |
| People | Public Schools — Substitute teacher's aide |
| People | Social Service Agencies — Part-time clerical work |
| | |
| *Code* | *Interests:* Self-assessed or inventoried interests. |
| People | Social interests as assessed by Strong-Campbell Interest Inventory |
| People | Likes working with people (especially children) |
| | |
| *Code* | *Personality Traits:* Dominant traits as assessed by self, inventories, or observations by others. |
| People | Courteous, polite, hardworking (self-assessed) |
| People | Sensitive (assessed by counselor) |
| | |
| *Code* | *Other:* Significant personal experiences and other employment-related information |
| People | Orthopedic handicap has made her sensitive to suffering of others |

Summary Notes:

First Choice: Working with People in Level-I or Level-II occupations

Second Choice: Working with data in Level-II occupations in a people-serving industry.

☐ Personality traits — dominant traits as assessed by client along with inventories or observations by others

☐ Other — significant personal experiences and other employment-related information

The employability profiles may reveal that clients are employable in several occupational levels and areas. Figure 7-2 presents a case study indicating that the client was employable in at least two occupational areas. Her associate's degree in business and her clerical experience suggested that she was qualified for jobs working with data (i.e, office occupations). On the other hand, her volunteer experience as a Sunday-school teacher, her substitute work as a teacher's aide, and her interests in children provided a second profile, qualifying her to seek jobs working with people (i.e., child-care worker, teacher's aide).

## SELECTING JOBS TO PURSUE

A model for selecting specific jobs to pursue in the search for employment is presented in Figure 7-3. The model classifies three levels of occupations. Professional occupations normally require four or more years of college or commensurate experience. Skilled occupations usually require one or two years of education or training beyond high school, an extended apprenticeship program, or several years of on-the-job experience. Unskilled and semiskilled occupations usually require little formal training and can usually be learned on the job in a relatively short time.

Because the entry-level requirements for the same job may vary from employer to employer, the levels cannot be viewed as strict classifications. Consequently, some jobs are listed in more than one level. Some occupations such as supervisor may be obtained through the progressive accumulation of on-the-job experience. Other occupations such as those requiring licenses will not be accessible without the appropriate educational requirements. Therefore, the occupational levels should be viewed as generalizations in which exceptions are found.

Occupations are further classified into subareas within each level. Levels I and II are divided into three subareas: data, people, and things. Data occupations include jobs that primarily involve working with numerical or written information. Workers might be required to compare, copy, compute, compile, analyze, coordinate, or synthesize numerical or written information. People occupations include jobs that primarily involve working with other people. Workers might be required to help, serve, give information, persuade, entertain, supervise, instruct, negotiate with, or counsel other people. Things occupations include jobs that primarily involve working with objects. Workers might be required to handle materials, tend machines, work with tools, drive vehicles, operate machinery, operate precision

**Figure 7-3. Model for selecting jobs to pursue in search for employment**

| **Level III: Professional Occupations** | | |
|---|---|---|
| Includes such jobs as managers, engineers, scientists, social workers, lawyers, teachers, health practitioners, registered nurses, and writers | | |

| **Level II: Skilled Occupations** | | |
|---|---|---|
| Data | People | Things |
| Includes such jobs as computer operators, court stenographers, accounting clerks, and secretaries | Includes such jobs as physical therapist assistants, licensed practical nurses, and dental hygienists | Includes such jobs as aircraft mechanics, electricians, chefs, plumbers, jewelers, and carpenters |

| **Level I: Unskilled or Semiskilled Occupations** | | |
|---|---|---|
| Data | People | Things |
| Includes such jobs as receptionists, file clerks, postal clerks, and bookkeepers | Includes such jobs as teacher aides, nurse aides, retail-sales workers, and child-care workers | Includes such jobs as janitors, food-preparation workers, cooks, painters, and bookbinders |

*STEP 1: Select Level of Employability:* Based on current education, training, and other credentials.

*STEP 2: Select Subarea of Level:* Based on training, current level of education, abilities, and interests.

*STEP 3: Select Job(s) to Pursue from Subarea:* Based on desirability to individual and availability of positions in local labor market.

instruments, or set up and repair equipment. The subareas have been adapted from the classification system used in the Dictionary of Occupational Titles (U.S. Department of Labor, Employment and Training Administration, 1977). Similar to the classification of levels, the subareas also represent generalizations in which exceptions can be found. Many jobs require workers to perform tasks involving two or all three of the subareas. For example, a cashier works with data (counting money and recording purchases), people (greeting customers), and things (working the cash register). It is classified as a data job because the primary work activities involve working with data. However, some occupations can also be dually classified.

Professional occupations are not divided into these subdivisions because such occupations often require workers to perform complex mixtures of tasks involving data, people, and things. Rather, professional occupations are grouped into twelve occupational clusters adopted from the Occupational Outlook Handbook (U.S. Department of Labor, Bureau of Labor Statistics, 1987). People who qualify for professional occupations will have credentials, usually college experience or a degree, that will significantly contribute to determining which of the twelve clusters they should examine in order to select desirable employment alternatives.

## LIST OF OCCUPATIONS

An extended list of over 200 occupations, grouped into the aforementioned levels and subareas, is included in this section. Each occupational listing is followed by a number in parentheses. This number represents the predicted numerical change in employment from 1984 to 1995 that has been estimated by the Bureau of Labor Statistics (The Job Outlook, Spring, 1986). Additional occupational information can be obtained from the Dictionary of Occupational Titles (U.S. Department of Labor, Employment and Training Administration, 1977) and the Occupational Outlook Handbook (U.S. Department of Labor, Bureau of Labor Statistics, 1987). Each occupational profile in the Occupational Outlook Handbook includes descriptions of the nature of work, working conditions, employment, training requirements, job outlook, earnings, related occupations, and sources of additional information.

### Level III: Professional Occupations

**Executive, administrative, and managerial occupations** include bank officers and managers (119,000); health services managers (147,000); hotel managers and assistants (21,000); school principals and assistant principals (12,000); accountants and auditors (307,000); construction and building inspectors (4,100); inspectors and compliance officers other than construction (9,7000); personnel, training, and labor-relations specialists (34,000); purchasing agents (36,000); underwriters (17,000); and wholesale and retail buyers (28,000).

**Engineering, surveying, and architectural occupations** include architects (25,000); surveyors (6,100); engineers (480,000); aerospace engineers (14,000); chemical engineers (13,000); civil engineers (46,000); electrical and electronics engineers (206,000); industrial engineers (37,000); mechanical engineers (81,000); metallurgical, ceramic, and materials engineers (4,300); mining engineers (less than 500); nuclear engineers (800); and petroleum engineers (3,800).

**Natural science and mathematical occupations** include actuaries (4,000), computer systems analysts (212,000), mathematicians (4,000), statisticians (3,800), chemists (8,500), geologists and geophysicists (6,900), meteorologists (900), physicists and astronomers (1,700), agricultural scientists (2,800), biological scientists (9,500), and foresters and conservation scientists (1,800).

**Social science, social work, religious and legal occupations** include lawyers (174,000), economists (7,300), psychologists (21,000), sociologists (less than 500), urban and regional planners (1,600), social workers (75,000), recreation workers (26,000), protestant ministers (N/A), rabbis (N/A), and roman catholic priests (N/A).

**Teaching, counseling, library and archival occupations** include kindergarten and elementary school teachers (281,000), secondary school teachers (48,000), adult and vocational education teachers (48,000), college and university faculty (−77,000*), counselors (29,000), librarians (16,000), and archivists and curators (800).

**Health diagnosing and treating occupations** include chiropractors (9,100), dentists (39,000), optometrists (7,700), physicians (109,000), podiatrists (4,300), and veterinarians (8,800).

**Nursing, pharmacological, dietetic, therapeutic, and physician assistant occupations** include dieticians and nutritionists (12,000), occupational therapists (8,000), pharmacists (15,000), physical therapists (25,000), physician assistants (10,000), recreational therapists (3,900), registered nurses (452,000), respiratory therapists (11,000), and speech pathologists and audiologists (8,000).

**Health technology occupations** include clinical laboratory technologists and technicians (18,000).

**Writing, art, and entertainment occupations** include public relations specialists (30,000); radio and television announcers and newscasters (6,300); reporters and correspondents (13,000); writers and editors (54,000); designers (46,000); graphic and fine artists (60,000); actors, directors, and producers (11,000); dancers and choreographers (2,100); and musicians (26,000).

**Nonhealth technological occupations** include air traffic controllers (less than 500), broadcast technicians (5,100), computer programmers (245,000), and legal assistants (51,000).

**Marketing and sales occupations** include insurance sales workers (34,000), manufacturers' sales workers (51,000), real estate agents and brokers (52,000), securities and financial services sales

*Represents a decrease in total employment.

workers (32,000), and wholesale trade sales workers (369,000).

**Transportation occupations** include aircraft pilots (18,000).

## Level II: Skilled Occupations

**Occupations working primarily with data** include medical record technicians (10,000), radio and television announcers and newscasters (6,300), drafters (39,000), broadcast technicians (5,100), computer programmers (245,000), legal assistants (51,000), library technicians (3,800), bank tellers (24,000), bookkeepers and accounting clerks (118,000), computer and peripheral equipment operators (143,000), reservation and transportation ticket agents and travel clerks (6,900), secretaries (268,000), statistical clerks ( – 12,000), and stenographers ( – 96,000).

**Occupations working primarily with people** include recreation workers (26,000); protestant ministers (N/A); physician assistants (10,000); recreational therapists (3,900); respiratory therapists (11,000); dental hygienists (22,000); electrocardiograph technicians (3,300); electroencephalographic technologists and technicians (1,100); emergency medical technicians (3,400); licensed practical nurses (106,000); actors, directors and producers (11,000); dancers and choreographers (2,100); musicians (26,000); insurance sales workers (34,000); manufacturers's sales workers (51,000); real estate agents and brokers (52,000); travel agents (32,000); wholesale trade sales workers (369,000); police and detectives (66,000); nursing aides (348,000); psychiatric aides (5,100); and blue-collar worker supervisors (85,000).

**Occupations working primarily with things** include dispensing opticians (9,600); radiologic technologists (27,000); surgical technicians (5,200); photographers and camera operators (29,000); electrical and electronics technicians (202,000); engineering technicians (90,000); science technicians (40,000); tool programmers, numerical control (3,400); chefs and cooks, except short order (210,000); barbers and hairstylists (4,200); cosmetologists and related workers (150,000); farm operators and managers ( – 62,000); aircraft mechanics and engine specialists (18,000); automotive and motorcycle mechanics (185,000); automotive body repairers (32,000); diesel mechanics (48,000); farm equipment mechanics (1,700); mobile heavy equipment mechanics (12,000); commercial and industrial electronic equipment repairers (8,000); communications equipment mechanics (2,700); computer service technicians (28,000); electronic home entertainment equipment repairers (6,900); home appliance and power tool repairers (9,100); general maintenance mechanics (137,000); heating, air-conditioning, and refrigeration mechanics (29,000); industrial machinery repairers (34,000); millwrights (5,500); office machine and cash register servicers (16,000); bricklayers and stonemasons (15,000); carpenters (101,000); concrete masons and terrazzo workers (17,000); drywall workers and latherers (11,000); electricians (88,000); glaziers (7,700); plasters (800); plumbers and pipefitters (61,000); boilermakers (3,900); dental laboratory technicians (9,900); jewelers (2,700); machinists (37,000); tool-and-die makers (16,000); upholsterers (6,300); and welders and cutters (41,000).

## Level I: Unskilled and Semiskilled Occupations

**Occupations working primarily with data** include legal assistants (51,000); library technicians (3,800); cashiers (556,000); bank tellers (24,000); bookkeepers and accounting clerks (118,000); data entry keyers (9,900); mail carriers (8,000); postal clerks (−27,000); receptionists and information clerks (83,000); reservation and transportation ticket agents and travel clerks (6,900); traffic, shipping, and receiving clerks (61,000); typists (11,000); flight attendants (13,000); file clerks (N/A); word processing typists (N/A); braille typists (N/A); mail clerks (N/A); registration clerks (N/A); duplicating machine operators (N/A); and personnel clerks (N/A).

**Occupations working primarily with people** include recreation workers (26,000); electrocardiograph technicians (3,300); electroencephalographic technologists and technicians (1,100); actors, directors, and producers (11,000); dancers and choreographers (2,100); musicians (26,000); cashiers (556,000); insurance sales workers (34,000); manufacturers' sales workers (51,000); retail sales workers (583,000); travel agents (32,000); wholesale trade sales workers (369,000); receptionists and information clerks (83,000); teacher aides (88,000); telephone operators (89,000); correction officers (45,000); police and detectives (66,000); bartenders (112,000); waiters and waitresses (424,000); dental assistants (48,000); nursing aides (348,000); psychiatric aides (5,100); and child-care workers (55,000).

**Occupations working primarily with things** include dispensing opticians (9,600); radiologic technologists (27,000); photographers and camera operators (29,000); electrical and electronics technicians (202,000); tool programmers, numerical control (3,400); firefighting occupations (48,000); guards (188,000); chefs and cooks, except short order (210,000); janitors and cleaners (443,000); automotive and motorcycle mechanics (185,000); automotive body repairers (32,000); diesel mechanics (48,000); farm equipment mechanics (1,700); mobile heavy equipment mechanics (12,000); electronic home entertainment equipment repairers (6,900); home appliance and power tool repairers (9,100); line installers and cable splicers (24,000); telephone installers and repairers (−19,000); general maintenance mechanics (137,000); heating, air-conditioning, and refrigeration mechanics (29,000); industrial machinery repairers (34,000); millwrights (5,500); musical instrument repairers and tuners (900); office machine and cash register servicers (16,000); vending machine servicers and repairers (4,900); carpet installers (11,000); drywall workers and lathers (11,000); glaziers (7,700); insulation workers (7,100); painters and paperhangers (17,000); roofers (16,000); sheet-metal workers (16,000); structural and reinforcing metal workers (16,000); tilesetters (3,000); roustabouts (less than 500); bookbinding workers (14,000); butchers and meatcutters

(−9,000); compositors and typesetters (14,000); dental laboratory technicians (9,900); lithographic and photoengraving workers (13,000); machinists (37,000); photographic process workers (14,000); shoe and leather workers and repairers (−8,100); upholsterers (6,300); stationary engineers (3,800); water and sewage treatment plant operators (9,400); metalworking and plastic working machine operators (3,200); numerical-control machine operators (17,000); precision assemblers (66,000); transportation equipment painters (9,100); welders and cutters (41,000); busdrivers (77,000); construction machinery operators (32,000); industrial truck and tractor operators (−46,000); truckdrivers (428,000); and construction trades helpers (27,000).

## SELECTING INDUSTRIES FOR THE JOB SEARCH

The industrial structure of a local economy is not apparent through casual observation. Employment seekers will become familiar with selected industries through their roles as consumers or through previous work experience. However, many job vacancies exist in small manufacturing plants or service companies and are obvious only to their employees and to the people who reside in the same neighborhood. Table 7-3 provides a profile of the employment listed by industrial classifications for the United States (Personick, 1985). The table includes actual numbers of people employed in each industry for the years 1959, 1969, 1979, and 1984, as well as offering employment projections for 1990 and 1995.

After selecting a job or a cluster of jobs to pursue in the search for employment, clients should examine the extended list of industries to identify those industries that employ people in the jobs they are hoping to obtain. Some jobs are available in only one industry while others are available in virtually all industries. Table 7-2 identifies the industries in which the 37 most-available occupations might be found. The figure indicates that wholesale-trade salespeople can only be found in wholesale-trade industries, whereas secretaries can be found within all major industrial classifications. Employment seekers will find some industries to be more desirable than others because they offer more job security, greater pay, or increased chances for advancement. Therefore, after identifying the industries in which they might find the jobs they have selected to pursue, clients should rank the industries according to their desirability and availability in the local economy.

Part III of the model form "Selecting an Employment Objective" lists a grid of the major industrial classifications. Employment seekers should review the list of industries in Table 7-3 and write the names of potential industries in the appropriate section of the grid. The form also instructs clients to select the four most desirable industries by evaluating such variables as working conditions, salary,

# Table 7-3. U.S. Employment by Industry

(In thousands)

| Industry | Actual | | | | Projected | | | | | |
|---|---|---|---|---|---|---|---|---|---|---|
| | | | | | 1990 | | | 1995 | | |
| | 1959 | 1969 | 1979 | 1984 | Low | Moderate | High | Low | Moderate | High |
| **Agriculture, forestry and fisheries:** | | | | | | | | | | |
| Dairy and poultry products . . . . . . . . . . . . . . . . . . | 1,479 | 754 | 449 | 374 | 318 | 324 | 327 | 297 | 305 | 310 |
| Meat animals and livestock . . . . . . . . . . . . . . . . | 933 | 701 | 527 | 472 | 439 | 448 | 452 | 398 | 404 | 415 |
| Cotton. . . . . . . . . . . . . . . . . . . . . . . . . . . . . . . . . | 539 | 159 | 58 | 46 | 33 | 31 | 38 | 24 | 29 | 33 |
| Food and feed grains . . . . . . . . . . . . . . . . . . . . . | 915 | 589 | 583 | 604 | 536 | 555 | 561 | 500 | 506 | 515 |
| Agricultural products, n.e.c. . . . . . . . . . . . . . . . . . | 1,369 | 1,037 | 1,155 | 1,155 | 1,150 | 1,155 | 1,167 | 1,135 | 1,157 | 1,168 |
| Forestry and fishery products. . . . . . . . . . . . . . . . | 63 | 55 | 80 | 78 | 73 | 77 | 78 | 76 | 82 | 89 |
| Agricultural services . . . . . . . . . . . . . . . . . . . . . | 285 | 327 | 488 | 564 | 575 | 574 | 578 | 540 | 576 | 598 |
| **Mining:** | | | | | | | | | | |
| Iron and ferroalloy ores mining . . . . . . . . . . . . . | 33 | 30 | 31 | 17 | 14 | 15 | 16 | 12 | 13 | 15 |
| Copper ore mining . . . . . . . . . . . . . . . . . . . . . . | 23 | 34 | 33 | 16 | 14 | 16 | 18 | 12 | 14 | 16 |
| Nonferrous metal ores mining . . . . . . . . . . . . . . . | 31 | 25 | 38 | 24 | 21 | 22 | 24 | 16 | 18 | 19 |
| Coal mining . . . . . . . . . . . . . . . . . . . . . . . . . . . . | 201 | 138 | 261 | 198 | 191 | 199 | 203 | 181 | 185 | 189 |
| Crude petroleum and natural gas . . . . . . . . . . . | 202 | 157 | 212 | 285 | 283 | 291 | 296 | 274 | 289 | 303 |
| Stone and clay mining and quarrying . . . . . . . . | 105 | 99 | 104 | 90 | 91 | 96 | 97 | 87 | 92 | 97 |
| Chemical and fertilizer mineral mining . . . . . . . . | 19 | 18 | 25 | 21 | 19 | 21 | 22 | 18 | 20 | 22 |
| **Construction:** | | | | | | | | | | |
| Maintenance and repair construction . . . . . . . . . | 870 | 868 | 1,339 | 1,246 | 1,275 | 1,332 | 1,358 | 1,373 | 1,404 | 1,430 |
| New construction . . . . . . . . . . . . . . . . . . . . . . . . . | 3,040 | 3,506 | 4,540 | 4,674 | 4,635 | 4,857 | 4,918 | 4,957 | 5,232 | 5,427 |
| **Manufacturing:** | | | | | | | | | | |
| *Durable goods:* | | | | | | | | | | |
| Ordnance. . . . . . . . . . . . . . . . . . . . . . . . . . . . . . . | 50 | 175 | 73 | 95 | 103 | 108 | 110 | 105 | 111 | 118 |
| Guided missiles and space vehicles . . . . . . . . . . | 94 | 107 | 81 | 120 | 143 | 149 | 151 | 143 | 152 | 158 |
| Logging . . . . . . . . . . . . . . . . . . . . . . . . . . . . . . . . | 149 | 137 | 149 | 125 | 107 | 111 | 114 | 100 | 107 | 114 |
| Sawmills and planing mills . . . . . . . . . . . . . . . . . | 305 | 230 | 237 | 203 | 184 | 192 | 195 | 183 | 190 | 195 |
| Millwork, plywood, and wood products, n.e.c. . . . | 264 | 310 | 393 | 360 | 366 | 380 | 385 | 363 | 381 | 394 |
| Wooden containers . . . . . . . . . . . . . . . . . . . . . . . | 43 | 36 | 19 | 14 | 11 | 12 | 13 | 8 | 9 | 10 |
| Household furniture . . . . . . . . . . . . . . . . . . . . . . . | 259 | 316 | 329 | 295 | 303 | 317 | 322 | 303 | 321 | 332 |
| Furniture and fixtures, ecept household . . . . . . . . | 126 | 153 | 176 | 211 | 241 | 247 | 254 | 249 | 262 | 275 |
| Glass. . . . . . . . . . . . . . . . . . . . . . . . . . . . . . . . . . . | 153 | 188 | 202 | 169 | 167 | 171 | 175 | 164 | 173 | 179 |
| Cement and concrete products . . . . . . . . . . . . . . | 210 | 228 | 255 | 231 | 238 | 245 | 248 | 238 | 249 | 255 |
| Structural clay products. . . . . . . . . . . . . . . . . . . . . | 78 | 64 | 52 | 38 | 32 | 35 | 36 | 26 | 30 | 33 |
| Pottery and related products. . . . . . . . . . . . . . . . . | 49 | 45 | 52 | 45 | 44 | 47 | 48 | 46 | 47 | 50 |
| Stone and other mineral products, n.e.c. . . . . . . . | 125 | 140 | 165 | 133 | 146 | 150 | 154 | 144 | 149 | 156 |
| Blast furnaces and basic steel products. . . . . . . . | 588 | 644 | 571 | 335 | 283 | 311 | 339 | 235 | 261 | 325 |
| Iron and steel foundries and forgings . . . . . . . . . . | 269 | 312 | 324 | 209 | 192 | 205 | 208 | 182 | 194 | 204 |
| Primary copper and copper products . . . . . . . . . | 137 | 160 | 161 | 133 | 132 | 137 | 140 | 127 | 133 | 140 |
| Primary aluminum and aluminum products. . . . . . | 111 | 153 | 170 | 147 | 147 | 153 | 157 | 150 | 158 | 162 |
| Primary nonferrous metals and products . . . . . . . | 78 | 93 | 93 | 77 | 71 | 75 | 76 | 66 | 70 | 74 |
| Metal cans and containers. . . . . . . . . . . . . . . . . . | 75 | 87 | 80 | 58 | 54 | 58 | 59 | 48 | 52 | 55 |
| Heating equipment and plumbing fixtures . . . . . . | 71 | 76 | 76 | 63 | 60 | 63 | 64 | 57 | 60 | 62 |
| Fabricated structural metal products . . . . . . . . . . | 345 | 440 | 535 | 448 | 479 | 496 | 507 | 501 | 525 | 542 |
| Screw machine products. . . . . . . . . . . . . . . . . . . . | 88 | 114 | 117 | 97 | 99 | 106 | 108 | 101 | 108 | 113 |
| Metal stampings . . . . . . . . . . . . . . . . . . . . . . . . . | 189 | 255 | 245 | 211 | 219 | 229 | 231 | 224 | 232 | 240 |
| Cutlery, handtools, and general hardware . . . . . . | 135 | 165 | 185 | 148 | 155 | 161 | 163 | 156 | 164 | 169 |
| Fabricated metal products, n.e.c. . . . . . . . . . . . . | 232 | 315 | 376 | 344 | 372 | 387 | 393 | 381 | 402 | 423 |
| Engines and turbines . . . . . . . . . . . . . . . . . . . . . . | 90 | 112 | 145 | 116 | 115 | 121 | 123 | 117 | 124 | 130 |
| Farm and garden machinery . . . . . . . . . . . . . . . . | 128 | 141 | 184 | 111 | 125 | 131 | 135 | 129 | 136 | 145 |
| Construction, mining, oilfield machinery . . . . . . . . | 162 | 202 | 276 | 178 | 203 | 208 | 211 | 206 | 216 | 226 |
| Materials handling equipment . . . . . . . . . . . . . . . . | 65 | 95 | 106 | 80 | 99 | 104 | 105 | 113 | 119 | 123 |
| Metalworking machinery . . . . . . . . . . . . . . . . . . . | 252 | 347 | 379 | 313 | 346 | 360 | 366 | 357 | 377 | 392 |
| Special industry machinery. . . . . . . . . . . . . . . . . . . | 164 | 206 | 205 | 168 | 176 | 187 | 190 | 186 | 197 | 204 |
| General industrial machinery . . . . . . . . . . . . . . . . | 221 | 291 | 329 | 273 | 292 | 309 | 313 | 308 | 325 | 336 |
| Nonelectrical machinery, n.e.c. . . . . . . . . . . . . . . | 168 | 246 | 312 | 301 | 326 | 338 | 344 | 337 | 356 | 366 |
| Computers and peripheral equipment . . . . . . . . . | 111 | 224 | 339 | 479 | 614 | 640 | 648 | 680 | 713 | 741 |
| Typewriters and other office machines . . . . . . . . . | 28 | 52 | 59 | 48 | 46 | 50 | 50 | 41 | 44 | 47 |
| Service industry machines. . . . . . . . . . . . . . . . . . . . | 97 | 147 | 188 | 171 | 178 | 187 | 191 | 186 | 194 | 201 |
| Electrical transmission equipment . . . . . . . . . . . . . | 157 | 207 | 221 | 224 | 221 | 228 | 230 | 221 | 231 | 238 |
| Electrical industrial apparatus . . . . . . . . . . . . . . . . | 176 | 223 | 251 | 206 | 223 | 230 | 232 | 229 | 241 | 250 |
| Household appliances . . . . . . . . . . . . . . . . . . . . . | 157 | 187 | 178 | 150 | 147 | 153 | 155 | 146 | 150 | 156 |
| Electric lighting and writing equipment . . . . . . . . | 134 | 205 | 225 | 201 | 212 | 221 | 223 | 213 | 223 | 234 |

See footnotes at end of table.

Continued

## Table 7-3. (continued)

(In thousands)

| Industry | Actual | | | | Projected | | | | | |
|---|---|---|---|---|---|---|---|---|---|---|
| | | | | | 1990 | | | 1995 | | |
| | 1959 | 1969 | 1979 | 1984 | Low | Moderate | High | Low | Moderate | High |
| **Manufacturing:-Continued:** | | | | | | | | | | |
| *Durable goods:-Continued* | | | | | | | | | | |
| Radio and television receiving equipment ...... | 114 | 156 | 116 | 93 | 89 | 90 | 95 | 83 | 87 | 91 |
| Telephone and telegraph apparatus........... | 105 | 146 | 165 | 144 | 168 | 171 | 173 | 176 | 180 | 184 |
| Radio and communication equipment ......... | 252 | 409 | 357 | 472 | 537 | 556 | 564 | 584 | 607 | 622 |
| Electronic components and accessories ....... | 213 | 394 | 525 | 673 | 750 | 797 | 808 | 802 | 846 | 877 |
| Electrical machinery and supplies, n.e.c........ | 112 | 125 | 176 | 163 | 181 | 183 | 189 | 186 | 194 | 205 |
| Motor vehicles .................... | 696 | 912 | 991 | 863 | 820 | 852 | 863 | 795 | 828 | 861 |
| Aircraft ............................. | 722 | 805 | 632 | 634 | 666 | 692 | 710 | 680 | 714 | 737 |
| Ship and boat building and repair............. | 152 | 193 | 230 | 199 | 206 | 222 | 225 | 215 | 225 | 237 |
| Railroad equipment...................... | 41 | 51 | 74 | 36 | 36 | 36 | 39 | 35 | 36 | 38 |
| Motorcycles, bicycles, and parts ........... | 9 | 14 | 20 | 16 | 15 | 17 | 18 | 14 | 16 | 19 |
| | | | | | | | | | | |
| Transportation equipment, n.e.c............... | 23 | 89 | 103 | 86 | 98 | 102 | 105 | 99 | 106 | 114 |
| Scientific and controlling instruments ........... | 166 | 195 | 215 | 222 | 263 | 268 | 274 | 287 | 304 | 315 |
| Medical instruments and supplies ............ | 45 | 82 | 144 | 172 | 207 | 216 | 220 | 223 | 234 | 244 |
| Optical and ophthalmic equipment .......... | 85 | 75 | 81 | 77 | 76 | 80 | 82 | 73 | 78 | 81 |
| Photographic equipment and supplies ........ | 69 | 111 | 134 | 124 | 130 | 133 | 134 | 130 | 136 | 143 |
| Watches and clocks ..................... | 30 | 35 | 28 | 15 | 15 | 16 | 17 | 14 | 15 | 17 |
| Jewelry and silverware .................... | 67 | 78 | 92 | 78 | 75 | 78 | 82 | 73 | 78 | 81 |
| Musical instruments and sporting goods ....... | 116 | 149 | 145 | 141 | 136 | 143 | 144 | 136 | 143 | 149 |
| Manufactured products, n.e.c. ............... | 232 | 233 | 244 | 208 | 208 | 211 | 215 | 195 | 203 | 210 |
| | | | | | | | | | | |
| *Nondurable goods:* | | | | | | | | | | |
| Meat products ........................ | 325 | 344 | 363 | 361 | 335 | 345 | 350 | 320 | 331 | 339 |
| Dairy products ........................ | 327 | 260 | 189 | 164 | 129 | 134 | 138 | 122 | 127 | 133 |
| Canned and frozen foods................. | 249 | 291 | 316 | 286 | 273 | 287 | 293 | 261 | 275 | 284 |
| Grain mill products ..................... | 140 | 137 | 147 | 130 | 128 | 132 | 135 | 124 | 128 | 135 |
| Bakery products........................ | 314 | 286 | 238 | 218 | 191 | 197 | 200 | 182 | 188 | 194 |
| Sugar ............................... | 38 | 36 | 31 | 25 | 21 | 22 | 23 | 18 | 19 | 20 |
| Confectionery products................... | 79 | 87 | 80 | 77 | 67 | 71 | 73 | 61 | 66 | 71 |
| Alcoholic beverages .................... | 107 | 97 | 86 | 72 | 61 | 63 | 65 | 51 | 58 | 64 |
| Soft drinks and flavorings.................. | 111 | 142 | 153 | 144 | 134 | 139 | 141 | 127 | 134 | 154 |
| | | | | | | | | | | |
| Food products, n.e.c. .................... | 144 | 151 | 160 | 157 | 146 | 150 | 151 | 139 | 148 | 154 |
| Tobacco manufacturing .................. | 95 | 83 | 70 | 65 | 59 | 61 | 61 | 54 | 56 | 58 |
| Fabric, yarn, and thread mills .............. | 619 | 616 | 531 | 440 | 390 | 406 | 408 | 343 | 361 | 381 |
| Floor covering mills ..................... | 39 | 58 | 61 | 54 | 44 | 47 | 49 | 41 | 44 | 45 |
| Textile mill products, n.e.c. ............... | 74 | 82 | 71 | 56 | 49 | 52 | 54 | 44 | 47 | 49 |
| Hosiery and knit goods .................. | 221 | 251 | 227 | 206 | 179 | 185 | 186 | 160 | 169 | 177 |
| Apparel .............................. | 1,101 | 1,244 | 1,125 | 1,023 | 883 | 92 | 937 | 775 | 818 | 851 |
| Fabricated textile products, n.e.c............. | 144 | 182 | 198 | 194 | 184 | 191 | 200 | 177 | 186 | 197 |
| | | | | | | | | | | |
| Paper products........................ | 415 | 483 | 494 | 486 | 465 | 486 | 492 | 455 | 480 | 498 |
| Paperboard containers and boxes........... | 175 | 231 | 214 | 196 | 179 | 190 | 192 | 173 | 184 | 190 |
| Newspaper printing and publishing........... | 329 | 376 | 432 | 463 | 497 | 512 | 522 | 526 | 548 | 565 |
| Periodical and book printing and publishing .... | 156 | 210 | 230 | 274 | 289 | 298 | 307 | 296 | 313 | 325 |
| Printing and publishing, n.e.c............... | 450 | 549 | 639 | 725 | 792 | 826 | 839 | 856 | 890 | 925 |
| Industrial chemicals...................... | 260 | 296 | 328 | 300 | 291 | 302 | 307 | 287 | 306 | 322 |
| Agricultural chemicals ................... | 54 | 65 | 70 | 61 | 61 | 62 | 64 | 60 | 62 | 64 |
| Chemical products, n.e.c. ................ | 82 | 124 | 99 | 99 | 95 | 102 | 104 | 96 | 102 | 105 |
| Plastic materials and synthetic rubber ........ | 81 | 108 | 100 | 88 | 83 | 87 | 89 | 79 | 83 | 86 |
| Synthetic fibers......................... | 79 | 132 | 112 | 88 | 75 | 82 | 89 | 74 | 79 | 82 |
| Drugs ................................ | 106 | 143 | 193 | 206 | 222 | 229 | 235 | 234 | 245 | 254 |
| | | | | | | | | | | |
| Cleaning and toilet preparations ............ | 89 | 123 | 140 | 145 | 149 | 154 | 156 | 154 | 160 | 166 |
| Paints and allied products................. | 62 | 72 | 69 | 62 | 57 | 60 | 61 | 54 | 58 | 60 |
| Petroleum refining and related products ........ | 217 | 182 | 210 | 189 | 179 | 183 | 185 | 168 | 175 | 182 |
| Tires and inner tubes .................... | 105 | 119 | 127 | 94 | 87 | 90 | 92 | 82 | 86 | 92 |
| Rubber products, except tires and tubes ....... | 178 | 162 | 167 | 148 | 140 | 145 | 148 | 126 | 132 | 137 |
| Plastics products, n.e.c. .................. | 94 | 320 | 494 | 544 | 620 | 659 | 676 | 670 | 712 | 753 |
| Leather tanning and finishing................ | 36 | 29 | 20 | 17 | 13 | 15 | 15 | 11 | 13 | 13 |
| Leather products including footwear .......... | 341 | 316 | 232 | 178 | 145 | 152 | 161 | 121 | 130 | 139 |

See footnotes at end of table.

| Industry | Actual | | | | Projected | | | | | |
|---|---|---|---|---|---|---|---|---|---|---|
| | 1959 | 1969 | 1979 | 1984 | 1990 | | | 1995 | | |
| | | | | | Low | Moderate | High | Low | Moderate | High |
| **Transportation:** | | | | | | | | | | |
| Railroad transportation . . . . . . . . . . . . . . . . . . . . . | 930 | 651 | 559 | 378 | 314 | 323 | 325 | 272 | 283 | 298 |
| Local transit and intercity buses . . . . . . . . . . . . . | 315 | 314 | 302 | 317 | 316 | 325 | 332 | 323 | 330 | 338 |
| Truck transportation . . . . . . . . . . . . . . . . . . . . . . . | 1,019 | 1,212 | 1,551 | 1,560 | 1,673 | 1,750 | 1,783 | 1,766 | 1,868 | 1,950 |
| Water transportation . . . . . . . . . . . . . . . . . . . . . . | 239 | 234 | 222 | 206 | 207 | 218 | 222 | 220 | 230 | 239 |
| Air transportation . . . . . . . . . . . . . . . . . . . . . . . . | 185 | 357 | 443 | 498 | 516 | 538 | 545 | 556 | 579 | 607 |
| Pipelines, except natural gas . . . . . . . . . . . . . . . | 24 | 18 | 20 | 19 | 19 | 20 | 21 | 20 | 20 | 22 |
| Transportation services . . . . . . . . . . . . . . . . . . . . | 71 | 111 | 198 | 262 | 318 | 333 | 339 | 362 | 382 | 399 |
| **Communications:** | | | | | | | | | | |
| Radio and television broadcasting . . . . . . . . . . . | 90 | 131 | 191 | 237 | 253 | 263 | 268 | 278 | 290 | 303 |
| Communications, except radio and tv . . . . . . . . . | 749 | 919 | 1,121 | 1,116 | 1,176 | 1,222 | 1,243 | 1,228 | 1,295 | 1,353 |
| **Public utilities:** | | | | | | | | | | |
| Electric utilities, public and private . . . . . . . . . . . | 430 | 460 | 608 | 702 | 738 | 763 | 778 | 784 | 827 | 863 |
| Gas utilities . . . . . . . . . . . . . . . . . . . . . . . . . . . . . | 215 | 220 | 220 | 223 | 218 | 227 | 233 | 214 | 226 | 235 |
| Water and sanitary services . . . . . . . . . . . . . . . . | 63 | 88 | 94 | 115 | 118 | 121 | 124 | 118 | 124 | 133 |
| **Trade:** | | | | | | | | | | |
| Wholesale trade . . . . . . . . . . . . . . . . . . . . . . . . . | 3,380 | 4,159 | 5,501 | 5,897 | 6,471 | 6,710 | 6,827 | 6,632 | 6,985 | 7,291 |
| Eating and drinking places . . . . . . . . . . . . . . . . . | 2,002 | 2,806 | 4,857 | 5,733 | 6,190 | 6,470 | 6,597 | 6,625 | 6,936 | 7,250 |
| Retail trade, except eating and drinking places . . | 8,110 | 9,706 | 11,953 | 12,660 | 13,329 | 13,926 | 14,282 | 13,590 | 14,351 | 15,004 |
| **Finance, insurance, and real estate:** | | | | | | | | | | |
| Banking . . . . . . . . . . . . . . . . . . . . . . . . . . . . . . . . | 644 | 987 | 1,498 | 1,678 | 1,706 | 1,780 | 1,857 | 1,777 | 1,865 | 1,946 |
| Credit agencies and financial brokers . . . . . . . . . | 391 | 652 | 900 | 1,239 | 1,400 | 1,467 | 1,492 | 1,538 | 1,621 | 1,689 |
| Insurance . . . . . . . . . . . . . . . . . . . . . . . . . . . . . . . | 1,150 | 1,368 | 1,748 | 1,904 | 2,075 | 2,150 | 2,173 | 2,112 | 2,237 | 2,335 |
| Real estate . . . . . . . . . . . . . . . . . . . . . . . . . . . . . . | 774 | 852 | 1,368 | 1,475 | 1,518 | 1,594 | 1,624 | 1,598 | 1,675 | 1,747 |
| **Services:** | | | | | | | | | | |
| Hotels and lodging places . . . . . . . . . . . . . . . . . | 906 | 1,060 | 1,543 | 1,914 | 2,063 | 2,146 | 2,198 | 2,153 | 2,299 | 2,420 |
| Personal and repair services . . . . . . . . . . . . . . . . | 1,202 | 1,226 | 1,231 | 1,388 | 1,486 | 1,535 | 1,572 | 1,579 | 1,664 | 1,732 |
| Beauty and barber shops . . . . . . . . . . . . . . . . . . | 576 | 629 | 626 | 663 | 638 | 670 | 671 | 636 | 675 | 709 |
| Business services . . . . . . . . . . . . . . . . . . . . . . . . . | 830 | 1,688 | 3,173 | 4,612 | 5,995 | 6,200 | 6,310 | 6,887 | 7,245 | 7,535 |
| Advertising . . . . . . . . . . . . . . . . . . . . . . . . . . . . . . | 123 | 134 | 165 | 213 | 246 | 250 | 253 | 260 | 267 | 277 |
| Professional services, n.e.c. . . . . . . . . . . . . . . . . . | 785 | 1,041 | 1,804 | 2,295 | 2,702 | 2,823 | 2,876 | 3,170 | 3,335 | 3,483 |
| Automobile repair and services . . . . . . . . . . . . . | 443 | 566 | 834 | 1,022 | 1,015 | 1,079 | 1,102 | 1,123 | 1,194 | 1,249 |
| Motion pictures . . . . . . . . . . . . . . . . . . . . . . . . . . | 232 | 247 | 309 | 328 | 346 | 358 | 366 | 377 | 390 | 408 |
| Amusements and recreation services . . . . . . . . . | 378 | 496 | 768 | 869 | 1,003 | 1,045 | 1,066 | 1,084 | 1,135 | 1,181 |
| Doctors' and dentists' services . . . . . . . . . . . . . . . | 642 | 801 | 1,346 | 1,650 | 1,902 | 1,949 | 1,989 | 2,120 | 2,190 | 2,284 |
| Hospitals . . . . . . . . . . . . . . . . . . . . . . . . . . . . . . . | 975 | 1,776 | 2,614 | 3,001 | 3,093 | 3,242 | 3,300 | 3,071 | 3,256 | 3,400 |
| Medical services, n.e.c. . . . . . . . . . . . . . . . . . . . . | 313 | 671 | 1,432 | 1,821 | 2,347 | 2,449 | 2,495 | 2,725 | 2,886 | 3,023 |
| Educational services . . . . . . . . . . . . . . . . . . . . . . | 853 | 1,227 | 1,718 | 1,928 | 1,983 | 2,057 | 2,085 | 2,025 | 2,147 | 2,235 |
| Noncommercial organizations . . . . . . . . . . . . . . . | 1,333 | 1,764 | 2,072 | 2,182 | 2,261 | 2,339 | 2,380 | 2,396 | 2,486 | 2,602 |
| Household industry . . . . . . . . . . . . . . . . . . . . . . . . | 2,279 | 1,856 | 1,326 | 1,242 | 1,106 | 1,148 | 1,174 | 982 | 1,023 | 1,060 |
| **Government enterprises:** | | | | | | | | | | |
| U.S. Postal Service . . . . . . . . . . . . . . . . . . . . . . . . | 574 | 732 | 661 | 703 | 657 | 699 | 712 | 640 | 677 | 721 |
| Federal enterprises, n.e.c. . . . . . . . . . . . . . . . . . . | 104 | 152 | 155 | 123 | 129 | 134 | 136 | 133 | 140 | 145 |
| Local government passenger transit . . . . . . . . . . . | 71 | 87 | 130 | 174 | 194 | 197 | 200 | 202 | 209 | 219 |
| State and local enterprises, n.e.c. . . . . . . . . . . . . | 225 | 351 | 541 | 485 | 493 | 513 | 525 | 509 | 536 | 568 |

¹Includes wage and salary jobs, the self-employed, and unpaid family workers.
n.e.c. = not elsewhere classified.

job security, growth industry, and personal interest. In Part V of the form, clients are directed to write five employment objectives, each listing a job title, industrial classification, and geographical location. A complete case study is provided in Figure 7-4.

## JOBS PRESENTLY HELD BY PEOPLE
## WITH HANDICAPS

The President's Committee on Employment of the Handicapped (Disabled Adults in America, 1985) indicated that disabled workers and nondisabled workers are similarly distributed among major occupational groups. Figure 7-5 indicates that nondisabled workers are somewhat more likely to be employed in professional, technical, and clerical occupations. The report also indicated that workers with disabilities were almost twice as likely as nondisabled workers to be self-employed. While it is true that, as a group, workers with disabilities can be found in virtually all occupational categories, the uniqueness of individuals and their disabilities will necessitate the careful selection of employment objectives. Some disabilities may eliminate some occupational choices, but in other occupations, disabilities may give people with handicaps an advantage. Granovetter (1979) observed that ... certain types of disabilities may result in higher productivity in some jobs. Persons with mental retardation, for example, tend to be very reliable and may well be desirable to employers in jobs that normally have high turnover.

The Association for Retarded Citizens identified a variety of jobs that workers with mental retardation have obtained through the On-the-Job Training Project. These jobs, presented in Table 7-4, should be viewed as a list of *possibilities* rather than a list of *limitations*. The authors have found that light-assembly jobs within electronic and other high tech industries are a good source of job opportunities for individuals with mental retardation. Cook, Dahl, and Gale (1978) conducted a study of jobs held by people with handicaps from 11 selected categories. Their report includes 63 tables based on the occupational divisions in the fourth edition of the Dictionary of Occupational Titles (DOT) (U.S. Department of Labor, Employment and Training Administration, 1977). Each table includes descriptions of jobs in the DOT division, jobs held by people with selected handicaps, other jobs in the division, and suggestions for people with handicaps who are interested in jobs listed in the division. The reader may wish to consult this resource for further information on jobs held by individuals who are handicapped.

**Figure 7-4. Case study: selecting an employment objective**

# SELECTING AN EMPLOYMENT OBJECTIVE

Name _____ Mark Xxxx _____ Date ___ 9/7/87 ___

Organization _____ Staff Member _____

## PART I. EMPLOYABILITY PROFILE

Many factors can be used in estimating employability. Highlights of employment-related information in each of the following eight categories will help to match an individual's employability with employment alternatives. Each entry should be coded for factors that differentiate levels (Unskilled/Semiskilled, Skilled, Professional) or areas (Data, People, Things) of employability. At the end of this section, selected factors can be used to develop a profile for one or more employment alternatives.

| Code | |
|---|---|
| | *Education:* Degrees, training, certificates, licenses, favorite courses, home-study courses, self-study. |
| — | Completed nine years of formal education |
| Things | Most enjoyable coursework: Machine shop |
| | |

| Code | |
|---|---|
| | *Work Experience:* Actual experience obtained through paid employment. |
| Things | Auto-parts stock clerk |
| Things | Food-preparation worker |
| Things | Factory worker for a food-processing company |
| Things | Repaired lawn mowers |

| Code | |
|---|---|
| | *Work Skills and Abilities:* Summary of the most employable skills and abilities. |
| Things | Repairing engines |
| Things | Storing materials |
| Things | Preparing food for cooking |
| | |

| Code | |
|---|---|
| | *Transferable Nonemployment Skills:* Skills learned through hobbies, volunteer activities, and other life roles (e.g., child care). |
| Things | Rebuilds motorcycles as a hobby |
| Things | Rebuilt a car engine |

**Continued**

**Figure 7-4 Continued**

| Code | *Knowledge of Selected Industries:* Information on industries learned through employment or other experiences. |
|------|------|
| Things | Auto-parts stores |
| Things | Restaurants |
| | |

| Code | *Interests:* Self-assessed or inventoried interests. |
|------|------|
| Things | Enjoys working on small engines |
| Things | Especially interested in working with motorcycles |
| | |

| Code | *Personality Traits:* Dominant traits as assessed by self, inventories, or observations by others. |
|------|------|
| Things | Mechanically inclined |
| | |
| | |

| Code | *Other:* Significant personal experiences and other employment-related information. |
|------|------|
| | |
| | |
| | |

Summary Notes:

Mark should seek Level-I or Level-II occupations working with things.

## PART II. SELECTING JOBS TO PURSUE

*STEP 1: Select Level of Employability:* __X__ I, __X__ II, or _____ III.
(Based on current education, training, and other credentials)

*STEP 2: Select Subarea of Level:* _____ Data, _____ People, or __X__ Things.
(Based on training, current level of education, abilities, and interests)

*STEP 3: Review Job(s) to Pursue from Selected Level and Subarea*

*STEP 4: Select the three most desirable jobs:* 1) _____Motorcycle mechanic_____ ,
2) _____Machinist_____ , and 3) _____Auto-parts stock clerk_____ .
(Based on desirability to individual and availability of positions in local labor market)

*Levels and Subareas of Occupations*

| Level III: Professional Occupations | | |
|---|---|---|
| Includes such jobs as managers, engineers, scientists, social workers, lawyers, teachers, health practitioners, registered nurses, and writers | | |
| **Level II: Skilled Occupations** | | |
| Data | People | Things |
| Includes such jobs as computer operators, court stenographers, accounting clerks, and secretaries | Includes such jobs as physical therapist assistants, licensed practical nurses, and dental hygienists | Includes such jobs as aircraft mechanics, electricians, chefs, plumbers, jewelers, and carpenters |
| **Level I: Unskilled or Semiskilled Occupations** | | |
| Data | People | Things |
| Includes such jobs as receptionists, file clerks, postal clerks, and bookkeepers | Includes such jobs as teacher aides, nurse aides, retail-sales workers, and child-care workers | Includes such jobs as janitors, food-preparation workers, cooks, painters, and bookbinders |

Continued

**Figure 7-4 Continued**

## PART III. SELECTING INDUSTRIES FOR THE JOB SEARCH

In each major classification, identify the industries in which job vacancies are likely to exist for the position of _____ Motorcycle mechanic _____

_____ (your first choice).

| Agriculture, forestry, fishing | Mining |
|---|---|
| | |
| Construction | Manufacturing<br><br>Motorcycle Manufacturers<br>(none located in community) |
| Transportation, communications, and public utilities | Wholesale trade |
| Retail trade<br><br>Motorcycle Dealerships | Finance, insurance, and real estate |
| Services<br><br>Motorcycle-Repair Shops | Public administration |

Select six of the most desirable industries (based on working conditions, salary, job security, growth industries, personal interest):

1. _____ Motorcycle Dealerships _____   2. _____ Motorcycle Repair Shops _____
3. _____   4. _____
5. _____   6. _____

## PART IV. WRITING EMPLOYMENT OBJECTIVES

Write five employment objectives according to their desirability to the employment seeker and the availability of the job in the labor market. Each objective should include a job title, industrial classification, and geographical area. The objective can be changed by substituting one or more of the three elements of the objective. The objectives will give direction and priority to the individual's search for employment.

### First Employment Objective

Job Title: __Motorcycle mechanic__

Industrial Classification: __Motorcycle dealership__

Geographical Area: __Hometown, USA__

### Second Employment Objective

Job Title: __Motorcycle mechanic__

Industrial Classification: __Motorcycle repair shops__

Geographical Area: __Hometown, USA__

### Third Employment Objective

Job Title: __Machinist__

Industrial Classification: __Tool manufacturing companies__

Geographical Area: __Hometown, USA__

### Fourth Employment Objective

Job Title: __Auto-parts stock clerk__

Industrial Classification: __New-car dealerships__

Geographical Area: __Hometown, USA__

### Fifth Employment Objective

Job Title: __Auto-parts stock clerk__

Industrial Classification: __Auto-parts stores__

Geographical Area: __Hometown, USA__

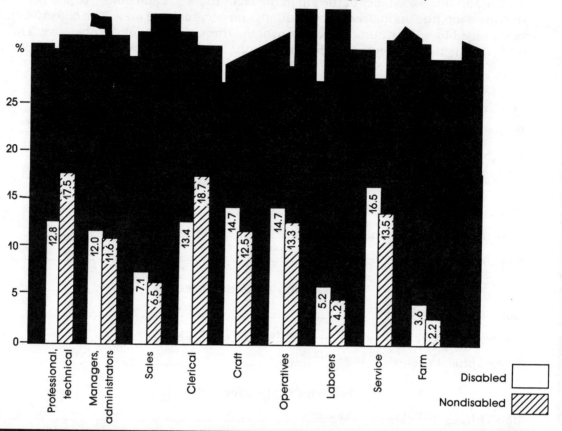

Figure 7-5. Occupations held by disabled and non-disabled workers. (From: *Disabled adults in America*. Washington, D.C.: President's Committee on Employment of the Handicapped, 1985.)

Legend:
- Disabled
- Nondisabled

Values:
- Professional, technical: 12.8 / 17.5
- Managers, administrators: 12.0 / 11.6
- Sales: 7.1 / 6.5
- Clerical: 13.4 / 18.7
- Craft: 14.7 / 12.5
- Operatives: 14.7 / 13.3
- Laborers: 5.2 / 4.2
- Service: 16.5 / 13.5
- Farm: 3.6 / 2.2

**Table 7-4.** Sample List of Jobs Held by Workers with Mental Retardation

| | | |
|---|---|---|
| Laundry worker | Farm laborer | Domestic worker |
| Library assistant | Food service worker | Baker |
| Mail clerk | Presser | Packer |
| Medical technician | Printing plant worker | Textile machine tender |
| Clerical aide | Furniture repairman | Manicurist |
| Cook | Maintenance worker | Usher |
| Messenger | Stock clerk | Dayworker |
| Nursery worker | Janitor | Upholsterer |
| Office machine operator | Telephone operator | Photocopy operator |
| Dishwasher | Laborer | Assembler |
| Painter | Warehouseman | Ward attendant |

Reprinted from: Association for Retarded Citizens. *Pamphlet: This isn't kindness. It's good business.* Arlington, Tx.: AARC.

# 8

# Job Analyses and Job Accommodations

**H**abilitation and rehabilitation professionals will encounter some clients whose employability is incomplete because their disabilities restrict them from performing fully all of the tasks that compose a given job. Consequently, the employability of these clients may depend on the willingness of employers to provide or to allow either some type of job accommodation or an extended period of on-the-job training. In such cases, a job analysis will help clients identify functional limitations and develop job-accommodation strategies before beginning their search for employment. The objective of developing job-accommodation strategies is to eliminate, or at least reduce, the functional barriers that are caused by the handicaps of clients. The types of job accommodations include the use of specialized products, job restructuring, and worksite alterations.

Many employers, especially those who underestimate the employability of clients, will not know that job-accommodation strategies can improve the work potentials of individuals with handicaps. In all likelihood, they have never heard of job accommodations and, unless they are told, they will never know that the productivity of workers with handicaps can be improved through such measures. Therefore clients, professionals, and other advocates should be fully prepared to provide this information to potential employers.

Job analyses can also be used to verify the appropriateness of vocational choices made by clients. Because many clients choose employment objectives based on incomplete and selective job information, they often find that the job includes undesirable assignments, or they learn that they are not qualified for the positions they seek. In such cases, a job analysis will help to insure that clients are pursuing the jobs they really want and that they have acceptable qualifications for their employment objectives.

Figure 8-1 presents a model for conducting job analyses and making job accommodations. Using the procedures for selecting employment objectives described in Chapter 7, professionals can assist clients in identifying an employment alternative for the job

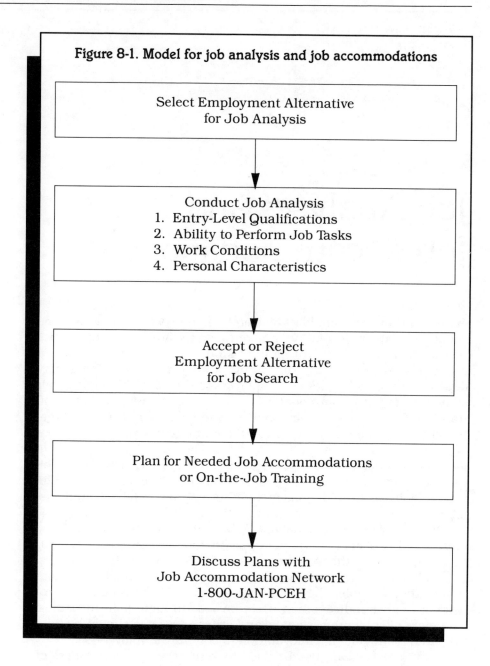

Figure 8-1. Model for job analysis and job accommodations

Select Employment Alternative
for Job Analysis

Conduct Job Analysis
1. Entry-Level Qualifications
2. Ability to Perform Job Tasks
3. Work Conditions
4. Personal Characteristics

Accept or Reject
Employment Alternative
for Job Search

Plan for Needed Job Accommodations
or On-the-Job Training

Discuss Plans with
Job Accommodation Network
1-800-JAN-PCEH

analysis. A "Job Analysis and Job Accommodation" form based on this model has been developed for client use. The job analysis includes the traditional concerns of assessing job tasks and work conditions, as well as that of assessing traditional vocational decision-making criteria of entry-level qualifications and personality characteristics. This chapter includes sections on job analysis, on job accommodations, and on the Job Accommodation Network. Figure 8-2 presents a case study using the model "Job Analysis and Job Accommodation" form.

Figure 8-2. Case study: job analysis and job accommodation

# JOB ANALYSIS AND JOB ACCOMMODATION

Name _____ Allen Xxxx _____ Date ___ 9/27/87 ___

Organization _____ Staff Member _____

This form will help employment seekers determine whether a selected job alternative is appropriate for them. It includes sections on: entry-level qualifications, ability to perform job tasks, work conditions, personal characteristics, decision making, and need for job accommodations or on-the-job training.

## I. GENERAL INFORMATION

Selected employment alternative to be analyzed: _____ Janitor _____

Reason for selecting this employment alternative: __Discussed plans with vocational__

__counselor.__ _____

Sources of information for job analysis:

__x__ Occupational descriptions from the *Dictionary of Occupational Titles*, the *Occupational Outlook Handbook*, or other formal sources.

__x__ Job description and other information provided by employer.

____ Discussions with people knowledgeable about this job.

Based on information gathered from occupational descriptions, list the names of jobs that are similar to the one being assessed:

1) Maintenance worker   2) Porter _____

## II. ENTRY-LEVEL QUALIFICATIONS

*Instructions:* (1) Based on the information obtained for the analysis, list the entry-level requirements for this job. (2) By placing a check mark in either the yes or the no column, indicate whether or not the individual has these entry requirements.

Yes     No

__x__   ____   Required degrees: __Usually not required__

__x__   ____   Licenses/certificates: __None required__

__x__   ____   Apprenticeships/specialized training: __None required__

__x__   ____   Experience: __Some experience is helpful__

**Continued**

Figure 8-2 Continued

## III. ABILITY TO PERFORM JOB TASKS

*Instructions:* (1) List the tasks that a worker will normally have to perform in this job. (2) By placing a check mark in either the yes or the no column, indicate whether or not the individual has any impairments or disabilities that will limit the ability to perform the job tasks. (3) Identify the general area of the functional limitation by placing a check mark in one of the five columns at the right of the page.

| Yes | No | | Cognitive Abilities | Motor-Mobile Abilities | Communication Abilities | Sensory Abilities | General Health |
|-----|-----|-----|-----|-----|-----|-----|-----|
| x | ___ | Task #1: __Sweeping floors__ | ___ | ___ | ___ | ___ | ___ |
| x | ___ | Task #2: __Vacuuming rugs__ | ___ | ___ | ___ | ___ | ___ |
| x | ___ | Task #3: __Emptying trash cans__ | ___ | ___ | ___ | ___ | ___ |
| x | ___ | Task #4: __Cleaning restrooms__ | ___ | ___ | ___ | ___ | ___ |
| ___ | x | Task #5: __Participating in monthly inventorying of stock (at a retail store)__ | x | ___ | ___ | ___ | ___ |
| ___ | ___ | Task #6: _____ | ___ | ___ | ___ | ___ | ___ |

## IV. WORK CONDITIONS

*Instructions:* By placing a check mark in either the yes or the no column, indicate whether the working conditions are appropriate for the individual.

Yes  No

x  ___  *Architectural accessibility:* Will the architectural accessibility (parking, low curbs, ramps, elevators, wide doorways, restrooms with wide stalls and handle bars) of the work environment be appropriate for the individual?

x  ___  *Work schedule:* Will the work schedule (hours, shift, shift rotations) be appropriate for the individual?

x  ___  *Work environment:* Will the work environment (cleanliness, indoors/outdoors, pollutants) be appropriate for the individual?

| Yes | No | |
|-----|----|----|
| x | ___ | *Training and supervision:* Will there be adequate training and supervision for the individual? |
| x | ___ | *Salary and benefits:* Are the starting salary and the benefits acceptable to the individual? |
| x | ___ | *Job Availability:* Are there local industries that employ people in this job? |

## V. PERSONAL CHARACTERISTICS

*Instructions:* By placing a check mark in either the yes or the no column, indicate whether the individual has the appropriate personal characteristics for this employment alternative.

| Yes | No | |
|-----|----|----|
| x | ___ | *Appearance:* Is the individual's appearance (cleanliness, grooming, and manner of dress) appropriate for this occupation? |
| x | ___ | *Social Skills:* Are the individual's social skills (meeting people, working with others, lack of inappropriate behavior) appropriate for this occupation? |
| x | ___ | *Work Attitudes:* Are the individual's work attitudes (respect for authority, willingness to follow directions, reliability, and punctuality) appropriate for this occupation? |

## VI. DECISION MAKING

*Instructions:* Based on the analysis of each of the sections, indicate with a check mark whether this employment alternative is: (1) Appropriate, (2) Appropriate with job accommodations or on-the-job training, or (3) Inappropriate.

| | Appropriate | Appropriate w/Accommodations | Inappropriate |
|---|---|---|---|
| 1. *Entry-Level Qualifications* | x | | |
| 2. Ability to Perform Job Tasks | | x | |
| 3. Work Conditions | x | | |
| 4. Personal Characteristics | x | | |

Jobs evaluated as appropriate or appropriate with job accommodations or on-the-job training should be considered for the employment search. Jobs evaluated as inappropriate should not be considered for the employment search.

Continued

**Figure 8-2 Continued**

## VII. NEED FOR JOB ACCOMMODATIONS OR ON-THE-JOB TRAINING

*Instructions:* (1) In the left column, describe the need for job accommodations. (2) In the right column, list the possible job accommodations (products, job restructuring, worksite modifications) or on-the-job training that might be needed to improve the individual's employability for this occupation.

| Job-Accommodation Needs | Possible Accommodations or On-The-Job Training |
|---|---|
| Without training, Allen will have difficulty working with computerized systems used in inventory control. | (1) <u>On-the-Job Training:</u> Allen could be taught to enter data on the computer terminal.<br><br>(2) <u>Job Restructuring:</u> Without data-entry training, Allen should perform inventorying tasks that do not require data-entry skills. |

Call the Job Accommodation Network for expert consultation: 1-800-JAN-PCEH

# JOB ANALYSIS

A job analysis is a structured, systematic, and thorough assessment of the characteristics of a given job. In addition to measuring job requirements, the job-analysis model used in this text also includes an analysis of worker characteristics. This job-analysis model compares the characteristics of a selected job with the characteristics of a client in four categories: entry-level qualifications, ability to perform job tasks, working conditions, and personality characteristics. The objective of conducting a job analysis is to insure that clients have an accurate understanding of the job tasks, the work conditions, and the desirable worker qualifications. With this information, professionals and clients can verify vocational choices, plan job-accommodation strategies, prepare on-the-job training programs, highlight qualifications for employment searches, and improve job skills to qualify for advancements and promotions.

Information about job requirements can be obtained from career literature such as the *Occupational Outlook Handbook* (U.S. Department of Labor, Bureau of Labor Statistics, 1987) and the *Dictionary of Occupational Titles* (U.S. Department of Labor, Employment and Training Administration, 1977). Other sources of information include job descriptions from employers, interviews with people knowledgeable about the selected occupation, computerized career-planning programs, and various career associations. Information about clients can be gathered from the model forms provided in this book (i.e., Work Readiness Assessment, Survey of Employment Barriers), educational records, health and rehabilitation records, previous habilitation or rehabilitation assessments, evaluations made by former employers and teachers, client references, client self-reports, and observations by professionals. More thorough or specific client assessments may be needed for clients with multiple handicaps.

A "Job Analysis and Job Accommodation" form has been developed based on the model presented in Figure 8-1. The form will help to identify those areas in which characteristics of the job match the characteristics of clients. These matched areas represent client qualifications. The form will also help to identify those areas in which characteristics of the job and the individual do not match. These unmatched areas represent potential barriers to employment. In some cases, clients might be well advised to consider other career alternatives. In other cases, the most appropriate plan of action might be to develop job accommodations and other strategies for those areas in which clients are underqualified for their selected employment objectives. The form concludes with a section on assessing the need for job accommodations or on-the-job training. After developing these strategies, it is recommmended that professionals discuss these plans with a staff member of the Job Accommodation Network. Information on the Job Accommodation Network is provided in a subsequent section of this chapter.

## JOB ACCOMMODATIONS

The employment of people with handicaps may require employers to provide some type of job accommodation or an extended period of on-the-job training. Job accommodations may involve the use of specialized products or equipment, job restructuring, or worksite modifications. For example, specialized products might include talking calculators for unsighted individuals or a teletype for people with hearing impairments. Job restructuring might involve removing telephone-answering responsibilities from hearing-impaired clerical workers and assigning additional filing responsibilities. Worksite modifications might include the provision of special parking and ramps for people with orthopedic impairments. Table 8-1 lists some examples of job accommodations. This list provides only a small sample of the potential job accommodations that can improve the employability of people with handicaps. A more comprehensive list is not included in this text because of space limitations and because technological developments in the manufacturing of specialized products will quickly render many suggestions obsolete. Therefore, once an accommodation need has been identified, it is recommended that professionals or employers telephone the Job Accommodation Network to develop further accommodation strategies. This national service, available through a toll-free telephone number, is the most comprehensive and up-to-date resource center for job accommodations.

It is important to note that job accommodations are not made just for new applicants. Table 8-2 summarizes the results of a recent evaluation survey of The Job Accommodation Network. The survey reported that, in addition to providing services to new applicants, employers also provided these services to currently employed workers for purposes of job retention, improved productivity, promotion, and other reasons. In fact, in a national survey of individuals with disabilities, it was reported that "thirty-five percent of disabled people who work now or who have worked full-time while disabled say that their employer made some sort of accommodation for their disability" (Louis Harris and Associates, 1986, p. 73). Although these findings suggest that most workers with disabilities do not need job accommodations, the employability of many disabled workers will still require accommodations at the worksite.

For many years, employers have assumed that the cost of accommodating workers with handicaps was prohibitive. It has been found, however, that most job accommodations can be implemented with little or no expense to employers. A national survey of employers indicated that "overwhelming majorities of top managers (81%), Equal Employment Opportunity (EEO) officers (79%), department heads/ line managers (75%), and small business managers (64%) say that the average cost of employing a disabled person is about the same as the cost of employing non-disabled persons" (Louis Harris and Associates, 1987, p. 60). The fact that job accommodations are generally

---

**Table 8-1.** Sample List of Job Accommodations

---

**Job Accommodation Products**
- Telephone amplifiers for workers with hearing impairments
- Headset telephones for workers with cerebral palsy
- Vibrating signal systems that convert auditory alarm signals into vibrations on a transmitter worn by workers with hearing impairments
- Talking calculators for workers with visual impairments

**Job Restructuring**
- Providing flexible working hours, rest periods, or assignments to be completed in the home
- Allowing retail sales workers with an inability to perform mathematical calculations to let other workers record sales and operate the cash register
- Reassigning telephone-answering responsibilities of clerical workers with hearing impairments to other office workers in exchange for additional typing responsibilities
- Removing the responsibilities of writing analytical monthly reports from stock clerks with mental retardation.

**Worksite Modifications**
- Reorganizing furniture to allow workers in wheelchairs to have greater mobility within the office
- Moving the jobsite to a ground-level floor, allowing greater accessibility to workers with orthopedic impairments
- Installing ramps and widening doorways for workers in wheelchairs
- Providing handicapped parking spaces, allowing easy access for workers with orthopedic impairments

---

not expensive is also supported in the report of the Job Accommodations Network. Table 8-2 indicates that 50% of the job accommodations surveyed in the report cost $50 or less and many cost nothing at all. The table also indicates that most accommodations covered in the report were made for people with sensory (47%) or motor (30%) disabilities. The Harris survey reported that employers made the following types of accommodations for their workers with disabilities: 90% removed architectural barriers, 50% purchased special equipment, 50% adjusted work hours or restructured jobs, 23% provided readers or interpreters to help blind or speech- and hearing-impaired employees, and 10% made other types of accommodations.

The President's Committee on Employment of the Handicapped suggested the following steps to implement job accommodations:

☐ Involve the newly hired disabled person in decisions on accommodations.
☐ Ask disabled job applicants what accommodations would assist their placement.

**Table 8-2.** Selected Evaluation Survey Highlights of the Job Accommodation Network (JAN)

**1. Status of Individual About Whom JAN Was Called**

| | |
|---|---|
| New Applicant | 39% |
| Current Employee | 61% |
|    Job retention (26%) | |
|    Improved productivity (19%) | |
|    Promotion (9%) | |
|    Other (7%) | |

**2. Cost of Job Accommodation to Employer**

| | |
|---|---|
| No cost | 31% |
| Between $1 and $50 | 19% |
| Between $50 and $500 | 19% |
| Between $500 and $1,000 | 19% |
| Between $1,000 and $5,000 | 12% |

**3. Disabilities of Individuals Accommodated**

| | |
|---|---|
| Sensory | 47% |
|    Vision (24%) | |
|    Hearing (21%) | |
|    Other (2%) | |
| Motor | 30% |
| Neurological Functioning | 3% |
| Multiple Handicaps | 7% |
| Other Bodily Systems | 13% |

From the *Job Accommodation Network Evaluation Study: Executive Summary.* (1987, April). Morgantown, WV: Job Accommodation Network.

□ Encourage managers and supervisors to identify jobs or tasks in which changes would be minimal.

□ Develop an orientation program for the handicapped worker.

□ Hold preemployment discussions with supervisors and co-workers.

□ Handle any on-the-job problems immediately (Employer Guide, 1984)

One form of job accommodation, perhaps not thought of as an accommodation, is providing an extended period of on-the-job training through one of the models of supported employment. This strategy has proven to be particularly useful for people with mental retardation. These workers are placed in positions and are provided with an extensive and systematic training program. Job coaches may be assigned to assist them in learning job tasks, working with other people, and functioning within the work environment. Work-adjustment strategies are discussed in greater detail in Chapter 11.

The Association for Retarded Citizens (ARC) of the United States has provided over 36,000 individuals labeled mentally retarded with job training and employment opportunities through their National Employment and Training Project, formerly called On-the-Job Training Project. ARC reimburses employers for a set percentage of the entry-level wages for clients who participate in the 320-hour on-the-job training project. More information on ARC's National Employment and Training Project is included in Chapter 12.

## JOB ACCOMMODATION NETWORK

In 1984 the Job Accommodation Network (JAN) began offering information and consulting services on individualized job-accommodation solutions to employers and others desiring to hire, retain, or promote individuals with disabilities. The development of this network has been achieved through the collaborative efforts of the President's Committee on Employment of the Handicapped (PCEH), the West Virginia Research and Training Center at West Virginia University, the U.S. National Institute for Handicapped Research, the U.S. Rehabilitation Services Administration, and private industry. This service represents the most comprehensive resource for job accommodations currently available in the United States.

The job-accommodation information and consulting services provided by JAN are free to employers, professionals, and individuals with handicaps. This network provides a data base that catalogs and stores information on job accommodations successfully used in the workplace by employers. The data base also contains other information concerning job accommodations such as accommodation resources, including the names and addresses of individuals and organizations experienced in the modification of work environments for persons with disabilities.

Access to the Job Accommodation Network is presently available through the toll-free telephone number 1-800-JAN-PCEH. Between July 1984 and December 1986, JAN received 4,816 inquiries (Job Accommodation Network, 1987, p. 1). Desired information is retrieved and transmitted by individuals who are skilled in translating expressed job-accommodation needs into specific job-accommodation strategies or techniques. Individuals using the network also have access to other information resources such as the National Rehabilitation Information Center and ABLEDATA, which contains information on job-accommodation products and equipment. A network of expert consultants is also available to discuss unusual or difficult accommodation problems. It is recommended that professionals telephone JAN for accommodation ideas or for reviewing their job-accommodation strategies.

# 9

# Characterizing Clients as Qualified Workers

**V**irtually all people searching for employment have felt the feelings of powerlessness and frustration that result from having other people controlling the decisions that so profoundly affect their lives. Although it is clearly the employers who possess the decision-making powers, it is the job seekers who control the amount and quality of information received by the employers. This information is often the only decision-making resource used by employers when selecting people for employment. Many employers would agree that the people who get hired are not always the individuals best suited for the job. The candidates who do get hired are usually the ones who have provided the most persuasive information to the decision makers.

An error often made by employment seekers is providing inadequate job-related information that fails to characterize them as qualified workers. An additional error often made by employment seekers with disabilities is not fully appreciating the importance of providing detailed descriptions of their employability. Without this information, employers are left in an information vacuum, which is all too often filled with stereotypical impressions. Disabled applicants who fail to provide quality information to employers will have diminished chances of obtaining a good job in a competitive labor market. It is important to remember that employers want to make good choices when selecting workers because they often have to work a long time with the people they select. Clients must understand that the effectiveness of employer hiring decisions is often limited to the quantity and quality of information received from job applicants.

Figure 9-1 presents a model for identifying job-related information. The foundation for this process is the selection of appropriate employment alternatives for the job search. Chapter 7 provides detailed instructions for selecting employment objectives. The remainder of this chapter discusses how to identify job-related information and how to present it effectively to employers through written communications and job interviews. Professionals are likely to

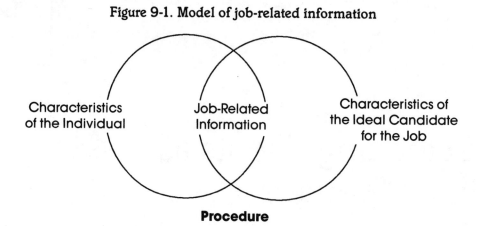

Figure 9-1. Model of job-related information

**Procedure**

1. Select an employment alternative for the job search.

2. Identify or estimate the characteristics of an ideal candidate for the selected employment alternative.

3. Identify and highlight client information that matches the characteristics of an ideal candidate.

observe the crystalization of a vocational self-concept and improved self-confidence as clients describe their qualifications for their selected employment objectives.

## JOB RELATED INFORMATION

The criteria used by employers for hiring applicants can usually be estimated with a fair degree of accuracy if clients are searching for specific jobs. In other words, clients can usually predict the information employers hope to receive from their job applicants. Employers usually have a list of qualifications an ideal candidate. Although employers' personal preferences will make this estimation somewhat incomplete, the core tasks of a given job are knowable. With information about the essential job tasks, clients can identify the job-related information that qualifies them for their employment objectives.

Job titles are names given to groups of tasks or work assignments that are commonly performed by the employees who work at them. Although subtle differences may be observed in the work assignments for the same job at different places of employment, there are core job tasks that remain fairly constant. For example, the position of receptionist will entail essential job tasks that cause it to be titled receptionist.

Information about jobs is readily available from a variety of sources. Job or career information can be found in career literature available in most libraries. Among the more commonly used career resources are the *Dictionary of Occupational Titles* (DOT) (U.S. Department of Labor, Employment and Training Administration, 1977) and the *Occupational Outlook Handbook* (OOH) (U.S. Department of Labor, 1987). Information about jobs can also be identified by conducting information interviews with employers and other knowledgeable people.

The essential information employers need for their decision making is listed in Table 9-1. The four categories should serve as the major themes of all written and verbal descriptions of client employability. Both the client and the professional should list the client's job-related information in each category. For example, in the category of education, list the degrees, training, licenses, certificates, courses, and other formal and informal educational experiences that contribute to qualifying clients for their objectives. In the experience category, list the paid, volunteer, and on-the-job-training experiences that contribute to qualifying clients for their objectives. The competencies category should include a list of clients' knowledge, skills, and abilities that qualify them for their objectives. In the personal characteristics category, list the personality traits, values, or attitudes that qualify clients for their objectives.

Clients with little training or work experience should be informed that for some jobs, personality traits and attitudes are the primary qualifications for employment. Some employers find it easy to train new workers for unskilled or semiskilled employment but find it

---

**Table 9-1.** Job Related Information Needed for Employer Decision Making

| Category | What the employer needs to know |
|---|---|
| Education | Do you have any training or education for this job? |
| Experience | Do you have experience working in this job or jobs similar to it? |
| Competencies | What knowledge, skills, and abilities do you possess for this job? |
| Personal characteristics | Do you have any personality traits, values, or attitudes that might qualify you for this job? |

almost impossible to instill traits of cooperativeness and reliability in people who do not already possess those traits. In such cases, personality traits represent job-related information.

Information that is not job related should be excluded from employment-search communications. For example, one client searching for a clerical job wanted to know if she should include information that she can operate a sewing machine on her résumé. This type of information would serve only to distort her characterization as a clerical worker.

## COMMUNICATING QUALIFICATIONS IN WRITING

Communicating employment qualifications through writing provides a valuable resource for both clients and employers. These resources can include résumés, letters, and job-application forms. Employers often rely on these written sources as a time- and cost-efficient way of selecting a smaller number of candidates from a larger group of applicants. It is common practice for employers to eliminate most applicants from employment consideration based solely on the written descriptions of their qualifications. Even among the applicants selected to receive job interviews, written descriptions of applicant qualifications will help shape employer perceptions and help employers remember an applicant's qualifying assets. Stereotypical impressions of individuals with handicaps should always be considered as a potential barrier to employment for individuals with disabilities. Written descriptions of qualifications are especially important for individuals with handicaps because they help employers look beyond stereotypes and see applicants' true work potentials. Therefore, it is strongly recommended that professionals encourage their clients to use a written profile of their qualifications as they search for employment. In some instances, professionals or significant others may need to write the profiles for clients who have limited writing abilities.

Written communications can be categorized as applicant-initiated descriptions or as employer-initiated descriptions. Written descriptions of qualifications initiated by applicants generally include résumés and letters of application. Employer-initiated descriptions usually include job applications obtained in personnel offices or at the worksites. Written descriptions initiated by applicants offer clients the greatest control over the amount, quality, organization, and appearance of their job-related information.

Filling out job applications often offers an inadequate medium for characterizing clients as qualified applicants. Qualifications for many unskilled, semiskilled, and skilled jobs may include information not normally asked for in job applications. Figure 9-2 indicates that William's primary qualifications for the position of nurse aide are his reaction to his own illness and his experience of caring for his

**Figure 9-2. Sample résumé for William.**

William is pursuing an unskilled job working with people. William has had epilepsy throughout his life, and at one point, his seizures increased so that he had to quit his job as a meat packer. As a result of a change in his medication, he has been seizure free for several years. He no longer wants to work in a manufacturing job. His qualifications for his employment objective are his sensitivity gained through his own illness and through his experience in caring for his aging parents. (employment level: unskilled; area: people)

WILLIAM XXXXXXXX
248 Second Street
Hometown, USA 00000
(000) 000-0000

| | |
|---|---|
| EMPLOYMENT OBJECTIVE | Nurse Aide or Orderly |
| EXPERIENCE | Care for aging parents by helping with shaving, bathing, assist in walking, transportation, setting medication schedules, grooming, dressing, and feeding. |
| INTEREST IN HELPING PEOPLE | After personal illness, I decided to pursue a career in helping people. The illness has been controlled through medication and is no longer a problem. |
| | Experience of caring for aging parents gave reassurance that I would like a career in helping people. |
| PERSONALITY TRAITS | Reliable, dependable, conscientious, and sensitive to the needs of others. |
| WORK EXPERIENCE | Worked for sixteen years as a meat packer for Local Meats, Inc., Hometown, USA During those years I had an excellent work record. |
| EDUCATION | HS Diploma from Hometown High School |
| REFERENCES | Available on request |

elderly parents, and Figure 9-3 documents that Mark's primary qualifications for the position of motorcycle mechanic come from his hobby of rebuilding and reselling motorcycles. Their characterizations as qualified workers could not have been achieved through employer job applications. In other cases, an individual's qualifications may be composed of selected information from a variety of experiences. For example, Figure 9-4 identifies Paul's qualifications to work in recreation or sports management as a combination of vari-

**Figure 9-3. Sample letter of application for Mark.**

Mark is seeking a skilled job working as a motorcycle mechanic. Mark has a learning disability that limits his ability to read and write. His qualifications for his employment objective come primarily from his hobby of rebuilding and reselling used motorcycles. It was decided to summarize his qualifications in a letter. (employment level: skilled; area: things)

MARK XXXXXXXX
100 East Street, Hometown, USA 00000
(000) 000-0000

January 30, 1988

Mr. William Xxxxxxxx
Suzuki Motorcycle
100 Center Avenue
Hometown, USA 00000

RE: Job-Application: Motorcycle Mechanic

Dear Mr Xxxxxxxx:

   Please consider me for employment in or leading to the position of motorcycle mechanic.

   I am very mechanically inclined. Over the last six years I have bought approximately fifty used motorcycles, rebuilt them, and resold them.

   Working with motorcycles is a hobby I would like to turn into a career. If you would like more information, I can be reached at the above telephone number. Thank you.

Sincerely yours,


Mark Xxxxxxxx

ous work experiences and of his interest in sports. The richness of his characterization as a recreation or sports manager could never be accomplished in a typical job application.

The importance of writing clear descriptions of qualifications for selected employment objectives cannot be overstated. Professionals should insure that clients are achieving maximum quality, as well as clarity, in their written communications. Employers use these written descriptions to judge the work quality of applicants because résumés and letters of application are, in effect, work samples of the

**Figure 9-4. Sample résumé for Paul.**

Paul is seeking a skilled-level job working with people. A former athlete, he now has limited physical capabilities as the result of a heart condition. He is seeking employment in recreation or sports management. His qualifications for this employment objective are his knowledge and interest in sports and his management skills learned through a variety of jobs that are only slightly related to his objective. Job-related skills that were learned in those jobs are explained in great detail. He also decided to expand his credentials by returning to college as a part-time student. (employment level: skilled; area: people)

---

### PAUL XXXXXXXX
100 Tenth Avenue, Hometown, USA 00000
(000) 000-0000

EMPLOYMENT OBJECTIVE: To obtain a position in recreation or sports management

EDUCATION: Pursuing a Bachelors of Science Degree in Management from Local College. Part-time evenings, twenty one credits completed.

#### COMPETENCIES

| | |
|---|---|
| Recreation & Sports | • Played short-stop in the minor league for a National League Team.<br>• Played organized sports of soccer, flag football, and individual sports of golf, karate, swimming, jogging, weight lifting, and nautilus. |
| Program Development | • Started the "Over Thirty" Basketball League for the Hometown City Recreation Dept. The leage has ten teams and over 100 participants.<br>• Implemented the first city-wide baseball clinic involving four presentations with over 200 participants.<br>• Directed the Hometown American Legion Baseball Program |
| Planning & Organizing | • Billed and collected funds from hundreds of Hometown businesses for the Office of Licenses and Inspections.<br>• Organized schedules and kept statistics for ten teams and approximately 180 players as President of the Hometown Baseball Association. |
| Writing | • Served as sports editor for the Hometown College newspaper.<br>• Publicized Hometown Baseball Association through local newspapers. |
| Fund Raising | • Raised approximately $4,500 for the Falcons Youth Football Team and $2,000 annually for the American Legion Teams. |
| Supervision | • Supervised the daily work activities of seven recreational aides for the Recreational Dept. of the City of Hometown.<br>• Supervised work details of twenty workers in the Dept. of Highway for the City of Hometown. |

#### EXPERIENCE

Foreman, Dept. of Public Works, City of Hometown, 1982-87
Health Inspector, Dept. of Health, City of Hometown, 1977-82
Compliance Officer, License and Inspection Dept., City of Hometown, 1975-77
Recreational Aide, Dept. of Parks & Recreation, City of Hometown, 1973-75
Production Worker, RCA, Hometown, USA, 1971-73
Semi-Professional Baseball Player, National League Team, 1968-71

applicants who submitted them. This is especially true for individuals who are seeking clerical positions.

Eight written samples of applicant qualifications appearing in Figures 9-2 through 9-8 demonstrate effective methods of presenting job-related information for selected employment objectives. The samples include written profiles of individuals with handicaps who were seeking jobs at all levels and types of employment. Use of a model "Employment Application" form is demonstrated in Figure 9-9. The following are suggestions for effectively communicating qualifications through writing.

☐ Encourage clients to use résumés, letters of application, or the model "Employment Application" form as their primary methods of communicating qualifications. Often employers will not require applicants to complete job applications if their résumés or other documents effectively describe their qualifications.

☐ Since job applications usually offer an inadequate format for describing applicant qualifications, clients should try to substitute their résumés or other written correspondence for job applications whenever possible. If an employer indicates that applicants must complete job applications for employment consideration, direct clients to submit their résumés or other written correspondence with their job applications.

☐ Discourage clients from dropping in on employers to complete job applications. This is especially important for clients with limited reading and writing abilities. They should complete applications at home and have someone check it for spelling, grammar, and general impression. They can obtain job applications either by requesting them over the telephone or by picking them up at the places of employment.

☐ High-quality paper and a good typewriter should be used in the preparation of résumés and other written correspondence. Word processors, now widely available, are an excellent tool for formating and phrasing written communications. Résumé-preparation services are available in many communities.

☐ Use white or slightly off-white paper. Do not use attention-getting colors such as yellow or pink.

☐ Do not lie or use obvious exaggerations in language.

☐ Résumés should generally be on one page and should be easy to read. The most important features in a résumé should be obvious by simply looking at it. Use of selective underlining, capitalizing, and highlighting will help to accomplish this task.

☐ Résumé contents should include primarily job-related information. Unrelated information should be omitted or understated. For example, a history of six different jobs held during the high school years could be summarized

## Figure 9-5. Sample résumé for Allen.

Allen is seeking an unskilled job as a maintenance worker. He is 34 years old and has mild to moderate mental retardation. His primary qualifications for this work are his reliability, maturity, good attitude, and good health. These traits are listed in his qualification highlights, and his job-related experiences are described in the experience category. Because employers rarely find a good working attitude among workers for this position, his personality traits are a primary qualification for this job. (employment level: unskilled; area: things)

---

**ALLEN XXXXXXXX**
505 N. First Street
Hometown, USA 00000
(000) 000-0000

| | |
|---|---|
| EMPLOYMENT OBJECTIVE | Maintenance Worker |
| QUALIFICATION HIGHLIGHTS | • Reliable and punctual<br>• Mature and hardworking<br>• Good general health |
| EXPERIENCE | Local Hospital, Hometown, USA 1978-85<br>Position: Orderly |
| | Duties included transporting patients to various departments, assisting nurses, and helping the maintenance department in cleaning floors. |
| | Hometown Tribune, Hometown, USA 1968-71<br>Position: Teletype copyboy |
| | Duties included taking teletype materials from nine teletype machines and delivering them to the printers. |
| EDUCATION | Hometown High School, Hometown, USA |
| | Local Community College, Hometown, USA<br>Ten Week GED Program, Passed the GED Test |
| PERSONAL TRAITS | Hardworking, punctual, reliable, loyal |
| REFERENCES | Available on request |

**Figure 9-6. Sample résumé for Mary.**

Mary is seeking employment working in unskilled clerical positions. Mary has mild to moderate mental retardation and has been working as a dishwasher for a local restaurant. Her primary qualifications for her objective are her desire to be employed in the clerical field and her reliability that was established in her dishwashing job. To increase her qualifications, she secured a volunteer position assisting a desk clerk at a local hotel. In that volunteering experience, she was taught some elementary office skills. (employment level: unskilled; area: data)

---

MARY XXXXXXXX
111 Central Avenue
Hometown, USA 00000
(000) 000-0000

| | |
|---|---|
| EMPLOYMENT OBJECTIVE | Clerical positions such as mail clerk, file clerk, stock clerk, desk clerk, and other general clerical positions. |
| RELATED EXPERIENCE | To gain clerical experience, I am currently volunteering as a desk clerk at the Local Hotel. |
| EDUCATION | Hometown High School, Graduated 1983<br>Local Community College, one course in English. |
| EMPLOYMENT | Local Restaurant, Hometown USA, Dishwasher, March, 1986 to present. |
| INTERST & WILLINGNESS TO LEARN | In addition to volunteering at the Local Hotel, I am planning to take a typing course to improve my clerical skills. |
| RELIABILITY | In my present job, I have only missed one day of work in the last year. On that day I arranged for someone else to cover my job. |
| ABILITIES | General office duties of filing, sorting mail, preparing outgoing mail, xeroxing, using an adding machine, stocking inventories, and answering telephones. |
| PERSONAL TRAITS | Neat in appearance, courteous, and organized. |

---

**Figure 9-7. Sample résumé for Patricia.**

Patricia is seeking a skilled position working with data. More specifically, she is seeking employment as an accounting or bookkeeping clerk. Patricia has been out of the labor market for more than 20 years while raising a family and coping with general health problems that have left her in a weakened condition with limited endurance. Her qualifications include her associate degree, the competencies she possesses, and her employment as a time clerk. (employment level: skilled; area: data)

---

PATRICIA XXXXXXXX
411 South Street, Hometown, USA 00000
(000) 000-0000

EMPLOYMENT OBJECTIVE

An accounting or bookkeeping position with an opportunity for professional development.

EDUCATION

Associate of Science Degree in Accounting from Local Community College, Hometown, USA, 1986

Accounting Courses: Principles of Accounting I, Principles of Accounting II, Intermediate Accounting I, Intermediate Accounting II, Cost Accounting.

Related Courses: Business Math, College Math, Statistics, Introduction to Data Processing, Business Communications.

Grade Point Average: 3.12 CQPA

Activities: Served as treasurer for the Student Government

COMPETENCIES

| Accounting | • Post accounts receivables and accounts payables<br>• Prepare invoices, balance sheets, billing statements, and bank reconciliations |
| Computation | • Accurately calculate mathematical and statistical statements and reports |
| Data Entry | • Type and enter data into computer terminals |
| Writing | • Write business correspondence and reports |

RELATED EXPERIENCE

Time Clerk, Local Manufacturing Corp., Hometown, USA Prepared employee time records to payroll department, recorded production of pressroom and finishing departments, and filed and answered telephones. 1959-64.

— References Available on Request —

**Figure 9-8. Sample résumé for Sandra.**

Sandra is seeking a professional position in communications or public relations. She has spina bifida and walks with the aid of crutches and braces. Her qualifications for her employment objective include her degree, the competencies she learned in her college curriculum, and a brief student internship. Unrelated part-time jobs she held were omitted. To add to her experience, she sought some volunteer work at the local public television station. (employment level: professional; area: communications)

---

### SANDRA XXXXXXXX
111 Main Street, Hometown, USA 00000
(000) 000-0000

#### EMPLOYMENT OBJECTIVE

An entry level communications position in advertising or public relations

#### EDUCATION

Bachelor of Arts Degree in English/Communications from the University of Hometown, Hometown, USA. Graduated 1986.

Related Courses: Basic Television Production, Advanced Television Production, Mass Communications Management, Writing for Television, Written Communications, Oral Communications, Educational Television.

#### COMPETENCIES

| | |
|---|---|
| Writing | • Wrote approximately twelve feature television entertainment scripts. Curriculum requirements.<br>• Wrote newsletter articles for the "Hometown Extra" Newsletter, Hometown Property Owners Association. |
| Video Production | • Set up physical environment, directed camera shots, and edited a video tape. Curriculum requirements. |
| Audio Production | • Operated an audio board to control broadcast microphones and musical intro's and outro's. Curriculum requirement. |
| Graphics | • Prepared graphic chyron displays for a video broadcast. Curriculum requirement.<br>• Designed layouts for a newsletter and activities calandar for the Hometown Property Owners Association. |
| Advertising Accounts | • Sold advertisement space to new and existing accounts for the Hometown newsletter, Hometown Property Owners Association. |

#### EXPERIENCE

Community Relations Assistant, Hometown Property Owners Association, Lake Peaceful, USA. Paid student internship. November to December, 1986.

Video Camera Operator, WWWW-TV, Hometown, USA. Volunteer. Spring, 1987

— References Available on Request —

**Figure 9-9. Sample employment application for Thomas.**

Thomas is seeking an unskilled job working as a warehouse-materials handler. He has moderate mental retardation and is 23 years of age. A simple "Employment Application" form helps to communicate his essential qualifications for this job: his good physical condition, his ability to work in a structured manner, and his reliability as a worker. (employment level: unskilled; area: things)

# EMPLOYMENT APPLICATION

Name ___ Thomas Xxxxxxxx _____

Address __ 1000 Main Street _____

City _____ Hometown _____

State _____ USA _____ Zip Code ___ 00000 ___

Telephone Number ___ (000) 000-0000 _____

Employment Objective: _____ Warehouse Materials Handler _____

_____

_____

| **Qualification Highlights** |
|---|
| PHYSICAL WORKER: In excellent physical condition and enjoy manual labor |
| |
| ORGANIZED WORKER: Able to work with materials in an orderly fashion within an organized work environment |
| |
| RELIABLE WORKER: Punctual, honest, and very dependable |
| |
| |
| |
| |

by stating, "Held a number of unrelated jobs during years in high school." Listing these jobs individually would confuse the theme of the client's characterization as a qualified worker.

☐ Use the category heading "Related Experience" to report job-related work experiences. The reader will assume that there are unrelated experiences.

☐ Increase qualifications by taking courses or by volunteering in order to obtain experience.

☐ There is mixed support for listing references on a résumé. If listed, the names, addresses, telephone numbers, and positions of three references should be listed at the end of the résumé. If not listed on the résumé, the references should be presented on a separate page, and a notation on the résumé should read "References Available on Request."

☐ References should include three people who can comment on the applicant's quality of work and personal character. At least two of the references should know candidates from past educational or employment experiences.

☐ The model "Employment Application" form should be reserved for clients seeking unskilled or semiskilled employment.

## COMMUNICATING QUALIFICATIONS IN JOB INTERVIEWS

Job interviews are the second and often the final step in the hiring process. Clients should appreciate that most applicants who receive job interviews are being seriously considered for employment. These candidates usually have been selected as the most qualified people among a larger group of applicants. In the interview, employers will gather additional information about the candidates. By doing a little investigative homework, interviewees can obtain closer estimates of the attributes employers are hoping to find in candidates. Professionals should instruct their clients to learn as much as possible about the available position, the company, and the employer's description of an ideal candidate for the position. This information can be obtained by requesting job descriptions from employers, by conducting information interviews with people knowledgeable about the company, and by conducting information interviews with people knowledgeable about similar positions.

Job interviews are also complex interpersonal interactions between interviewers and job candidates. Therefore, in addition to seeking job-related information, interviewers will want to meet the applicants to determine whether they will fit into the interpersonal environment of the work setting. It will be extremely difficult to predict the personality preferences of the interviewers. It is best to advise clients to be themselves and to avoid exaggerating characteristics that are not their own.

A model "Pre-Interview Preparation" form will help clients gather important interview information, highlight their qualifications for the position, identify a catchword or catchphrase as an aid to remembering their qualifications, and develop solutions to problems perceived by interviewers. A checklist of activities is also included on the form to remind clients of the important preparatory steps for a job interview. A case study using this form is included in Figure 9-10. To identify their qualification highlights, clients should focus on the central questions listed in Table 9-1. Most clients find extensive interview preparation, such as answering 50 commonly asked questions, to be too long for practical use. On the other hand, if they focus on the four primary categories of job-related information, they will have a controllable amount of information that is less likely to overwhelm them during the interview.

As an aid to remembering job-related information, it is recommended that clients develop and memorize catchwords or catchphrases to summarize their qualification highlights. Such memory aids are commonly used in study techniques. Catchwords are either actual or nonsense words composed of the first letter of each key word in the list of qualification highlights. Similar to catchwords, catchphrases are developed from the first letter of each key word in the list of qualification highlights. To identify catchwords or catchphrases, first list the qualification highlights for the position as directed in section II of the "Pre-Interview Preparation" form. Second, circle one word for each qualification highlight that most clearly identifies the respective qualification. Third, take the first letter of each key word and construct a catchword. Scrambling the words may help to develop an actual word. In some instances, especially when no vowels are present, an actual word cannot be constructed. In such cases, a nonsense catchword may be used, or a catchphrase can be developed. A catchphrase can be constructed by developing a personalized phrase based on the first letter in each keyword. A sample is provided in the case study in Figure 9-10.

As stated, the primary purpose of the job interview is for the employers to obtain additional information from the job candidates. Clients may be surprised to find that the people who conduct job interviews may not be very good at it. Interviewers are often department heads or line supervisors who are not trained or skilled in acquiring information through the interview process. Therefore, clients should be prepared to provide important job-related information even if interviewers are not good at asking for it. Clients should also be ready to provide extended descriptions and summaries of their qualifications.

Professionals can help clients improve their interview skills by conducting role-playing interviews. In the interviews, clients can gain insight into employer decision-making strategies by playing the roles of both the interviewer and the interviewee.

Figure 9-10. Case study: pre-interview preparation

# PRE-INTERVIEW PREPARATION

Name ___Thomas Xxxxxxxx_____ Date ___9/7/87_____

Organization _____ Staff Member _____

## I. INTERVIEW INFORMATION

Date of Interview __9/9/87__ Time ___1PM___ Name of Position ___Materials Handler__

Name of Company ___Wholesale Warehouse, Inc._____ Phone ___000-0000___

Company Address ____100 First St., Hometown, USA_____

Name and Title of Interviewer(s) ___Mr. Jones_____

## II. QUALIFICATION HIGHLIGHTS

List three to five of your most important qualifications for this job:

1. ___Excellent physical condition_____
2. ___Work in an organized manner_____
3. ___Reliable_____
4. _____
5. _____

(Circle a key word for each qualification and develop a catchword or catchphrase to aid you in remembering your qualification highlights:

Catchword ___P O R_____
Catchphrase ___Plan On Rain_____

## III. SOLUTIONS TO PROBLEMS PERCEIVED BY INTERVIEWER

Identify potential problems that might be perceived by employers and develop a response that might satisfy their concerns.

Problem ___Lack of work history may be a barrier_____

Solution __Discuss patterns of reliability established in other life roles, such as his__

__excellent attendance record in school_____

Problem ___His shyness may serve as an interview disadvantage.___

Solution ___The counselor and Thomas will role play job interviews. The counselor will___
___encourage him to make eye contact and speak assertively.___

## IV. INTERVIEW CHECKLIST

*BEFORE THE INTERVIEW:*

_X_ Complete a pre-interview preparation form.
_X_ Memorize the catchword or catchphrase that summarizes your qualification
highlights.
_X_ Practice your description of your qualifications either to another person
or privately aloud to yourself.
_X_ Insure that you are appropriately groomed and dressed.
_X_ Bring a copy of your resume or application.
_X_ Arrive on time for the interview.

*DURING THE INTERVIEW:*

_X_ Sit with good posture, face the interviewer, make eye contact, and avoid
nervous habits.
_X_ Listen to the introductions and to the interviewer's description of the job.
_X_ Describe your qualifications when given the opportunity.
_X_ Explain how your disability (if it is a relevent or an obvious one) will affect your
job performance if the interviewer fails to ask you about it.
_X_ Express your interest and desire directly (e.g., "This is a good job. I am very
interested in having it.").
_X_ Ask about the salary and benefits for the job.
_X_ Ask how long it will take to select the person for the job.
_X_ Insure that you have the names of the interviewer(s).

*AFTER THE INTERVIEW:*

_X_ Send a thank-you note to the interviewer immediately after the interview.

Interviewers are likely to remember experiences at the beginning and end of interviews. Studies on memory indicate that the beginning and end of serial information is most remembered (Wallace, Goldstein, and Nathan, 1987, p. 194). With this thought in mind, clients should attempt to leave a good impression at the beginning and end of their interviews. In the beginning of an interview, clients should not be too quick to begin talking. Encourage them to begin their interviews by sitting comfortably, facing the interviewer, making eye contact, and listening. Listening is an important element of communication. It demonstrates respect for the speaker and will take clients' minds off of themselves. If clients are listening to the interviewer, they will be unable to focus on their interview anxieties. They should listen to introductions of people, company profiles, and descriptions of the job. Clients should be taught to paraphrase descriptions given by interviewers in order to test the accuracy of their understanding. Listening and paraphrasing information will also give them a little time to calm themselves and to vent some anxiety. Clients should fully understand the description of the job tasks before they begin describing their qualifications for it. They should close interviews by making a brief summary statement of their qualifications and expressing their desire to be hired for the position. Although they might show a little anxiety in doing so, they should be encouraged to close the interview with an enthusiastic statement of their desire for the job. Something like "This job sounds very interesting. I hope that you will seriously consider me for it. I would be happy to work with you!" will serve as a lasting impression. As they depart, clients should shake hands with interviewers and thank them for the opportunity to discuss their qualifications.

# 10

# Strategies for Obtaining Employment

**I**f the employment search has been approached as a process, by this point clients will have assessed their job readiness, developed strategies for removing employment barriers, selected employment objectives based on their abilities, completed job analyses, developed strategies for needed job accommodations, identified their job-related information, prepared written descriptions characterizing them as qualified workers, and developed their interviewing skills. Having experienced these preparatory activities, clients should feel ready to begin the actual job-search activities.

Figure 10-1 presents an employment-seeking model that emphasizes the problem-solving, decision-making, and communication aspects of an employment search. In the search for employment, clients should focus on the problem of employers needing qualified workers. Focusing solely on their own problems associated with needing a job often prevents clients from appreciating the concerns of employers. Therefore, professionals should sensitize clients to employer problems and viewpoints, and should stress that employers often prefer to hire applicants who are perceived as offering solutions to employer problems over those applicants who are perceived as seeking solutions to their own problems.

Viewing the employment search as a decision-making model will help clients appreciate the respective roles of applicants and employers in the hiring process. Succinctly stated, applicants provide information, and employers make decisions. Employers make hiring decisions almost exclusively on the information provided by applicants; they generally do not add to applicant information. More frequently, employers seek only to verify applicant information. Employer decisions can only be as good as the information they receive from applicants. Employment seekers who feel that employers do not fully understand their true level of employability are often those who have failed to provide information that describes their true level of employability. Providing job-related information to employers is an applicant's most important avenue of influencing the decision-making

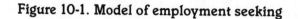

## Figure 10-1. Model of employment seeking

Message:
I can solve your problem
My qualifications are. . .

Sender:
Applicant
with
solution

Medium: Resumes,
applications, and
interviews in person
or by telephone

Receiver:
Employer
with
problem

Elements of the Model:

PROBLEM:    Employers need for qualified workers

SOLUTION:    Applicants who are qualified workers

SENDER:    Applicant (Information Provider)

RECEIVER:    Employer (Decision Maker)

MESSAGE:    Applicants communicating that they are qualified workers and can
solve the problem of needing qualified workers

MEDIUM:    Resumes, letters of application, job applications, telephone,
conversations, and personal interviews

process. It is critical that clients understand the decision-making process and assume the responsibility of communicating their qualifications to employers.

Viewed as a communication model, the dynamic elements of the employment search include a sender, a receiver, a message, and a medium. Applicants are the senders and employers are the receivers. The written correspondence and interpersonal communications used in the search strategies are the mediums. In these communications, senders are attempting to send messages to receivers through various mediums for the purpose of providing decision-making information to employers. Their messages should communicate that clients are qualified workers who want to help employers solve their problems. This chapter focuses on the selection of the most effective mediums for communicating messages to employers and for monitoring the frequency at which those messages are sent by applicants.

This chapter includes descriptions of employment-search strategies, of planning weekly job-search activities, and of placement strategies for professionals.

## JOB-SEARCH PLAN OF ACTION

Employment-search activities encompass two objectives: first, to locate job vacancies; and second, to become candidates for the available positions. To achieve candidacy, applicants must avoid elimination in the screening process used by employers to reduce a larger group of applicants to a small group of candidates. Employers will eliminate from consideration those applicants who do not appear to meet their criteria for the positions. Chapter 9 includes information on how to identify job-related information and how to effectively characterize clients as qualified workers.

To achieve the objective of locating job vacancies, clients must search for unannounced job vacancies as well as for vacancies that are advertised or announced by employers. Throughout a given geographical location, job vacancies routinely become available either as a result of the need to replace workers who have vacated their positions or as a result of the need to hire workers for newly created jobs. As mentioned in previous chapters, there is evidence suggesting that only 15% of those vacancies will be announced in want ads. Table 10-1 lists recommended strategies for obtaining employment. To maximize the thoroughness of their job searches, clients should use a combination of all recommended strategies. Clients who have restricted communication abilities may need to rely more heavily on the assistance of their advocates. Table 10-2 summarizes the results of a survey conducted by the Census Bureau (Job Search, 1976). The survey summarizes the use and effectiveness of job-search methods of some ten million job-seekers. Clearly, the most commonly used

**Table 10-1.** Recommended Strategies for Obtaining Employment

| Strategy | Methods |
|---|---|
| Direct-to-employer applications | • Telephone employers to inquire about vacancies<br>• Mail written correspondence to employers<br>• Conduct interviews with prospective employers |
| Networking | • Telephone selected people to inquire about jobs they know to be available<br>• Mail written correspondence to selected people to inquire about jobs they know to be available<br>• Conduct interviews among selected people to inquire about jobs they know to be available |
| Want ads | • Apply for job vacancies advertised in newspapers and trade journals |
| Third parties | • Apply for jobs announced as available at the Office of Employment Security<br>• Inquire among private employment agencies for desirable job opportunities<br>• Apply for temporary jobs at temporary employment agencies<br>• Inquire among nonprofit agencies for job vacancies |
| Advocacy and placement assistance | • Have friends, family, and others assist clients in the above search strategies<br>• Have professionals locate job vacancies for clients |

**Table 10-2.** Use and Effectiveness of Job-Search Methods

| Method | % of total job-seekers using this method | Effectiveness Rate |
|---|---|---|
| Applied directly to employer | 66.0% | 47.7% |
| Asked friends: | | |
|     about jobs where they work | 50.8% | 22.1% |
|     about jobs elsewhere | 41.8% | 11.9% |
| Asked relatives: | | |
|     about jobs where they work | 28.4% | 19.3% |
|     about jobs elsewhere | 27.3% | 7.4% |
| Answered newspaper ads: | | |
|     local | 45.9% | 23.9% |
|     nonlocal | 11.7% | 10.0% |
| Private employment agency | 21.0% | 24.2% |
| Federal/state employment service | 33.5% | 13.7% |
| School placement office | 12.5% | 21.4% |
| Civil service test | 15.3% | 12.5% |
| Asked teacher or professor | 10.4% | 12.1% |
| Went to place where employers come to pick up people | 1.4% | 8.2% |
| Placed newspaper ads: | | |
|     local | 1.6% | 12.9% |
|     nonlocal | .5% | [b] |
| Answered ads in professional or trade journals | 4.9% | 7.3% |
| Union hiring hall | 6.0% | 22.2% |
| Contracted local organization | 5.6% | 12.7% |
| Placed ads in professional or trade journals | .6% | [b] |
| Other | 11.8% | 39.7% |

[a]Effectiveness rate percentage was obtained by dividing the number of jobseekers who found work using the method by the total number of jobseekers who used the method, whether successfully or not.

[b]Base less than 75,000.

From Job Search: There's a Method in the Madness. (Spring, 1976). Occupational Outlook Quarterly, 18-19.

and effective method of obtaining employment is applying directly to employers. This strategy also appears to be the method by which most workers with disabilities have obtained their jobs. A nationwide survey of employers indicated that "68 percent of their disabled workers obtained their jobs through their own efforts and by word-of-mouth" (Louis Harris and Associates, 1987, p. 40).

The types of jobs sought by clients and the balance of supply and demand for the labor to fill those jobs will determine the intensity of effort required to locate job vacancies. Position vacancies for which the labor demand outweighs the number of qualified or interested applicants are the easiest to locate. They are more likely to be announced in want ads and available through third-party agencies. Chapter 7 includes a list of the 37 most-available jobs (Silvestri and Lukasiewicz, 1985). Positions that are in high demand by workers are the most difficult to find. Locating these vacancies requires applicants to conduct an intensive search of the labor market. This is especially true of positions that are not widely available and that have low turnover rates. Searching for such high-demand positions requires applicants to use a networking strategy to get to know employers and employees within the targeted industries. Clients may request volunteer work or internships as a means of gaining experience and meeting important people in selected industries. Generally speaking, the better the job, the harder it will be to locate the vacancy, compete for candidacy, and obtain the position. This does not mean that good jobs are impossible to get. It simply means that employment seekers will have to work harder to locate and obtain them.

The amount of frustration experienced in the employment search can be reduced if employment seekers budget their time and efforts appropriately. For example, the task of locating job vacancies among employers who do not advertise their positions can be efficiently accomplished by telephoning those employers. An employment seeker can telephone ten employers within one hour and locate as many job vacancies as another employment seeker who spends a whole week filling out job applications at the worksites. Although they may achieve the same end, the person who conducted the search by telephone completed the task in a more efficient manner.

Figure 10-2 presents a recommended weekly job-search plan of action that can be used by clients. It includes strategies for locating job vacancies that are unannounced as well as for locating those vacancies that are advertised and announced. The recommended plan suggests that clients invest 50% of their time and effort in direct-to-employer applications, 20% in networking, 15% in responding to want ads, and 15% in third party agencies or organizations. A "Weekly Job-Search Plan of Action" form is modeled in the case study in Figure 10-3. This plan will help clients structure their weekly job-search efforts, set goals for the volume of search activities, and monitor the achievement of their weekly job-search goals.

It is important to impress upon clients that once they have selected appropriate employment objectives and are capable of characterizing themselves as qualified workers, the only thing that stands between them and employment is the volume of search activity. Bolles (1985) pointed out that there are two types of employers: those who will hire them and those who will not hire them. Clients must search among employers until they find those who will hire them. As clients conduct their weekly search activities, encourage them to focus their attention on completing their search goals rather than on the outcomes of their searches. Virtually all client initial inquiries for employment will receive responses that are either negative or indifferent. Unfortunately, that is the nature of the employment search. Focusing too closely on the outcome of their search activities (i.e.,

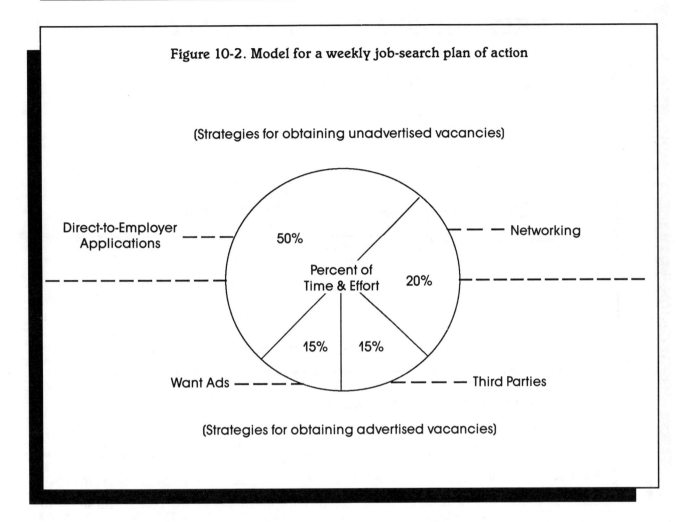

**Figure 10-2. Model for a weekly job-search plan of action**

(Strategies for obtaining unadvertised vacancies)

Direct-to-Employer Applications

Networking

Percent of Time & Effort

50%

20%

15%    15%

Want Ads

Third Parties

(Strategies for obtaining advertised vacancies)

getting hired) will begin to disrupt their ability to persevere in their efforts. Encourage them to reward themselves for completing the weekly search activities.

## DIRECT-TO-EMPLOYER APPLICATIONS

Applying directly to employers is the most common and most successful method of obtaining employment. Therefore, it is recommended that clients invest at least 50% of their job-search time and effort in applying directly to employers. This strategy, however, requires that clients contact selected employers regardless of whether or not job vacancies are known to exist. This strategy can be very confusing and time consuming if it is not conducted in a system-

Figure 10-3. Case study: weekly job-search plan of action

# WEEKLY JOB-SEARCH PLAN OF ACTION

Name _____ Patricia Xxxx _____ Week of _____ 9/7/87 _____

(Strategies for obtaining unadvertised vacancies)

Direct-to-Employer Applications — — — 50% — — — Networking

Percent of Time & Effort    20%

Want Ads — — — 15%   15% — — — Third Parties

(Strategies for obtaining advertised vacancies)

1. **DIRECT-TO-EMPLOYER APPLICATIONS** (50% of Your Search Time and Effort)

   *Goal Statement:* This week I will complete _____25_____ (number) job inquiries

   for the position of _____bookkeeper_____ (job title).

   I will search among _____school districts_____ (type of industry) in

   _____Hometown, USA_____ (geographical area). I will contact these

   employers by _____telephone_____ (telephone, mail, interviews, other).

   *Preparation:* Write a list of your targeted industries that are located within your specified geographical area. Use the telephone book, industrial guides, and chamber of commerce membership lists to gather this information. Consult your local librarian for additional information resources.

2. **NETWORKING** (20% of Your Search Time and Effort)

   *Goal Statement:* This week I will contact _____20_____ (number) people

   to inform them that I am searching for employment. I will contact these people by

   _____telephone_____ (telephone, mail, interviews, other).

   *Preparation:* Write a list of the people you will contact this week. These people should be selected from family members, friends, acquaintances, former co-workers and classmates, teachers, former employers, and other people that are referred to you.

3. **WANT ADS** (15% of Your Search Time and Effort)

   *Goal Statement:* This week I will review the daily want ads of _____2_____ (number) newspapers in search of advertised job vacancies. The newspapers will include

   _____Hometown Tribune and Hometown Times_____ .

   *Preparation:* Subscribe to, purchase, or borrow the selected newspapers.

4. **THIRD PARTIES** (15% of Your Search Time and Effort)

   *Goal Statement:* This week I will contact _____4_____ (number) representatives from third-party agencies. I will contact these people by _____telephone_____ . (telephone, mail).

   *Preparation:* Write a list of the representatives you will contact this week. The list might include federal or state employment offices, private employment agencies, temporary employment agencies, and school placement offices.

---

### SUMMARY OF THIS WEEK'S JOB SEARCH ACTIVITIES
(To be completed at the end of the week)

*Instructions:* For each strategy, list the number of contacts made in the goal statements, list the actual number of contacts made, and indicate whether or not the goal was achieved.

| Strategy: | Goal | Actual Contacts | Goal Achieved | |
|---|---|---|---|---|
| 1. Direct-to-Employer Applications | 25 | 25 | Yes | No |
| 2. Networking | 20 | 20 | Yes | No |
| 3. Want Ads (Papers actually read) | 14 | 14 | Yes | No |
| 4. Third Parties | 4 | 4 | Yes | No |

For successfully achieving my goals I will reward myself by _____
__Going out to dinner with a friend._____

atic and efficient manner. The model "Weekly Job-Search Plan of Action" form directs clients to complete a goal statement that includes the number of contacts to be made during the week, and it defines the employers to be contacted by listing the job title, industry, and geographical area of the client's employment objective. Chapter 7 provides detailed instructions on developing employment objectives.

## Writing Goal Statements

A sample goal statement for conducting **direct-to-employer** applications might read:

This week I will complete _____25_____ (number) job inquiries for the position of _____clerical aide_____ (job title).

I will search among _____banks_____ (type of industry) in _____Baltimore, MD_____ (geographical area).

I will contact these employers by _____telephone followed by written correspondence_____ (telephone, mail, interviews, other).

After contacting all of the banks in Baltimore, Maryland, the client should redirect the search activities by changing one, two, or all three elements of the employment objective. By changing the industry, the new goal statement might read:

This week I will complete _____25_____ (number) job inquiries for the position of _____clerical aide_____ (job title).

I will search among _____insurance companies_____ (type of industry) in _____Baltimore, MD_____ (geographical area).

I will contact these employers by _____telephone followed by written correspondence_____ (telephone, mail, interviews, other).

A change in job title and type of industry could completely the direction of the job search:

This week I will complete _____25_____ (number) job inquiries for the position of _____teacher's aide_____ (job title).

I will search among _____elementary schools_____ (type of industry) in _____Baltimore, MD_____ (geographical area).

I will contact these employers by _____telephone followed by written correspondence_____ (telephone, mail, interviews, other).

## Preparation

To complete the first goal statement, the employment seeker must first develop a list of 25 banks in Baltimore, Maryland. The list should include names, addresses, and telephone numbers. The list should be prepared on lined loose-leaf paper for proper record keeping. Employer information can be obtained from the yellow pages of the telephone book, industrial guides available from the local chamber of commerce, government publications, and other community reference materials available in local libraries.

## Telephoning Employers

To determine accurately whether job vacancies exist among the listed employers, clients should communicate as directly as possible with the supervisors of the department in which they would work if they were employed at those companies. Telephoning department supervisors at each company is the most time-efficient manner of locating job vacancies among the listed employers. A "Script for Contacting Employers by Telephone" form is presented in Figure 10-4. It explains how to identify the name of the department supervisor, inquire about job vacancies, and ask for the names of other people who might know about job vacancies. Professionals should model this technique for clients as well as have them practice the technique by role-playing with other clients.

## Corresponding with Employers

Mailing cover letters with résumés, letters of application, or job applications will insure that an employer receives written descriptions of client employment qualifications. These documents are helpful in supplementing memory of telephone conversations and are sometimes kept for future vacancies. Clients should forward written descriptions of their qualifications to the supervisors they spoke with by telephone as well as to the supervisors they could not reach. The correspondence should always be sent to the attention of the department supervisors. Clients should avoid undirected mass mailings addressed: To Whom It May Concern. Such undirected methods of submitting applications have a poor success rate. The names of supervisors can be obtained from company telephone operators, receptionists, or anyone else who answers the telephone for the company. The sample cover letter in Figure 10-5 inquires about a position as a nurse aide at a nursing home. The letter has an opening statement, a brief summary of qualifications, and information on how the individual can be contacted for more information. A résumé would normally accompany this letter.

Figure 10-4. Script for contacting employers by telephone

# SCRIPT FOR CONTACTING EMPLOYERS BY TELEPHONE

| Notes | Script |
|---|---|
| **PURPOSE:** *Identify the supervisor of the department in which you wish to work.*<br><br>For example, a person seeking a maintenance position would want to speak to the supervisor of the maintenance department. Someone seeking a bookkeeping position would want to speak to the supervisor of the accounting department. If you cannot identify a department supervisor, ask to speak with the personnel manager. If it is a small company, ask to speak to the general manager or the owner. | HELLO. MY NAME IS _____Allen Xxxxxx_____ .<br>MAY I SPEAK TO THE PERSON IN CHARGE<br>OF _____Maintenance Department_____ ?<br>          (Name of department) |
| **PURPOSE:** *Inquire about job vacancies at that company.*<br><br>If no vacancies exist, you might ask: "Do you anticipate any vacancies in the near future?" If not, ask: "Do you know of other departments at your company that might have a vacancy?" | HELLO. MY NAME IS _____Allen Xxxxxx_____ .<br>I'M LOOKING FOR A JOB AS A _maintenance_<br>_____worker_____ DO YOU HAVE ANY<br>JOB VACANCIES? |
| **PURPOSE:** *To describe your qualification highlights to employers.*<br><br>List your three most important qualifications for the job you are seeking. | MY QUALIFICATION HIGHLIGHTS<br>INCLUDE:<br>1. Reliable and punctual<br>2. Mature and hardworking<br>3. Good general health |
| **PURPOSE:** *Ask for other employers who might have available positions.* | CAN YOU SUGGEST ANY OTHER<br>EMPLOYERS WHO MIGHT HAVE A JOB<br>VACANCY? |
| **PURPOSE:** *Thank the supervisors for talking with you.* | THANK YOU FOR YOUR TIME. |
| **PURPOSE:** *Ask if you can call back.* | MAY I CALL YOU BACK IN A MONTH OR TWO<br>TO INQUIRE ABOUT FUTURE VACANCIES? |

**Figure 10-5. Sample cover letter.**

September 10, 1987

Mr. William Xxxxxxxxx
248 Second Street
Hometown, USA 00000

Mr. Thomas Bxxxxxxx
Hometown Nursing Home
100 First Avenue
Hometown, USA 00000

RE: Application for Nurse Aide Position

Dear Mr. Bxxxxxxx:

Please consider me for a nurse aide position with your nursing home.

My qualifications for this position include a strong desire to help other people and experience in caring for my aging parents. A copy of my resume is enclosed for your consideration.

Please call me at (000) 000-0000 if you would like more information about my qualifications. Thank you.

Sincerely yours,

William Xxxxxxxxx

## Interviewing Employers

Interviewing employers about possible job vacancies is generally too time consuming, and many employers will not be available for such meetings. A small number of employers, however, may be willing to meet with clients to discuss employment alternatives and perhaps even to assume mentorship roles for them. As mentors, these employers can provide guidance and valuable advice that can come only from someone within an industry.

## Record Keeping

It is recommended that clients use a three ring binder and 8½ x 11-inch loose-leaf paper for maintaining records of their job-search strategies. A section divider should be used to separate the records for each search strategy used by clients. The records of direct-to-employer applications should include the weekly lists of employers to contact (their names, addresses, and telephone numbers) and notes on the method of communication, on the dates and the action taken with each employer, and on the job vacancies found through this employment-seeking strategy. A sample of such records appears in Figure 10-6. Also, the case study (Figure 10-3) includes an example of the recommended record keeping.

## NETWORKING

Word of mouth is the essential characteristic used in the networking strategy of locating job leads. Table 10-2 indicates that employment seekers routinely learn about job vacancies from relatives, friends, teachers, and professionals. The networking strategy simply expands on this informal manner of receiving information. Virtually everyone has a network of people they know from their families, from their neighborhoods, and through various life experiences. These people may be able to provide clients with information about job vacancies and should therefore be considered valuable information resources. If they cannot directly provide information about job vacancies, they can often lead clients to other people in key positions who can provide this information. The unique feature of the networking strategy is that the channels of information often transcend the chain of command structures of most companies. Such information channels are characterized by word-of-mouth exchanges among family members, friends, acquaintances, and strangers. These channels of information can circumvent company policy and go right to the board rooms of major corporations. For example, an employee may confide in a co-worker that he will be leaving his current job to take a better position with another company. This co-worker becomes a

**Figure 10-6. Sample records of direct-to-employer applications**

Section: *Records of Direct-to-Employer Applications*

Week of: _____9/7/87_____

Job ___Clerical Aide___ Industry _____Banks_____ Geographical Area _Baltimore, MD_

| Company Information | Notes |
| --- | --- |
| Mr. John Axxxxx,<br>Personnel Manager<br>First Hometown Bank<br>200 Main Street<br>Hometown, USA 00000<br>(000) 000-0000 | 9/10/87 — Called, no vacancies<br><br>— Mailed cover letter & resume |
| Mr. John Bxxxx,<br>Personnel Manager<br>Second Hometown Bank<br>300 Main Street<br>Hometown, USA 00000<br>(000) 000-0000 | 9/10/87 — Called, position available<br><br>9/11/87 — Mailed cover letter & resume<br><br>— Call back in two weeks |

valuable source of information for the position that is about to be vacated.

The networking strategy may be directed at obtaining information about jobs in specific industries. In such cases, clients would ideally speak directly with people who work at those specified companies. Using the directed networking strategy, clients should ask their personal acquaintances who work within their targeted industries about existing and future job vacancies. If they do not know anyone at those companies personally, they should ask their acquaintances to refer them to people who do work within those specific companies. Using an undirected strategy, clients will simply inquire among the people in their networks to learn of any suitable job leads.

The most time-efficient manner of obtaining information about job vacancies through networking is clients telephoning a selected number of people each week. In these telephone conversations they should inform the people in their networks that they are searching for employment and describe their employment objectives. Clients should also ask to be kept informed of existing and future job vacancies, as well as asking for the names of other people who might know about job vacancies defined by their employment objectives. Professionals should model telephone inquiry skills and have clients practice those techniques through role-playing. Clients who are uncomfortable with contacting people by telephone may find it easier to mail the "Job-Hunting by Word of Mouth" form modeled in Figure 10-7. This form letter might also be used to contact people who are difficult to reach by telephone.

## Goal Statement

The "Weekly Job-Search Plan of Action" form directs clients to prepare a list of people to be contacted through the **networking** strategy of locating job leads. A sample goal statement for using the networking strategy might read:

This week I will contact _____20_____ (number) people

to inform them that I am searching for employment and

to request information about existing and future job

vacancies. I will contact these people by ___telephone___

(telephone, mail, interviews, other).

## Preparation

For each week of their job search, clients should write a list of the people they plan to call. The people should be selected from their family members, friends, acquaintances, former co-workers and classmates, teachers, and former employers. These people can extend the network by referring employment seekers to people in their own network of family members, friends, and acquaintances.

## Record Keeping

The lists of people to be contacted each week should be maintained in a separate section of clients' three-ring binders. In addition to the names and phone numbers of the contacts, clients should record the dates the people were contacted and the information received from them including any job leads. Figure 10-8 includes record keeping examples for the networking strategy of obtaining employment.

## WANT ADS

Applying for job vacancies advertised in the help wanted sections of newspapers is another commonly used strategy for obtaining employment. It is recommended that employment seekers invest

**Figure 10-7. Job hunting by word-of-mouth form letter**

# JOB-HUNTING BY WORD-OF-MOUTH

Employment Seeker <u>Mary Xxxxxxxxx</u>

Telephone Number <u>(000) 000-0000</u>

Job(s) Sought <u>Clerical positions</u>

Preferred Industries <u>Banks, Insurance Companies</u>

Geographical Area <u>Baltimore, MD</u>

Date <u>January 28, 1988</u>

Dear <u>Karen</u> :

   I am in the process of looking for a job. This note is a request for help. Word-of-mouth is one of several methods that I am using to locate job opportunities. I would greatly appreciate it if you would help me by:

1.  Informing me of any job vacancies that you know to exist. My preference for jobs, industries, and geographical area is listed above.

2.  Giving me the names of people who might be knowledgeable of these and similar jobs.

   Please telephone me at the above number if you have any information about job vacancies that might exist now or in the future. Thank you.

   Sincerely yours,

   *Mary*
_____
Signature

**Figure 10-8. Sample records of networking contacts**

Section: *Records of Networking Contacts*

Week of: _____9/7/87_____

| Information | Notes |
| --- | --- |
| William Sxxx (uncle)<br>(000) 000-0000 | 9/10/87 — called, received two referrals |
| Mary Txxxxx (friend)<br>(000) 000-0000 | 9/10/87 — mailed letter |
| Bob Cxxxxxx (schoolmate)<br>(000) 000-0000 | 9/11/87 — called, gave information |

approximately 15% of their time and effort in responding to want ads. Although it is a commonly used job-search strategy, this method provides information on as little as 15% of the jobs available at any given time (Olympus Research Corporation, 1973). Furthermore, the competition for these advertised positions is very high. It is not uncommon for employers to receive a hundred or more applications for a single position. Some job advertisements may literally attract more than a thousand applications. In the first step of the employee selection process, employers review the résumés or applications to identify those applicants who do not fit the criteria for the position. Practically speaking, they use this step of the selection process to reduce larger amounts of paperwork into smaller and more manageable amounts of paperwork. Applicants who are not eliminated in this process become the job candidates. The candidates are generally invited to provide additional information in job interviews. The person selected for the job will be chosen from these job candidates. Becoming a job candidate can only be accomplished by avoiding elimination in the initial, and often superficial, screening activities conducted by employers.

Since most applicants will be screened out of the competition by employers who merely glance at their résumés, it is extremely important that clients provide job-related information that is likely to match the selection criteria of employers. Chapter 9 provides instructions on how to identify the job-related information about clients that will characterize them as qualified workers. Clients can also highlight their qualifications in a cover letter that would normally accompany a résumé. The cover letter should be addressed to the person indicated in the want ad. If no name is provided in the want ad, the letter should be addressed: To Whom It May Concern. Cover letters should include concise statements of purpose, qualification highlights, and information on how to be contacted for job interviews. Figure 10-9 presents a cover letter Mary used to apply for a job that was advertised in the want ads of her hometown newspaper.

## Goal Statement

The "Weekly Job-Search Plan of Action" form directs clients to review the daily **want ads** in selected newspapers. The goals statement might read:

This week I will review the daily want ads of _____2_____

(number) newspapers in search of advertised job vacancies. The newspapers will include _____The Hometown_____

Tribune and The Hometown Times _____ .

## Preparation

Clients should subscribe to, purchase, or borrow the daily editions of the newspapers they wish to review for employment opportunities. Copies of local newspapers are usually available in community and school libraries.

## Record Keeping

Copies of the actual want ads, a record of the date the advertisement appeared, and notes on the action taken by clients should be kept in a separate section of the three-ring binder. The want ads should be clipped out of the newspapers and taped (stapled or glued) to pages in the "Want Ad" section of their records. Figure 10-10 includes samples of how the records should be maintained by clients.

## THIRD PARTIES

*Third parties* refers to those agencies and organizations that play an intermediary role in matching workers with jobs. These third parties might include state and federal employment services, private employment agencies, temporary employment agencies, and non-profit organizations. It is recommended that clients invest no more than 15% of their job-search time and effort in this strategy for obtaining employment. Clients should first identify the third-party agencies and organizations that are available in their communities. After selecting the appropriate agencies and organizations, clients

**Figure 10-9. Sample cover letter response to help wanted ad**

September 10, 1987

Mary Xxxxxxxx
111 Central Avenue
Hometown, USA 00000
(000) 000-0000

Mr. Edward Sxxxxx
First Hometown Bank
100 Second Avenue
Hometown, USA 00000

RE: Employment Application — Mailroom Clerk

Dr. Mr. Sxxxxx:

Please consider me for the position of mailroom clerk that was recently advertised in the Hometown Tribune.

In addition to preparing outgoing mail and sorting incoming mail, I can file, use photocopying machines, and answer telephones. I am neat in appearance and can work in an organized manner. To increase my clerical skills I have been volunteering as a desk clerk at the Hotel Local.

Please call me at (000) 000-0000 if you would like to interview me for this position. Thank you.

Sincerely yours,

Mary Xxxxxxxxx

should call each agency and make an appointment to explain the type of employment they wish to obtain. It is important that clients present the third-party agents with the same job-related information that would be presented to employers. In addition to helping applicants find jobs, these agents often screen applicants for employers.

## Public Employment Services

Public employment services such as the local Office of Employment Security will provide information on job vacancies free of charge. They can also provide information on how to apply for state and federal civil-service employment.

**Figure 10-10. Sample records of help wanted ad responses**

Section: *Records of Help Wanted Ads and Responses*

Week of: _____9/7/87_____

Want Ad

| | |
|---|---|
| **RECEPTIONIST-SECRETARY** Wanted for Mid Valley area. Part or full-time. Pleasant office conditions. Write: Box 4116789 | |

Notes

Source: Hometown Tribune, appeared 9/10/87

9/11/87 — Mailed cover letter and resume

| | |
|---|---|
| **OFFICE ASSISTANT**-- Needed to start immediately. No exp. necessary. Call now 000-0000. | |

Source: Hometown Times, appeared 9/11/87

9/11/87 — Mailed cover letter and resume

## Private Employment Agencies

Private employment agencies may be able to match clients with suitable positions. However, these agencies usually require a fee for their services. The fees differ from state to state, and in some cases, the fees are paid by employers. If an agency's job announcement reads "fee paid," it means the employer will pay the commission; if it reads "fee negotiable," it means that the employment seeker will have to pay for part of the commission; and if it reads "fee," it means that the employment seeker will have to pay the entire fee. These agencies do not receive a large number of requests to fill unskilled jobs because such applicants do not generally want to pay a fee for these services. If clients wish to apply to private employment agencies, they should understand that they will be expected to sign a contract that may require them to pay a fee if the agency finds them a job.

## Temporary Employment Agencies

"Temp" agencies, as they are often called, place applicants in short-term assignments ranging from one day to several months. Employers will use these agencies to perform the temporary work assignments that result from a variety of employer needs. In one company, temporary assignments might result from an employee taking a sick leave, whereas in another company, the temporary assignment might result from a seasonal increase in work load. Some employers use the temporary agencies to try out employees for full-time employment. If they prove to be effective workers, they will be offered full-time jobs.

Temp agencies generally staff clerical and light industrial positions. These agencies are an excellent source of job opportunities for clients who lack work experience or who do not want to work full-time. Clients who wish to enter the world of work on a part-time basis will find temp agencies a good source of part-time employment opportunities. Applicants who receive these placement services are employed by the temp agencies rather than by the companies at which they are assigned to work. These agencies often offer benefit packages for their employees who work a minimum number of hours per week. Since temp agencies receive their fees from employers, their loyalty will rest with the companies they serve. Therefore, they will sometimes ask applicants to accept undesirable or difficult assignments. In an attempt to avoid the frustrations of quitting or being fired, clients should be encouraged to reject temporary work assignments that are not in their area of ability or interest.

## Goal Statement

The "Weekly Job-Search Plan of Action" form directs clients to contact a selected number of **third party agency** representatives during each week of their job searches. The goal statement might read:

This week I will contact _____6_____ (number) representatives from third-party agencies. I will contact these people by _____telephone_____ (telephone, mail).

## Preparation

Clients should prepare a weekly list of the agency representatives to be contacted each week of their job searches. The lists might include representatives from the Office of Employment Security, private employment agencies, temporary employment agencies, and school placement offices.

## Record Keeping

A separate section of the client's notebook should be reserved for recording contacts with third-party agencies. A single page should be prepared for each agency. It should include the name of the agency, the agency representative, the telephone number, and a record of contacts, inquiries, and discussions with the representative. Figures 10-11 and 10-12 provide samples of how these records should be maintained.

**Figure 10-11. Sample records of third party contacts**

Section: *Records of Third Party Contacts — Office of Employment Security*

Contact Person: _____Mr. John Wxxxxx_____ Phone: _____000-0000_____

| Date | Notes |
|------|-------|
| 9/11/87 | — Called and made an appointment for 9/14/87 |
| 9/14/87 | — Received two job leads |
|  | — Called employers and sent resumes |
| 9/21/87 | — Called, no leads |
| 9/28/87 | — Called, receive one job lead |
|  | — Called employer, arranged interview for 9/29/87 |

**Figure 10-12. Sample records of third party contacts**

Section: *Records of Third Party Contacts — Temporary Employment Agency*

Contact Person: _____Mrs. Sxxxxx_____ Phone: _____000-0000_____

| Date | Notes |
|------|-------|
| 9/14/87 | — Called, no leads |
| 9/21/87 | — Visited office, interviewed for part-time job |

# ADVOCACY AND PLACEMENT ASSISTANCE

A thorough search for employment requires clients to perform concurrently a complex mixture of tasks. These include writing correspondence, typing, searching for employer information, telephoning employers, visiting agencies, conducting information interviews, and keeping records. Searching for a job is no easy task. It consumes significant amounts of time and energy, provides little or no reinforcement for sustaining an active search, and often results in negative or indifferent responses from employers. Consequently, most clients will need, or at least appreciate, some degree of support and help from professionals and significant others.

Clients will need varying degrees of assistance as they conduct their job searches. Some clients will occasionally need guidance and advice, some will need direction provided on a daily basis, and some will occasionally need assistance in completing job-search tasks. Others will need to rely on friends or professionals to conduct most of the job-search activities.

The nature of a client's handicap will influence the type of employment-seeking assistance needed from other people. For example, clients with hearing impairments might use the assistance of an advocate to telephone employers; clients with learning disabilities might need someone to proofread their written correspondence; clients with motor impairments will need someone to type their letters; and clients with mental retardation might need an advocate to help them complete applications and write letters of application. To obtain some positions, clients must demonstrate a significant degree of independence and may, therefore, be limited in the amount of help they can accept from advocates. For example, clients seeking good-paying jobs that are highly desired in the labor market cannot expect to secure these positions without participating in the job search.

Clients can obtain employment-seeking assistance from family members and friends, habilitation and rehabilitation professionals, and advocacy agencies and groups. Collectively, these people can serve as support groups to clients who are completing their transitions into the world of work.

## Family Members and Friends

Family members and friends of clients can help by performing such job-search tasks as completing applications, writing letters, preparing lists of employers, telephoning employers, or reading want ads.

## Habilitation and Rehabilitation Professionals

Habilitation and rehabilitation professionals may be relied on to provide guidance and assistance in client-conducted job searches, or they may assume a larger role by providing placement services. In helping clients to conduct their own job searches, professionals should encourage clients to assume as much responsibility for completing their job-search activities as their handicaps permit. Professionals should facilitate, whenever possible, the development of client-support groups to assist clients with their search for employment.

Professionals who do provide placement assistance should approach the labor market with the same orientation that has been prescribed for clients conducting their own job searches. Serving in these brokering roles, professionals must be equally concerned with the problems of employers. Employers may be reluctant to accept referrals from placement personnel perceived as working in the exclusive interest of their clients. Therefore, professionals must present their clients as potential solutions to the employer's problem — the need for qualified workers. In the sample correspondence listed in Figure 10-13, the counselor presented clients as a valuable labor resource that has been largely untapped by most employers. The letter encourages employers to telephone the counselor to discuss the possibility of hiring these job candidates. The second page suggests three reasons why they should employ people with handicaps, and the third page lists brief profiles of workers with handicaps.

Although the correspondence mentions that tax benefits are available to employers who hire individuals with handicaps, the correspondence does not try to portray these workers as inexpensive labor. Professionals should avoid characterizing clients as cheap labor. Doing so may imply low productivity from these workers and may attract employers who are only interested in cheap labor.

## Advocacy Agencies and Groups

Clients may also be able to find employment-seeking assistance among community advocacy agencies and groups. Job-search and placement assistance is available at Offices of Vocational Rehabilitation as well as many social service agencies such as Goodwill Industries. However, groups and organizations such as Rotary Clubs, Kiwanis Clubs, Lions Clubs, churches, unions, college alumni associations, and chambers of commerce are excellent sources for recruiting advocacy groups members who can develop job opportunities for individuals with handicaps. Many advocacy groups providing employment assistance to people with handicaps may already exist within the community. McCarthy (1985) reviewed a variety of productive partnerships that have been developed to bridge the gap between the rehabilitation and the business communities. Some examples are programs sponsored by corporations such as IBM, by service clubs such as the Rotarians, and by unions and trade organizations such as the AFL-CIO. The memberships of such groups usually include many community business leaders. These people are valuable community resources who should be included in the development of advocacy groups and programs.

**Figure 10-13. Sample correspondence from placement counselor**

# CAREER AND EMPLOYMENT SERVICES, INC.

September 10, 1987

Mr. Joseph Xxxxxxxxx
First Hometown Bank
100 Center Avenue
Hometown, USA 00000

RE: Referral for Employment

Dear Mr. Xxxxxxxxx:

You now have access to an untapped pool of highly rated workers. They are people with handicaps. The results of recent Harris poll of employers indicated that most managers (91%) rated their disabled workers as either excellent or good.

The individuals whose worker profiles appear on the attached page are interested in working for your organization. The profiles are of handicapped individuals who have participated in an employment preparation program funded by the Hometown Job Training Partnership Act (JTPA).

These workers have been screened for work readiness and employability. Their employment objectives have been selected based on careful assessments of their abilities and credentials. They have received orientations of employer expectations and they have made plans to insure that work will receive a high priority in their lives.

Additionally, these workers will receive post-employment guidance for at least one month after they are hired. The counselor is also available to employers for information, advice, and problem solving assistance.

You will probably find that your other applicants cannot match this level of desire and preparation for work. Can you afford not to consider them for your job vacancies? Please telephone me at (000) 000-0000 if you would like to consider any of these workers for employment.

Sincerely,


Michael Bxxxxx
CAREER & EMPLOYMENT COUNSELOR

**Figure 10-13. Continued**

# THREE GOOD REASONS FOR EMPLOYING PEOPLE WITH HANDICAPS

I.   HIGHLY RATED WORK PERFORMANCE

In a 1987 national survey of employers, Louis Harris and Associates reported that most managers (91%) rated the work performance of their workers as excellent or good. Employers compared disabled workers to non-disabled on several key criteria:

*Willingness to Work Hard:* 46% rated as better; 33% as about the same
*Reliability:* 39% rated as better; 42% as about the same
*Attendance and Punctuality:* 39% rated as better; 40% as about the same
*Productivity:* 20% rated as better; 57% as about the same
*Desire for Promotion:* 23% rated as better; 55% as about the same
*Leadership Ability:* 10% rated as better; 62% as about the same

II.  HIGH LEVEL OF WORK PREPARATION

The attached list of workers participated in an employment program for handicapped workers funded by the Hometown Job Training Partnership Act (JTPA). Highlights of their work preparation activities include:

- Assessment of work readiness
- Assessment of employable abilities
- Selection of employment objective based on abilities
- Assessment of need for job accommodations
- Planned for work related life changes

III. EMPLOYER BENEFITS

In addition to selecting employees from this highly qualified group of workers, employers can benefit from:

- Availability of an employment counselor to provide information, advice, and problem solving assistance to handicapped workers and their employers
- Federal tax credits for hiring individuals with handicaps and, in some cases, partial salary reimbursements during initial training periods.
- Positive work attitudes among these workers

Figure 10-13. Continued

# WORKER PROFILES

These profiles are those of workers with handicaps. In most cases their handicaps have little or no effect on their ability to perform the jobs listed in their employment objectives. Please telephone Mr. Bxxxxx at (OOO) 000-0000 if you would like to consider one or more of these highly qualified workers for employment. Please identify the worker you are interested in by their initials.

* * * * * *

| | |
|---|---|
| Persons's Initials: | A.M. |
| Employment Objective: | Maintenance Worker |
| Qualification Highlights: | * Reliable and punctual |
| | * Mature and hardworking |
| | * Good general health |

* * * * * *

| | |
|---|---|
| Person's Initials: | P.T. |
| Employment Objective: | Bookkeeper |
| Qualification Highlights: | * Associates Degree in Accounting |
| | * Five years of related clerical experience |
| | * Typing and data entry skills |

* * * * * *

| | |
|---|---|
| Person's Initials: | T.S. |
| Employment Objective: | Warehouse Materials Handler |
| Qualification Highlights: | * Excellent physical condition |
| | * Able to work with materials in an orderly fashion |
| | * Punctual, honest, and very dependable |

* * * * * *

| | |
|---|---|
| Person's Initials: | M.B. |
| Employment Objective: | Office Clerical Position |
| Qualification Highlights: | * General clerical skills of filing, sorting, photocopying, and answering telephones |
| | * Performed volunteer work to obtain clerical experience |
| | * Neat in appearance, courteous, and organized |

# 11

# Adjustments to Employment

**T**he vocational habilitation or rehabilitation process should not end when clients obtain employment. The ultimate test of clients' employability begins on their first day of work. Client feelings of ambivalence that existed before obtaining employment should be expected to intensify when clients are offered jobs because the risks they take are no longer hypothetical. During the first days, weeks, and months of employment, clients will encounter a variety of life and work adjustments. How successfully they accomplish these adjustments may have an enduring effect on their future vocational behavior, as well as determining whether or not they will keep the jobs they have found.

In these initial periods of employment, clients are most vulnerable to quitting or being released from their jobs. In addition to job retention, professionals should appreciate that early experiences on the job may significantly contribute to defining clients' vocational self-concepts, which will, in turn, guide their future vocational behavior. Therefore, these early work experiences carry the potential of doing as much harm as good. Some clients who have difficulty adjusting to work, sometimes through no fault of their own, may draw private conclusions that they are unemployable. Once clients have secured jobs, professionals should, either directly or indirectly, help them make the necessary life and work adjustments commonly faced when employment is obtained.

"The basic assumption of work adjustment theory is that individuals seek to achieve and to maintain a positive relationship with their work environment" (Zunker, 1987, p. 67). According to Dawis and Lofquist (1984), individuals bring their requirements to a work environment, and the work environment has its requirements of individuals. Therefore, in addition to satisfying the requirements of their jobs, clients must seek jobs that will satisfy their psychological and life needs. This chapter includes sections on satisfying job requirements and completing individual life adjustments. The section "Supported Employment" describes four models of providing on-the-job training and supervision.

## SATISFYING JOB REQUIREMENTS

To satisfy job requirements, clients must successfully perform the tasks of the job, work with other people, and function within their work environments. Table 11-1 outlines the major adjustments clients must complete successfully. Dawis and Lofquist (1984) advocate that job placement is best accomplished when worker traits match requirements of the work environment. The ability of clients to satisfy employer job requirements largely depends on the selection of appropriate employment objectives for clients' job searches.

### Performing the Job Tasks

First, the distinction between two important terms should be clarified. *Element* is the smallest step into which it is practical to subdivide any work activity without analyzing the separate motions, movements, and mental processes involved. *Task* is one or more of these elements; it is one of the distinct activities that constitute the logical and necessary steps in the performance of work by the worker. A task is created whenever human effort, physical or mental, is exerted to accomplish a specific purpose (U.S. Department of Labor, 1972).

Each job will consist of one or more core tasks that must be performed by workers. For example, the position of janitor might include the following tasks: sweeping floors, vacuuming rugs, emptying trash cans, and cleaning restrooms. To perform each job task successfully, clients must complete a series of task elements. For example, sweeping floors might include the following elements: getting the broom and dust pan from the storage closet, sweeping designated areas, picking up dirt in the dust pan and disposing of it in the waste basket, and returning the broom and dust pan to the storage closet. The elements of a job task must usually be performed in some appropriate sequence. Even when task elements do not have to be performed in a prescribed sequence, doing so may help to make the job easier to learn.

Obviously, the complexity of job tasks and task elements will vary from position to position. Clients will also differ in the amount of time and practice they will need to learn their job tasks. These factors will contribute to determining the length of postemployment support and training. Once the job tasks have been learned, clients should seek to complete those tasks in accordance with performance standards set by employers. Supervisors at the worksite will define acceptable and unacceptable standards of work performance. When clients are deficient in their ability to perform selected job tasks, several courses of action might be facilitated by professionals. The first is to provide training in which clients will receive guidance from supervisors, co-workers, job coaches, or professionals. Clients should be encouraged to discreetly maintain a pocket notebook in which they

**Table 11-1. Satisfying Job Requirements**

I.  PERFORMING THE JOB TASKS
    A. Learning the Job Tasks
       1. Identify job tasks
       2. Define work elements of each job task
       3. Learn appropriate sequence of work elements
    B. Establishing Satisfactory Job Performance
       1. Define job performance criteria
       2. Identify proficiencies and deficiencies
       3. Develop plans to remove deficiencies
          a. Provide on-the-job training and supervision
          b. Consider job accommodations
       4. Establish ongoing evaluation intervals

II. WORKING WITH OTHER PEOPLE
    A. Managers and Supervisors
       1. Learn names and positions of managers
          and supervisors
       2. Learn appropriate ways of relating to managers
          and supervisors
       3. Discuss handicap with supervisors and health
          officers (if appropriate)
    B. Co-Workers
       1. Learn names and positions of co-workers
       2. Learn appropriate ways of socializing with
          co-workers
       3. Seek support from co-workers

III. FUNCTIONING WITHIN THE ORGANIZATION AND WORK
     ENVIRONMENT
    A. Learning about Important Organizational Procedures
       1. Pay structure and benefit packages
       2. Work shifts, lunches, breaks, vacations and
          procedures for taking sick days
    B. Learning about the Work Environment
       1. Learn location of work and establish reliable
          transportation
       2. Learn location of work station, rest rooms, cafeteria,
          break areas, restricted areas

can record job instructions and other important information. A second course of action for removing performance deficiencies is to provide some type of job accommodation. For example, supervisors might consider removing tasks that are difficult for clients to perform and substituting alternate tasks that can be performed by clients.

## Working with Other People

Most work environments require individuals to work with other people. Within their work environment, clients must learn appropriate ways of relating with managers, supervisors, and co-workers. When relating with managers and supervisors, clients must follow directions, learn company procedures for the performance of their jobs, accept constructive criticism, and seek advice. When relating with co-workers, clients must identify areas of shared responsibility, synchronize their work activities and, if wanted, socialize at the worksite. Professionals should help clients decide whether they should discuss their handicaps with supervisors or co-workers and, if so, how they should share this information. Clients with active health concerns affecting safety, such as individuals with seizure disorders who work with heavy equipment, should provide this information to supervisors and company health officers.

## Functioning Within the Organization and the Work Environment

Successful work adjustment requires clients to function within company organizational procedures and within the physical work environment. Clients should learn about such procedures as pay structure, promotion requirements, pay raises, benefit packages, job evaluations, reporting procedures, work shifts, starting and quitting times, break periods, and lunch periods. They should also learn about job-site facilities, including the location of work stations, rest rooms, cafeteria, break areas, and other departments. The "Job Fact Sheet" will also help them to identify these characteristics.

## INDIVIDUAL LIFE ADJUSTMENTS

When clients become employed, professionals should attempt to facilitate adaptive adjustments by helping them find satisfaction in their work, adjust their life roles to accommodate new work roles, plan for job security and continued career development, and counsel clients who cannot keep their jobs.

## Individual Needs

In addition to clients satisfying job requirements, successful employment tenure (i.e., job retention) requires that workers obtain personal satisfaction from their jobs. Several researchers offer insights into worker motivation and job satisfaction. In his theory of vocational choice, Holland (1973) indicated that job satisfaction should occur when individuals, based on their personality types, are matched with congruent work environments. Applying Holland's theory, professionals should insure that clients select employment objectives based on their unique profiles of employable traits.

Similarly, Festinger's (1957) theory of cognitive dissonance supports the need for clients to select employment objectives that are congruent with their self-perceptions. His theory is based on the assumption that individuals will behave consistently with their self-perceptions. Inconsistencies that occur between behavior and self-perceptions result in a cognitive dissonance that causes anxiety. This state of tension, in turn, motivates individuals to alter their behavior in order to return themselves to a more relaxed state of feeling and thinking. Festinger's theory would suggest that clients who accept jobs performing tasks (behaviors) that are inconsistent with their self-perceptions are likely to encounter work-related anxieties. When the anxieties become sufficiently intense, clients will feel compelled to reduce this tension. In these situations, clients may begin displaying avoidance patterns of absenteeism or tardiness, or they may simply quit their jobs. For example, one client who perceived herself as shy accepted a telemarketing position in which she had to sell products over the telephone. She became so upset with this job that she quit after the lunch break on her first day of work. Generally speaking, professionals can intervene by verifying the appropriateness of the jobs that clients accept and by facilitating more adaptive work adjustments.

Herzberg (1966), in his two-factor theory of work motivation, identified separate sources for job satisfaction and job dissatisfaction. In essence, clients can simultaneously experience job satisfaction and dissatisfaction. Sources of job satisfaction include such motivators as recognition, achievement, responsibility, and the performance of work activities. Herzberg postulated that causes of job dissatisfaction were related more to the job context or the work environment, and he included such factors as negative perceptions of administration, supervision, or company policies. In the context of Herzberg's theory, professionals should help clients maximize positive work experiences and minimize negative experiences in the work environment.

## Life-Role Adjustments

Prior to obtaining employment, clients will have distributed their time and energy among a number of nonworking life roles. Once they begin working, however, they will have to invest considerable time and energy in their jobs and distribute their remaining time among previously held commitments. In many instances, clients may have to reduce the amount of help provided at home as well the amount of time spent with other people. In doing so, they may encounter resistance among people who have relied on them for such work or companionship. This is especially true if clients have been assuming homemaking responsibilities that will, subsequent to their employment, be transferred to others who do not want them. It is hoped that professionals will anticipate and develop strategies for avoiding these potential employment barriers during the planning stage of the employment-seeking process. Additionally, once employment is accepted, the reduction of free time will make routine activities such as grocery shopping and banking more difficult and stressful to complete. Clients will need problem-solving assistance and emotional support during the first few weeks and months of employment as they develop new life routines. In addition to providing this assistance, professionals should facilitate the development of a self-sustaining client-support system consisting of co-workers and significant others.

## Job Security and Career Development

Technological advancements, corporate takeovers, unstable energy costs, movement to a global economy, and demographic changes in the population are just a few of the events that will sustain the dynamic nature of the labor market. Job security, once widely achieved by working for the same company for a lifetime, is no longer practical and is, to a large degree, no longer possible. As a natural reaction to the unreliability of our social institutions, such as corporations, Naisbitt (1984) indicated that Americans are forced to rely less on institutions and more on themselves. From a practical viewpoint, participating in a continuing process of career development becomes an essential element of job security. It is, perhaps, the most reliable and self-controllable method that workers have for safeguarding their continued employability.

Career development should be viewed as an ongoing process of self-development involving self-directed learning of skills on the job, continuing education, and the pursuit of upward job mobility. Clients should be encouraged to develop future career aspirations and to implement plans for achieving them. Without specialized training, some clients may be disappointed to learn they only qualify for unskilled or semiskilled jobs. Instruct such clients to view these job opportunities as potential "stepping-stones" that, with continued self-development, can be used to prepare themselves for better jobs. Professionals can help clients examine the jobs that might be achieved through on-the-job promotions.

## Job Attrition

Not all clients will be able to keep the jobs they obtain. Some may find the adjustment to be too difficult; others may encounter health problems, may not like the type of work they have found, may get fired, or may quit their jobs. When clients are forced or compelled to quit their jobs, professionals should help them interpret the meaning of this job loss. They may have a self-defeating tendency to view their losing a job as a verification of their unemployability. For example, one client quit his job as a materials handler in a warehouse because the work aggravated an old back injury. Having been unemployed for five years, he accused himself of being a quitter. The counselor presented an alternative perception of the situation: After being unemployed for five years, he finally interrupted the pattern of avoiding work; he demonstrated both a willingness to risk change and a sense of responsibility by personally notifying his supervisor that he was unable to keep the job.

This type of self-talk often goes unnoticed by professionals. Clients should be encouraged to describe the events that led up to their dismissals or to their quitting their jobs. In many cases, the job loss can be meaningfully interpreted as a small step that still leads in the direction of achieving their vocational goals. After clients have adjusted to their job loss, professionals should help them reassess their situations and make future vocational plans.

## SUPPORTED EMPLOYMENT

The term "supported employment" has become widely used during the last several years as a description of work options open for individuals who are handicapped. This term, as defined by the Developmental Disabilities Act of 1984 (Federal Register, 1984), means paid employment for individuals with developmental disabilities, who, as a result of their disabilities, would not be successful in competitive employment at or above the minimum wage. In addition, these clients require intensive and regular support for them to be effective workers. Supported employment is conducted in a variety of settings, with emphasis placed on selecting workplaces in which individuals without handicaps are employed. Examples of supported employment have *traditionally* included employment alternatives such as (1) the Supported Jobs Model, (2) the Enclave Model, (3) the Mobile Crew Model and (4) the Benchwork Model (Mank, Rhodes, and Bellamy, 1986).

1. In the Supported Jobs Model individuals with handicaps are placed in regular community jobs, and support is provided on the job as needed. In this way, if a person is having difficulty performing a specific task or job, help is immediately available.

2. The Enclave Model involves a group of individuals with handicaps (enclave) who receive training and supervision with individuals who are not handicapped. Because this is neither full competitive employment nor a sheltered employment, it is able to provide integrated employment benefits as well as necessary supervision.

3. The Mobile Crew Model, as the name implies, is a combination of service and business. The model consists of a group of individuals with handicaps, usually four or five clients, working in the community doing service jobs (e.g., groundskeeping or maintenance). Typically the crew works out of a van rather than a self-contained building or office area. There are special advantages in using this type of model, as in rural areas, where it is often difficult to support full-scale employment projects. There are, however, additional costs usually incurred using this model. For example, supervision is a major part of the program that often requires additional funds.

4. The Benchwork Model, as described by Mank, Rhodes, and Bellamy (1986), was originally "designed to provide employment in electronics assembly work in a service agency that also functioned as a business enterprise." Using this model, clients received training and supervision as they performed their contract tasks. The model was initially designed for individuals with severe disabilities but could be adapted for different populations.

Bellamy, Rhodes, Mank, and Albin (1987) have identified program quality as an integral part of the supported employment movement. They have been candid in pointing out that "compromises on quality made solely in the interest of cost or availability can be expected to hamper supported employment for years to come."

In summary, supported employment requires the use or support of any activity that helps sustain paid work by clients with disabilities. This support not only includes supervision and training but also the need for effective transportation, which traditionally is a major problem requiring a well-thought-out implementation plan.

# 12

# Locating Community Resources and Services

**C**lients are often unaware of the resources and services available in their communities. A national survey conducted among individuals with handicaps concluded that "most disabled persons are not familiar with some of the most widely available services for disabled persons, such as medical and rehabilitation services" (Louis Harris and Associates, 1986, p. 82). This chapter will serve as an introductory guide to services funded directly or indirectly by the federal government. Each state, operating within federal guidelines, has some flexibility in determining how the federal money is spent. Furthermore, additional services are likely to be provided by local governments and voluntary organizations. Consequently, the services provided to persons with handicaps may vary from community to community. To insure that clients are aware of services available to them, it is important to identify key people within the community who are knowledgeable about local social service systems.

## INFORMATION

Many communities have referral agencies that can be contacted for information about services available to individuals with handicaps. These agencies can direct clients to federally funded services and to services sponsored by local agencies and advocacy groups. Most information and referral agencies are listed in telephone directories under "Social Service Agencies." If no such services can be found, check Appendix B of this book for the names, addresses, and telephone numbers of State Vocational Rehabilitation Offices and Governor's Committees on the Employment of the Handicapped. These offices can serve as a starting point in the search for resources and services at local levels. Additional information about employment of individuals with handicaps can be obtained by writing to the President's Committee on Employment of the Handicapped; 1111 20th Street, NW, Room 636; Washington, DC 20036.

## VOCATIONAL REHABILITATION

Each state maintains vocational rehabilitation agencies to help individuals with handicaps become employable by providing a wide range of services, financial assistance, and training. Many states have commissions or rehabilitation units that provide specialized services for blind people. The services offered by vocational rehabilitation agencies might include the following:

- ☐ A medical examination to determine the extent of disability, suitability for employment, and specific medical help needed by clients.
- ☐ Counseling and guidance to assess employability and rehabilitation needs.
- ☐ Medical assistance to reduce or remove disabilities and restore employability. The assistance might include medical, surgical, psychiatric, and hospital services. They may also provide artificial limbs, braces, hearing devices, and eyeglasses needed for employment.
- ☐ Job training at trade schools, at rehabilitation centers, or at home.
- ☐ Financial assistance for college or vocational schools.
- ☐ Financial assistance during the rehabilitation period to pay for room and board, transportation, and other necessary assistance.
- ☐ Referral and job-placement assistance.
- ☐ On-the-job help, if needed, including expenses for getting to the job or for keeping the job.

Agencies are generally available at local levels. Check the local telephone directory under "Rehabilitation Services."

## EDUCATION AND JOB TRAINING

There are a variety of community resources to help with education and job training. The services include financial aid, special services for the visual and hearing-impaired, and job training programs.

## Student Financial Aid

In addition to student financial aid provided by the vocational rehabilitation offices, individuals with handicaps may take advantage of state and federal financial aid programs made available to all students. Financial assistance received from these sources can be used to pay for education and training at colleges and vocational schools. Student financial aid programs are also available from state governments. However, these programs differ considerably from state to state. Federal financial aid programs are based on the financial needs of students and their families. Federal financial aid programs include the following:

- ☐ Grants awarded on the basis of financial need, which if received, do not have to be repaid by students.
- ☐ Loans that must be repaid. However, repayment of these loans can be deferred until after students graduate from college or vocational programs.
- ☐ Work-study programs in which students receive pay for part-time jobs performed at the schools where they receive their education and training.
- ☐ Cash benefits such as the GI Bill or Social Security. These benefits do not have to be repaid by the recipients.

Applications for student financial aid programs can be obtained from high school counselors or financial aid offices of colleges and vocational schools.

## Library Services for Special Groups

The National Library Services for the Blind and Physically Handicapped has a network of cooperating regional libraries throughout the United States, Puerto Rico, and the Virgin Islands. Clients can receive an extensive collection of books, magazines, bibliographies, directories, and reference materials. These resources are available in braille and in recorded form along with the necessary playback equipment. Eligible persons are United States citizens who cannot hold or read standard printed materials. For further information about these services, write to National Library Service for the Blind and Physically Handicapped; Library of Congress; Washington, DC 20542.

## Schools for the Deaf

Gallaudet College provides higher educational opportunities for deaf persons and is funded by the federal government. In addition to its undergraduate programs, Gallaudet offers a graduate program for teacher preparation and a program for research. For more information write to Gallaudet College; 800 Florida Avenue, NE; Washington, DC 20002.

The National Technical Institute for the Deaf (NTID) in Rochester, New York, is a special technical college for deaf students from all states. Many NTID students receive financial assistance from their state vocational rehabilitation agencies. For more information, write to Office of Career Opportunities; National Technical Institute for the Deaf; One Lomb Memorial Drive; Rochester, NY 14623.

For more information on post-secondary programs serving deaf students write to Special Education Programs; Department of Education; Washington, DC 20202.

## Job Training Partnership Act

The Job Training Partnership Act (JTPA) replaced the Comprehensive Employment and Training Act (CETA) in 1983 as the national program to prepare youth and unskilled adults for the labor force and to afford job training to economically disadvantaged individuals and others facing serious barriers to employment. JTPA programs might include on-the-job training provided by employers as well as programs sponsored by local colleges and vocational schools. Information about job-training programs can be obtained by telephoning the local Office of Employment Security.

## ARC's National Employment and Training Project

Since 1966 the Association for Retarded Citizens (ARC) has provided job training and employment opportunities to more than 36,000 individuals with mental retardation through its National Employment and Training Project. The project, formerly referred to as ARC's On-the-Job Training Project, receives funding from the Department of Labor. Once clients are placed, ARC enters into a contract with employers to reimburse a set percentage of clients' salaries during a 320-hour training period. Employers are reimbursed 50% of the clients salary for the first 160 hours of employment and 25% for the second 160 hours. To obtain applications and more information about ARC's National Employment and Training Project write or telephone Association for Retarded Citizens; National Employment and Training Project; 2501 Avenue J; Arlington, Texas 76006: (817) 640-0204.

## EMPLOYMENT

Employment services are provided by state and federal agencies. Additionally, local groups may offer similar services.

### State Offices of Employment Security

There are over 2,000 Offices of Employment Security throughout the United States, which match applicants with job opportunities. Each office is mandated by law to have a specially trained person to assist individuals with handicaps in their efforts to obtain employment. These offices should be listed under "Employment Services" in local telephone directories.

### Federal Jobs

Normally, federal jobs are announced to the public and are filled on a competitive basis. There are, however, a small number of non-competitive appointments made for individuals with mental retardation or severe physical disabilities. Workers with handicaps can sometimes obtain a temporary appointment with the Federal government, which is a good way to obtain work experience. Federal job information centers are listed under "U.S. Government" in most telephone directories. Federal employment information will also be available in the state employment security offices.

## FINANCIAL ASSISTANCE

The Social Security Administration coordinates two important sources of financial assistance available to persons with handicaps.

### Social Security Disability Insurance

Social Security Disability Insurance (SSDI) benefits are paid to workers with handicaps and to their families when earnings are lost or reduced as a result of their disabilities. Individuals are considered disabled if they have a physical or mental impairment that prevents them from working and that is expected to last 12 months or to result in death.

### Supplemental Security Income

Supplemental Security Income (SSI) payments are made to aged, disabled, or blind individuals who have limited income and resources. To receive SSI payments, individuals must meet Social Security definitions of being disabled or blind. In contrast to SSDI benefits, individuals can obtain SSI payments without having been employed. Local Social Security offices are listed in telephone directories under "Social Security Administration."

## MEDICAL ASSISTANCE

Medical assistance is primarily available from the Medicare and Medicaid programs.

### Medicare

The Medicare health insurance program serves individuals over the age of 65 and persons under 65 who are disabled. The program is not based on income, and it provides basic insurance to help pay for care received in hospitals as well as voluntary insurance, with monthly premiums, to help pay for doctor bills and other approved expenses. Further information will be available from local Social Security offices.

### Medicaid

Medicaid is a joint federal and state program that provides physical and health-care services to individuals with low incomes. Each state determines its own eligibility requirements for Medicaid. Generally, individuals may be eligible for Medicaid if they are receiving welfare or other public assistance benefits. Additional information can be obtained from local welfare or public-assistance offices.

## CIVIL RIGHTS

Individuals with handicaps have legally guaranteed rights to education, employment, health care, senior citizen activities, welfare, and any other public or private programs that receive federal funding. The Office for Civil Rights in the Department of Education and the Office for Civil Rights in the Department of Health and Human Services enforces federal laws prohibiting discrimination against persons on the basis of race, color, national origin, sex, age, or handicaps. Individuals concerned with civil rights issues should contact the Governor's Committee in their home states for further information.

# HOUSING

Programs for loans for home improvements and rental assistance are available through the U.S. Department of Housing and Urban Development.

## Loans for Home Improvements

Individuals with handicaps may be eligible for a Title I Home Improvement Loan insured by the U.S. Department of Housing and Urban Development (HUD). HUD-insured loans can be used to remove architectual barriers, hazards, or inconvenient features in the home.

## Rent Assistance

Low income families may be eligible for housing assistance through payments from the U.S. Department of Housing and Urban Development (HUD). Payments are made directly to the owners of rental units to make up the difference between the rental amount approved by HUD and the amount the tenant is required to pay. Tenants are required to pay between 25% and 30% of their adjusted income.

Information on HUD programs are available from locally administered offices. Check telephone directory for "Housing" listed under "U.S. Government," or write to Special Advisor on the Handicapped; U.S. Department of Housing and Urban Development; Room 10184; Washington, DC 20410.

# TRANSPORTATION

The Federal Urban Mass Transportation Administration requires that community mass transportation services receiving federal funds make their transportation services accessible to individuals with handicaps. Mass transportation services may accomplish this objective by altering their existing coaches or by providing a parallel transportation service. In such cases, specially equipped vans would be used to provide alternate transportation. Local mass-transit offices should be contacted to receive further information.

## CONTINUED BENEFITS FOR THOSE WHO
## RETURN TO WORK

Individuals with handicaps who have been receiving Social Security benefits may continue to receive those benefits for a short period when they enter or return to the work world. Individuals receiving Supplemental Security Income (SSI), Social Security Disability Insurance (SSDI), Medicare, and Medicaid may be eligible to keep these subsidies and benefits during a trial work period lasting up to nine months. The trial work period is designed to allow individuals who are uncertain of their employability to work for a time without jeopardizing their benefits. For more information about trial work periods, contact the local Social Security office listed in the telephone directory under "Social Security Administration."

In summary, this chapter can serve as an introductory guide to locating community resources and services. Since the number and types of services differ from city to city, both clients and professionals should locate agencies and individuals within their communities who know about the local service systems.

# References

*ARC Facts, OJT Project.* (1987). Arlington, TX: Association for Retarded Citizens of the United States.

Association For Retarded Citizens. Pamphlet: This isn't kindness. It's good business. Arlington, TX: ARC.

Azrin, N. H., & Besalel, V. A. (1980). *Job Club Counselor's Manual: A Behavioral Approach to Vocational Counseling.* Baltimore, MD: University Park Press.

Banathy, B. H. (1973). *Developing a Systems View of Education.* Belmont, CA: Lear Siegler/Fearon.

Bandura, A. (1969). *Principles of Behavior Modification.* New York: Holt, Rinehart & Winston.

Bellamy, G. T., Horner, R. H., & Inman, D. P. (1979). *Vocational Habilitation of Severely Retarded Adults.* Austin, TX: PRO-ED.

Bellamy, G. T. (1983). Work and Work Related Services: Post-school options. In M. E. Snell (Ed.), *Systematic Instruction of the Moderately and Severely Handicapped* (2nd ed.) (pp. 490–502). Columbus, OH: Merrill.

Bellamy, G. T., Rhodes, L. E., Mank, D. M., & Albin, J. M. (1987). *Supported Employment: A Community Implementation Guide.* Baltimore, MD: Paul H. Brookes.

Bolles, R. N. (1985). *The 1985 What Color Is Your Parachute?* Berkeley, CA: Ten Speed Press.

Bowe, F. (1986). *Disabled in 1985.* Hot Springs, AR: University of Arkansas Research and Training Center in Vocational Rehabilitation.

Brolin, D. E. (1976). *Vocational Preparation of Retarded Citizens.* Columbus, OH: Merrill.

Brown, D. (1980). *Steps to Independence for People with Learning Disabilities.* Washington, DC: Closer Look Parents' Campaign For Handicapped Children & Youth.

Cleland, C., & Swartz, J. D. (1982). *Exceptionalities Through the Lifespan: An Introduction.* New York: MacMillan.

Cook, P. F., Dahl, P. R., & Gale, M. A. (1978). *Vocational Opportunities: Vocational Training and Placement of the Severely Handicapped.* Salt Lake City: Olympus.

*Disabled Adults in America,* Washington DC: President's Committee on Employment of the Handicapped, 1985.

Dawis, R. B., & Lofquist, L. (1984). *A psychological theory of work adjustment: An individual differences model and its application.* Minneapolis: University of Minnesota.

Du Pont de Nemours and Company. (1982). *Equal to the Task.* Wilmington, DE: Author.

*Employer Guide: Simple steps to job accommodation.* (1984). Washington, DC: The President's Committee on Employment of the Handicapped.

English, H. B., & English, A. C. (1958). *A Comprehensive Dictionary of Psychological & Psychoanalytic Terms.* New York: Longmans, Green & Co.

*Federal Register.* (1984, September 25). Developmental Disabilities Act of 1984. (Report no. 98-1074, Section 102 [11] [F]).

*Federal Register.* (1975). The Education for All Handicapped Children Act (Public Law 94-142) section 5(b)(4).

Festinger, L. (1957). *A Theory of Cognitive Dissonance.* Evanston, IL: Row, Peterson.

Gilliland, B. E., James, R. K., Roberts, G. T., & Bowman, J. T. (1984). *Theories and Strategies in Counseling and Psychotherapy.* Englewood Cliffs, NJ: Prentice-Hall.

Goode, E. (1984). *Sociology.* Englewood Cliffs, NJ: Prentice-Hall.

Granovetter, M. (1979). Placement as Brokerage — Information Problems in the Labor Market. In D. Vandergoot and D. Worrall, *Placement in Rehabilitation: A Career Development Perspective.* Baltimore, MD: University Park Press.

Grossman, H. J. (Ed.). (1983). *Classification in Mental Retardation.* Washington, DC: American Association on Mental Deficiency.

Hansen, J. C., Warner, R. W., & Smith, E. J. (1980). *Group Counseling* (2nd Ed.). Chicago: Rand McNally.

Hart, W. (1962). Effective approaches to employers. *Rehabilitation Record, 3,* 34-37.

Herzberg, F. (1966). *Work and the Nature of Man.* Cleveland, OH: World Book Company.

Holland, J. (1973). *Making Vocational Choices: A Theory of Careers.* Englewood Cliffs, NJ: Prentice-Hall.

Jackson, T., & Mayleas, D. (1981). *The Hidden Job Market for the Eighties.* New York: Quadrangle/The New York Times Book Co.

*Job Accommodation Network Evaluation Study: Executive Summary.* (1987). Morgantown, WV: Job Accommodation Network.

Job Search: There's a Method in the Madness. (Spring, 1976). *Occupational Outlook Quarterly,* 18-19.

Kazdin, A. E. (1978). *History of Behavior Modification: Experimental foundations of contemporary research.* Baltimore, MD: University Park Press.

Kiernan, W. E., & Stark, J. A. (1986). *Pathways to Employment for Adults with Developmental Disabilities.* Baltimore, MD: Brooks Publishing Co.

Lathrop, R. (1977). *Who's Hiring Who.* Berkeley, CA: Ten Speed Press.

Louis Harris and Associates. (1986). *The ICD Survey of Disabled Americans: Bringing Disabled Americans into the Mainstream.* New York: International Center for the Disabled.

Louis Harris and Associates. (1987). *The ICD Survey II: Employing Disabled Americans.* New York: International Center for the Disabled.

Mank, D. M., Rhodes, C. E., & Bellamy, G. T. (1986). For Supported Employment Alternatives. In W. E. Kiernan and J. A. Stark, *Pathways to Employment for Adults with Developmental Disabilities.* Baltimore, MD: Brooks Publishing Co.

Mainstream. (1985). *Putting Disabled People in Your Place: Focus on Blind and Vision-Impaired Individuals.* Washington, DC: Author.

McCarthy, H. (Ed.). (1985). *Complete Guide to Employing Persons with Disabilities.* Albertson, NY: National Center on Employment of the Handicapped.

Meichenbaum, D. (1977). *Cognitive-Behavior Modification: An integrative approach.* New York: Plenum.

Naisbitt, J. (1984). *Megatrends.* New York: Warner Books.

Nathanson, R. B. (1977). The disabled employee: Separating myth from fact. *Harvard Business Review,* May-June, 1–3.

National Council on The Handicapped. (1986). *Toward Independence.* Washington, DC: U.S. Government Printing Office.

Olympus Research Corporation. (1973). *A Study to Test the Feasibility of Determining Whether Classified Ads in Daily Newspapers are An Accurate Reflection of Local Labor Markets and of Significance to Employers and Job Seekers.* San Francisco, CA: Author.

*Out of the Job Market: A National Crisis.* (1987). Washington, DC: The President's Committee on Employment of the Handicapped.

Parsons, F. (1909). *Choosing a Vocation.* Boston: Houghton Mifflin.

Personick, V. A. (1985). A Second Look at Industry Output and Trends through 1995. *Monthly Labor Review,* November, 26–41.

Rusch, F. (1986). *Competitive Employment Issues and Strategies.* Baltimore, MD: Paul H. Brookes.

Silvestri, G. T. and Lukasiewicz, J. M., (1985). Occupational Employment Projections: The 1984–95 Outlook. *Monthly Labor Review,* November, 37–49.

The Job Outlook in Brief. (1986). *Occupational Outlook Quarterly,* Spring, 10–29.

Toffler, A. (1980). *The Third Wave.* New York: Morrow.

U.S. Department of Commerce. (1985, November). *Selected Characteristics of Persons with a Work Disability by State: 1980.* Washington, DC: Congressional Information Service.

U.S. Department of Health and Human Services. (1986). (Kiernan, W. E.) *National Employment Survey for Adults with Developmental Disabilities.* Washington, DC: Author.

U.S Department of Labor, Bureau of Labor Statistics. (1987). *Occupational Outlook Handbook.* Washington, DC: U.S. Government Printing Office.

U.S. Department of Labor, Employment and Training Administration. (1977). *Dictionary of Occupational Titles.* Washington, DC: U.S. Government Printing Office.

U.S. Department of Labor, Manpower Administration. (1972). *Handbook for Analyzing Jobs.* Washington, DC: U.S. Government Printing Office.

U.S. Office of Management and Budget. (1972). *Standard Industrial Classification Manual.* Washington, DC: U.S. Government Printing Office.

Vandergoot, D., & Worrall, D. (1979). *Placement in Rehabilitation: A Career Development Perspective.* Baltimore, MD: University Park Press.

Wallace, P. M., Goldstein, J. H., & Nathan, P. (1987). *Introduction to Psychology.* Dubuque, IA: Brown.

Watson, D. L., & Tharp, R. G. (1981). *Self-Directed Behavior: Self-modification for personal adjustment* (3rd ed.). Monterey, CA: Brooks/Cole.

Wehman, P. (1981). *Competitive Employment: New Horizons for Severely Disabled Individuals.* Baltimore, MD: Paul H. Brookes.

Williams, R. L., & Long, J. D. (1979). *Toward a Self-Managed Life Style* (2nd ed.). Boston: Houghton Mifflin.

Williamson, E. G. (1965). *Vocational Counseling: Some Historical, Philosophical, and Theoretical Perspectives.* New York: McGraw-Hill.

Wolpe, J. (1958). *Psychotherapy by Reciprocal Inhibition.* Stanford: Stanford University Press.

Zandy, J. J. (1979). Planning for Job Placement. In D. Vandergoot and D. Worrall, *Placement in Rehabilitation: A Career Development Perspective.* Baltimore: University Park Press.

Zunker, V. G. (1987). *Career Counseling: Applied Concepts of Life Planning.* Monterey, CA: Brooks/Cole.

# Suggested Resources by Topic

The resources listed in this section will guide readers to information describing the current employment status of persons with handicaps in the United States, as well as learning about efforts to improve their employability and levels of employment. Additionally, readers will find important information about the labor market, information and funding directories, and a list of national agencies providing assistance to disabled persons seeking employment.

## EMPLOYMENT STATUS REPORTS

*Black Adults with Disabilities.* (1985). Washington, DC: The President's Committee on Employment of the Handicapped.

Bowe, F. (1983). *Demography and Disability: A Chartbook for Rehabilitation.* Hot Springs, AR: Arkansas Rehabilitation Research and Training Center.

*Disabled Adults in America.* (1985). Washington, DC: The President's Committee on Employment of the Handicapped.

*Disabled Adults of Hispanic Origin.* (1985). Washington, DC: The President's Committee on Employment of the Handicapped.

*Disabled Americans at Work.* (1985). Washington, DC: The President's Committee on Employment of the Handicapped, and the Dole Foundation.

Bowe, F. *Disabled in 1985.* (1986). Hot Springs, AR: University of Arkansas Research and Training Center in Vocational Rehabilitation.

*Disabled Women in America.* (1984). Washington, DC: The President's Committee on Employment of the Handicapped.

Du Pont de Nemours and Company. (1982). *Equal to the Task.* Wilmington, DE: Author.

*Employment for Disabled Veterans: A Blueprint for Action.* (1986). Washington, DC: The President's Committee on Employment of the Handicapped.

*Job Accommodation Network Evaluation Study: Executive Summary.* (1987). Morgantown, WV: Job Accommodation Network.

Louis Harris and Associates. (1986). *The ICD Survey of Disabled Americans: Bringing Disabled Americans into the Mainstream.* New York: International Center for the Disabled.

Louis Harris and Associates. (1987). *The ICD Survey II: Employing Disabled Americans.* New York: International Center for the Disabled.

Nathanson, R. B. (1977). The disabled employee: Separating myth from fact. *Harvard Business Review,* May-June 1–3.

*Out of the Job Market: A National Crisis.* (1987). Washington, DC: The President's Committee on Employment of the Handicapped.

U.S. Department of Commerce. (1985, November). *Selected Characteristics of Persons with a Work Disability by State: 1980.* Washington, DC: Congressional Information Service.

## EMPLOYMENT OF PERSONS WITH HANDICAPS

Azrin, N. H. & Besalel, V. A. (1980). *Job Club Counselor's Manual: A Behavioral Approach to Vocational Counseling.* Baltimore, MD: University Park Press.

Bellamy, G. T., Horner, R. H., & Inman, D. P. (1979). *Vocational Habilitation of Severely Retarded Adults.* Austin, TX: PRO-ED.

Bellamy, G. T., Rhodes, L. E., Mank, D. M., & Albin, J. M. (1987). *Supported Employment: A Community Implementation Guide.* Baltimore, MD: Paul H. Brookes.

Bender, M., Dinson-Millburn, N. & Richmond, L. J. (1985). *Careers, Computers, & the Handicapped.* Austin, TX: PRO-ED.

Bowe, F. (1985). *Jobs for Disabled People.* New York: Public Affairs Committee.

Bowe, F., & Rochlin, J. (1984). *The Business-Rehabilitation Partnership.* Hot Springs, AR: Arkansas Rehabilitation Research and Training Center.

Brown, D. (1980). *Steps to Independence for People with Learning Disabilities.* Washington, DC: Closer Look Parents' Campaign For Handicapped Children & Youth.

Cook, P. F., Dahl, P. R., & Gale, M. A. (1978). *Vocational Opportunities: Vocational Training and Placement of the Severely Handicapped.* Salt Lake City: Olympus.

*Employer Guide: Simple steps to job accommodation.* (1984). Washington, DC: The President's Committee on Employment of the Handicapped.

Galloway, C. (1982). *Employers as Partners: A Guide to Negotiating Jobs for People with Disabilities.* Rohnert Park, CA: California Institute on Human Services, Sonoma State University.

Geletka, J. R. (1982). *A Creative Partnership: Guidelines for the Development of a Project With Industry.* Washington, DC: Electronic Industries Foundation.

Kiernan, W. E., & Stark, J. A. (1986). *Pathways to Employment for Adults with Developmental Disabilities.* Baltimore, MD: Brooks Publishing Co.

Manpower Demonstration Research Corporation. (1982). *Supported Work for the Mentally Retarded: Launching the STETS Demonstration.* New York: Author.

McCarthy, H. (Ed.). (1985). *Complete Guide to Employing Persons with Disabilities.* Albertson, NY: National Center on Employment of the Handicapped.

National Alliance of Business. (1985). Moving Disabled People into the Workforce [Special Issue]. *NAB Clearing House Quarterly, 1*(4).

Pati, G. C., & Adkins, J. I. Jr. (1981). *Managing and Employing the Handicapped: The Untapped Potential.* Lake Forest, IL: Brace-Park Press.

Riccio, J. A. & Price, M. L. (1984). *A Transitional Employment Strategy for the Mentally Retarded: The Final STETS Implementation Report.* New York: Manpower Demonstration Research Corporation.

Rusch, F. (1986). *Competitive Employment Issues and Strategies.* Baltimore, MD: Paul H. Brookes.

Tindall, L., Gugerty, J., & Dougherty, B. (1984). *Promising Programs Which Use Job Training Partnership Act Funds for the Vocational Education, Training, and Employment of Handicapped Youth.* Madison, WI: Vocational Studies Center, University of Wisconsin-Madison.

Tindall, L., Gugerty, J., & Dougherty, B. (1984). *Utilizing the Job Training Partnership Act Funds for the Vocational Education, Training and Employment of Special Needs Students.* Madison, WI: Vocational Studies Center, University of Wisconsin-Madison.

Vandergoot, D., & Worrall, D. (1979). *Placement in Rehabilitation: A Career Development Perspective.* Baltimore, MD: University Park Press.

Wehman, P., et al. *Vocational Evaluation and Cerebral Palsy.* (In Press)

## LABOR MARKET RESOURCES

Job Search: There's a Method in the Madness. (Spring, 1976). *Occupational Outlook Quarterly*, 18–19.

National Alliance of Business. (1986). *Employment Policies: Looking to the Year 2000.* Washington, DC: Author.

Silvestri, G. T., & Lukasiewicz, J. M. (1985). Occupational Employment Projections: The 1984–95 Outlook. *Monthly Labor Review*, November, 37–49.

Olympus Research Corporation. (1973). *A Study to Test the Feasibility of Determining Whether Classified Ads in Daily Newspapers are An Accurate Reflection of Local Labor Markets and of Significance to Employers and Job Seekers.* San Francisco, CA: Author.

Personick, V. A. (1985). A Second Look at Industry Output and Trends through 1995. *Monthly Labor Review*, November, 26–41.

The Job Outlook in Brief. (1986). *Occupational Outlook Quarterly*, Spring, 10–29.

U.S. Department of Labor, Bureau of Labor Statistics. (1987). *Occupational Outlook Handbook.* Washington, DC: U.S. Government Printing Office.

U.S. Department of Labor, Employment and Training Administration. (1977). *Dictionary of Occupational Titles.* Washington, DC: U.S. Government Printing Office.

U.S. Office of Management and Budget. (1972). *Standard Industrial Classification Manual.* Washington, DC: U.S. Government Printing Office.

## DIRECTORIES

*Directory of Organizations Interested in People with Disabilities.* (1986). Washington, DC: The President's Committee on Employment of the Handicapped.

Eckstein, R. M. (Ed.). (1987). *Handicapped Funding Directory, 1987–88 Edition.* Margate, FL: Research Grant Guides.

## AGENCIES

ABLEDATA, National Rehabilitation Information Center, The Catholic University of America; 4407 Eight Street, NE; Washington, DC 20017. (800) 34-NARIC.

> ABLEDATA provides information on commercially available rehabilitation and independent-living equipment for persons with disabilities.

Association of Retarded Citizens of the United States (ARC); 2501 Avenue J; Arlington, TX 76006. (817) 640-0204.

> ARC sponsors the National Training and Employment Project for persons with mental retardation. Through the project, employers can be reimbursed part of the salaries of workers with mental retardation during initial training periods.

Job Accommodation Network (JAN); Box 468; Morgantown, WV 26505; (800) 526-7234 or (800) 526-4698 (in WV).

> Established by the President's Committee on Employment of the Handicapped, JAN provides information on practical accommodations that have proven successful in business and industry.

Job Opportunities for the Blind; 1800 Johnson Street; Baltimore, MD 21230. (800) 638-7518.

> In addition to placement services, this organization provides labor-market and job-search information (primarily cassette recordings) on a loan basis.

National Center on Employment of the Deaf; National Technical Institute for the Deaf; One Lomb Memorial Drive; Rochester, NY 14623. (716) 475-6834 or (716) 475-6205 (TTY).

> The Center provides employment opportunities through an automated career-matching system.

National Rehabilitation Information Center (NARIC); The Catholic University of America; 4407 Eight Street, NE; Washington, DC 20017. (800) 34-NARIC.

NARIC is a rehabilitation information service and research library.

The President's Committee on Employment of the Handicapped; 1111 20th Street, NW, Room 636; Washington, DC 20036. (202) 653-5044.

This Federal agency is primarily concerned with improving the employability of and employment opportunities for persons with handicaps.

# State Vocational Agencies and Governor's Committees

Vocational Rehabilitation Offices and Governor's Committees on Employment of the Handicapped (listed in alphabetical order by state)

Office of Vocational Rehabilitation, Department of Education; Pouch F, Mail Stop 0581; State Office Building; Juneau, Alaska 99811. (907) 465-2814.

Governor's Committee on Employment of the Handicapped; 2600 Denali Street, Suite 701; Anchorage, Alaska 99503. (907) 279-0438.

Division of Rehabilitation and Crippled Children Service; Department of Education; 2129 East South Boulevard; P.O. Box 11586; Montgomery, Alabama 36111. (205) 281-8780.

Governor's Committee on Employment of the Handicapped; Division of Rehabilitation and Crippled Children; P.O. Box 11586; 2129 East South Boulevard; Montgomery, Alabama 36111-0586. (205) 281-8780.

Rehabilitation Services Division; Department of Human Services; 1401 Brookwood Drive; P.O. Box 3781; Little Rock, Arkansas 72203. (501) 371-2571.

Governor's Commission on People with Disabilities; 1401 Brookwood Drive; P.O. Box 3781; Little Rock, Arkansas 72202. (501) 371-2686 (voice/TDD).

State Services for the Blind; 411 Victory Street; P.O. Box 3237; Little Rock, Arkansas 72203. (501) 371-2587.

Rehabilitation Services Bureau; Department of Economic Security; 1300 West Washington; Phoenix, Arizona 85007. (602) 255-3332.

Governor's Commission on Employment of the Handicapped; 1601 W. Jefferson; Site: 086-Z-2; Phoenix, Arizona 85004. (602) 255-3826.

Department of Rehabilitation; Health and Welfare Agency; 830 K Street Mall; Sacramento, California 95814. (916) 445-3971.

Governor's Commmittee on Employment of the Handicapped; 800 Capitol Mall, Room 4036; Sacramento, California 95814. (916) 323-2545 (Voice/TDD).

Division of Rehabilitation; Department of Social Services; 717-17th Street; P.O. Box 181000; Denver, Colorado 80218-0899. (303) 294-2803.

Colorado Coalition for Persons with Disabilities; 1245 East Colfax, Room 219; Denver, Colorado 80218. (303) 863-0113 or (303) 861-2735 (TDD).

Division of Vocational Rehabilitation; State Board of Education; 600 Asylum Avenue; Hartford, Connecticut 06105. (203) 566-4440.

Governor's Committee on Employment of the Handicapped; 200 Folly Brook Boulevard; Wethersfield, Connecticut 06109. (203) 566-8061.

Board of Education and Services for the Blind; 170 Ridge Road; Wethersfield, Connecticut 06109. (203) 249-8525.

Vocational Rehabilitation Services Administration; Department of Human Resources; 605 G Street, Northwest; Washington, DC 20001. (202) 727-3227.

Mayor's Committee on Handicapped Individuals; 605 G Street, Northwest, Suite 1101; Washington, DC 20001. (202) 727-0924.

Vocational Rehabilitation Service; Department of Labor; Delaware Elwyn Building; 321 East 11th Street; Wilmington, Delaware 19801. (302) 571-2851.

Governor's Committee on Employment of the Handicapped; Delaware Elwyn Building; 321 East 11th Street; Wilmington, Delaware 19801. (302) 571-3915.

Bureau for the Visually Impaired; Division of Social Services; 305 West Eighth Street; Wilmington, Delaware 19801. (302) 571-3570.

Division of Vocational Rehabilitation; Department of Labor and Employment Security; 1709 Mahan Drive; Tallahassee, Florida 32308. (904) 488-6210.

Division of Blind Services; Department of Education; 2540 Executive Center Circle, West; Tallahassee, Florida 32399. (904) 488-1330.

Division of Rehabilitation Services; Department of Human Resources; 878 Peachtree Street, Northeast, Room 706; Atlanta, Georgia 30309. (404) 894-6671.

Governor's Committee on Employment of the Handicapped; 878 Peachtree Street, Northeast, Suite 707; Atlanta, Georgia 30309. (404) 894-7552.

Vocational Rehabilitation Services; Department of Social Services; P.O. Box 339; Honolulu, Hawaii 96809. (808) 548-4769.

Commission on the Handicapped; 335 Merchant Street, Room 353; Honolulu, Hawaii 96813. (808) 548-7606.

Division of Vocational Department Services; 510 East 12th Street; Des Moines, Iowa 50319. (515) 281-4311.

Commission on Persons with Disabilities; Lucas State Office Building; Des Moines, Iowa 50319. (515) 281-5969.

State Commission for the Blind; 524 Fourth Street; Des Moines, Iowa 50309. (515) 281-7999.

Division of Vocational Rehabilitation; State Board for Vocational Education; 650 West State, Room 150; Boise, Idaho 83720. (208) 334-3390.

Governor's Committee on Employment of the Handicapped; 317 Main; Boise, Idaho 83735. (208) 334-2714.

Commission for the Blind; State House; Boise, Idaho 83720. (208) 334-3220.

Department of Rehabilitation Services; 623 East Adams Street; Springfield, Illinois 62706. (217) 782-2093.

Indiana Rehabilitation Services; 251 North Illinois; P.O. Box 7083; Indianapolis, Indiana 46207-7083. (317) 232-6503.

State Commission for the Handicapped; P.O. Box 1964; 1330 West Michigan Street; Indianapolis, Indiana 46206. (317) 633-0286.

Department of Social and Rehabilitation Services; Biddle Building, 2nd Floor; 2700 West Sixth Street; Topeka, Kansas 66606. (913) 296-3911.

Kansas Advisory Committee on Employment of the Handicapped; 1430 South Topeka Avenue; Topeka, Kansas 66612-1877. (913) 232-7828.

Office of Rehabilitation Services; Department of Education; Capital Plaza Tower; Frankfort, Kentucky 40601. (502) 564-4440.

Kentucky Committee on Employment of the Handicapped; L and N Building; 908 West Broadway; 5th Floor, Room 508; Louisville, Kentucky 40203. (502) 588-4073.

Department for the Blind; Education and Arts Cabinet; 427 Versailles Road; Frankfort, Kentucky 40601. (502) 564-4754.

Division of Vocational Rehabilitation; Office of Human Development; 1755 Florida Boulevard; P.O. Box 44371; Baton Rouge, Louisiana 70804. (504) 342-2285.

Bureau of Handicapped Persons; P.O. Box 44371; 1755 Florida Boulevard; Baton Rouge, Louisiana 70804. (504) 342-2723.

Blind Services Program; Office of Human Development; 1755 Florida Boulevard; P.O. Box 28; Baton Rouge, Louisiana 70821. (504) 342-5282.

Massachusetts Rehabilitation Commission; Statler Office Building; 20 Park Plaza; Boston, Massachusetts 02116. (617) 727-2172.

Governor's Committee on Employment of the Handicapped; Hurley Building, Government Center; 19 Stamford Street; Boston, Massachusetts 02114. (617) 727-6580.

Commission for the Blind; 110 Tremont Street, 6th Floor; Boston, Massachusetts 02108. (617) 727-5580.

Division of Vocational Rehabilitation; State Department of Education; 200 West Baltimore Street; Baltimore, Maryland 21201. (301) 659-2294.

Governor's Committee on Employment of the Handicapped; 200 West Baltimore, 7th Floor; Baltimore, Maryland 21201. (301) 333-2264.

Bureau of Rehabilitation; Department of Health and Human Services; 32 Winthrop Street; Augusta, Maine 04330. (207) 289-2266.

Governor's Committee on Employment of the Handicapped; 32 Winthrop Street; Augusta, Maine 04330. (207) 289-3484.

Michigan Rehabilitation Services; State Department of Education; 608 West Allegan; P.O. Box 30010; Lansing, Michigan 48909. (517) 373-3391.

Commission on Handicapped Concerns; Box 30015; 309 North Washington Avenue; Lansing, Michigan 48909. (517) 373-8397.

Commission for the Blind; Department of Labor; 309 North Washington; P.O. Box 30015; Lansing, Michigan 48909. (517) 373-2062.

Division of Rehabilitation Services; Department of Jobs & Training; 390 North Robert Street, 5th Floor; St. Paul, Minnesota 55101. (612) 596-5616.

Minnesota State Council for the Handicapped; Metro Square, Suite 208; 7th & Roberts Streets; St. Paul, Minnesota. (612) 296-6785 or (800) 652-9747.

State Services for the Blind and Visually Handicapped; Department of Jobs & Training; 1745 University Avenue; St. Paul, Minnesota 55104. (612) 642-0500.

Division of Vocational Rehabilitation; Department of Elementary and Secondary Education; 2401 East McCarty Street; Jefferson City, Missouri 65101. (314) 751-4249.

Governor's Committee on Employment of the Handicapped; Box 1668; 1904 Missouri Boulevard; Jefferson City, Missouri 65102. (314) 751-2600.

Services for the Blind; Division of Family Services; Department of Social Services; 619 East Capital Avenue; Jefferson City, Missouri 65101. (314) 751-4249.

Department of Rehabilitation Services; P.O. Box 22086; Jackson, Mississippi 39225. (601) 922-6811.

Office of Handicapped Services; Governor's Office of Federal–State Programs; 301 West Pearl Street; Jackson, Mississippi 39203-3090. (601) 949-2012.

Vocational Rehabilitation Services for the Blind; P.O. Box 4872; Jackson, Mississippi 39216. (601) 354-6411.

Rehabilitative Services Division; Department of Social and Rehabilitation Services; P.O. Box 4210; Helena, Montana 59601. (406) 444-2590.

Governor's Committee on Employment of the Handicapped; Personnel Division; Mitchell Building, Room 130; Helena, Montana 59620. (406) 444-3871 or (406) 444-3886.

Division of Vocational Rehabilitation Services; Department of Human Resources; 620 North West Street; P.O. Box 26053; Raleigh, North Carolina 27611. (919) 733-3364.

Governor's Advocacy Council for Persons with Disabilities; 116 West Jones Street; Raleigh, North Carolina 27611. (919) 733-9250.

Department of Services for the Blind; Department of Human Resources; 309 Ashe Avenue; Raleigh, North Carolina 27606. (919) 733-9822.

Division of Vocational Rehabilitation; Department of Human Services; State Capitol; Bismarck, North Dakota 58505. (701) 224-2907.

Governor's Council on Human Resources; State Capitol, 3rd Floor; Bismarck, North Dakota 58505. (701) 224-2970.

Division of Rehabilitation Services; Department of Education; 301 Centennial Mall, South; P.O. Box 94987; Lincoln, Nebraska 68509. (402) 471-2961.

Governor's Committee on Employment of the Handicapped; Box 94600; 550 South 16th Street; Lincoln, Nebraska 68509. (402) 474-3183.

Division of Rehabilitation Services for the Visually Impaired; Department of Public Instructions; 4600 Valley Road; Lincoln, Nebraska 68510-4884. (402) 471-2891.

Vocational Rehabilitation Division; State Board of Education; 101 Pleasant Street; Concord, New Hampshire 03301. (603) 271-3121.

Governor's Commission for the Handicapped; 85 Manchester Street; Concord, New Hampshire 03301. (603) 271-2773.

Division of Vocational Rehabilitation; Department of Labor and Industry; 1005 Labor and Industry Building; John Fitch Plaza, CN 398; Trenton, New Jersey 08625. (609) 292-5987.

Governor's Committee on the Disabled; 108-110 North Broad Street; Trenton, New Jersey 08625. (609) 633-6959.

Division of Vocational Rehabilitation; Department of Education; 604 West San Mateo; Santa Fe, New Mexico 87503. (505) 982-4555.

Governor's Committee on Concerns of the Handicapped; Bataan Memorial Building, Room 171; Santa Fe, New Mexico 87503. (505) 827-6465.

Bureau of Vocational Rehabilitation; Nevada Rehabilitation Division; 505 East King Street, Room 503; State Capitol Complex; Carson City, Nevada 89710. (702) 885-4470.

Governor's Committee on Employment of the Handicapped; 505 King Street, Room 500; Carson City, Nevada 89710. (702) 885-5348.

Office of Vocational Rehabilitation; State Education Department; 99 Washington Avenue; Albany, New York 12230. (518) 474-2714 or (800) 222-5627 (statewide toll free).

Office of the State Advocate for the Disabled; 10th Floor, Empire State Plaza; Agency Building, #1; Albany, New York 12223. (518) 474-2825 or (800) 522-4369 (statewide toll free).

Commission for the Blind and Visually Handicapped; State Department of Social Services; 40 North Pearl Street; Albany, New York 12243. (518) 473-1801.

Rehabilitation Services Commission; 4656 Heaton Road Commission; Columbus, Ohio 43229. (800) 282-4536.

Governor's Council on Disabled Persons; 4656 Heaton Road; Columbus, Ohio 43229. (614) 438-1391 or (800) 282-4536.

Public Welfare Commission; Department of Institutions, Social and Rehabilitative Services; Sequogah Memorial Office Building; P.O. Box 25352; Oklahoma City, Oklahoma 73125. (405) 424-4311 Extension 2873.

Office of Handicapped Concerns; 4300 North Lincoln Boulevard, Suite 200; Oklahoma City, Oklahoma 73105. (405) 521-3756.

Department of Human Resources; 2045 Silverton Road, Northeast; Salem, Oregon 97310. (503) 378-3850.

State Commission for the Handicapped; 453C, State Capitol; Salem, Oregon 97310. (503) 378-4545.

State Commission for the Blind; 535 Southeast 12th Avenue; Portland, Oregon 97214. (503) 238-8375.

Office of Vocational Rehabilitation; Department of Labor and Industry; Labor and Industry Bldg., Rm 1300; 7th & Forster Streets; Harrisburg, Pennsylvania 17120. (717) 787-5244.

Governor's Committee on Employment of the Handicapped; Labor and Industry Building; 7th and Forster Streets; 13th Floor, Room 1315; Harrisburg, Pennsylvania 17120. (717) 787-5232.

Blindness and Visual Services; Department of Public Welfare; 300 Capitol Associates Building; 901 North 7th Street; P.O. Box 2675; Harrisburg, Pennsylvania 17105. (717) 787-6176.

Division of Vocational Rehabilitation; Social and Rehabilitative Services; 40 Fountain Street; Providence, Rhode Island 02903. (401) 421-7005.

Services for the Blind; Social and Rehabilitative Services; 46 Aborn Street; Providence, Rhode Island 02903. (401) 277-2300.

Vocational Rehabilitation Department; 1410 Boston Avenue; P.O. Box 15; West Columbia, South Carolina 29171. (803) 734-4300.

Governor's Committee on Employment of the Handicapped; P.O. Box 15; West Columbia, South Carolina 29171-0015. (803) 734-3508.

Commission for the Blind; 1430 Confederate Avenue; Columbia, South Carolina 29201. (803) 758-7524.

Department of Vocational Rehabilitation Office; Kneip State Office Building; 700 Governor's Drive; Pierre, South Dakota 57501. (605) 773-3125.

Division of Vocational Rehabilitation; Department of Human Services; Citizens Plaza Bank Building; 400 Deadrick Street, 11th Floor; Nashville, Tennessee 37219. (615) 741-2095.

Governor's Committee on Employment of the Handicapped; Citizens Plaza Bank Building; 400 Deadrick Street, 11th Floor; Nashville, Tennessee 37219. (615) 741-2095.

Texas Rehabilitation Commission; 118 East Riverside Drive; Austin, Texas 78704. (512) 445-8000 or (512) 445-8313 (TDD).

Governor's Committee for Disabled Persons; 118 Riverside Drive; Austin, Texas 78704. (512) 445-8276 or (512) 447-8346 (TDD).

Texas Commission for the Blind; TCB Administrative Building; 4800 North Lamar; P.O. Box 12866; Austin, Texas 78711. (512) 459-2500.

Division of Rehabilitation Services; Office of Education; 250 East Fifth South; Salt Lake City, Utah 84111. (801) 533-5991.

Governor's Committee on Employment of the Handicapped; 120 North 200 West, P.O. Box 45500; Salt Lake City, Utah 84145-0500. (801) 533-6770.

Services for the Visually Handicapped; 309 East 100 South; Salt Lake City, Utah 84111. (801) 533-9393.

Department of Rehabilitative Services; Board of Vocational Rehabilitation; P.O. Box 11045; Richmond, Virginia 23230. (804) 257-0318.

Board of the Department of Rights of the Disabled; 101 North Street, 17th Floor; Richmond, Virginia 23219. (804) 225-2042 or (804) 552-3962 (Voice/TDD).

Vocational Rehabilitation Division; Department of Social and Rehabilitation Services; Agency of Human Resources; 103 South Main Street; Waterbury, Vermont 05676. (802) 241-2186.

Division of Services for the Blind and Visually Impaired; Department of Social and Rehabilitative Services; Agency of Human Resources; 103 South Main Street; Waterbury, Vermont 05676. (802) 241-2211.

Department of Vocational Rehabilitation; Department of Social and Health Services; State Office Building, #2 (OB-21C); Olympia, Washington 98504. (206) 753-2544.

Governor's Committee on Employment of the Handicapped; Employment Security Department; Mail Stop KG-11; Olympia, Washington 98504. (206) 753-1547 or (206) 753-7185 (TDD).

Department of Services for the Blind; 921 Lakeridge Drive, Room 202; Olympia, Washington 98504-2921. (206) 586-1224.

Division of Vocational Rehabilitation; Department of Health and Social Services; 1 West Wilson Street, Room 850; P.O. Box 7852; Madison, Wisconsin 53707. (608) 266-5466.

Governor's Committee for People with Disabilities; 131 West Wilson Street, Room 1003; P.O. Box 7852; Madison, Wisconsin 53707. (608) 266-5378 or (608) 267-2082 (TDD).

Division of Vocational Rehabilitation; Board of Vocational Education; State Capitol; Charleston, West Virginia 25305. (304) 766-4600.

Governor's Commission on Disabled Persons; c/o Department of Human Services; State Capitol Building, Room B-617; 1900 West Washington Street, East; Charleston, West Virginia 25305. (304) 348-2400.

Division of Vocation Rehabilitation; Department of Health and Social Services; Room 327, Hathway State Office Building; Cheyenne, Wyoming 82002. (307) 777-7389.

Governor's Committee on Employment; Barrett Building, 4th Floor; Cheyenne, Wyoming 82002. (307) 777-7191.

# Subject Index

## B

Behavioral contract agreement, *39*

## C

Community resources,
  civil rights, 172
  continued benefits, 174
  education, 168–170
  employment, 170–171
  financial assistance, 171
  housing, 173
  information, 167–168
  medical assistance, 172
  transportation, 173
  vocational rehabilitation, 168
Competitive Employment
    Obtainment model, *18*

## D

Disabled worker occupations,
  94, *100*

## E

Employability profile, 80-81, *80*,
    84
Employment,
  adjustments, 159, 160, *161*,
      162
    life adjustments, 162–165
  barriers, 55, *56*, *59*
    ambivalence, 55, 60
    avoidance behaviors, 68–69
    basic academic skills,
        67–68
    dependents care, 70
    economic disincentives,
        70–71
    employer perceptions,
        74–75
    independent-living skills,
        66
    low self-esteem, 63–64
    poor appearance, 65
    problem work histories,
        60–62
    self-management skills, 67
    social skills, 65–66
    social support, 71–72
    survey, *57*, *58*
    transportation, 69
    visibility of handicap, 72,
        *73*

**NOTES**

# Vocational Evaluation in Special Education

## By Norman C. Hursh, Sc.D., & Allen F. Kerns, Ed.D.

This brand-new book provides a solid knowledge base for evaluating the career capabilities of clients with special needs. It includes case histories, skill-building exercises at the end of every chapter, work sheets, charts, tables, and lists. You will also find more than fifty pages of appendices, test descriptions, work samples, aptitude tests, and preparation and training required for a broad range of careers. You will learn:

- How to write good, workable Individualized Educational Plans and curricula
- How to develop school-based transition and job placement programs
- How to evaluate students' interests, behaviors, and abilities in terms of training and job needs
- How to fully utilize the new *Dictionary of Worker Traits*, the comprehensive occupational information resource.

Clearly and easily written, and packed with useful tips, *Vocational Evaluation and Special Education* is a resource you cannot afford to work without.

### CONTENTS

1. The Historical Development of Educational Services for Disabled Students. 2. Vocational Rehabilitation: Links to Education. 3. Vocational Evaluation Development. 4. Implementing Vocational Evaluation in Special Education. 5. Occupational Information Resources in the World of Work. 6. Test Selection Issues in Special Education. 7. Vocational Evaluation Tools: Psychometric Tests. 8. Simulated Work Evaluation: Work Sample Evaluation. 9. Commercial Work Sample System. 10. Situational Assessment and Job Site Evaluation. 11. Vocational Evaluation Issues with Learning Disabled Students. 12. Vocational Evaluation of Severely Emotionally Disturbed Students. *References. Appendices. Includes Subject Index.*

1988, 280 pages. Softcover, #0-316-58914-4, $24.50.

# The Hearing Impaired Employee: An Untapped Resource

## Coordinating Editors: Georgene Fritz & Nancy Smith

This is the most practical and informative manual and sourcebook ever offered to supervisors, trainers, and employers of hearing impaired persons. It is an invaluable aid for employment counselors and agencies, and for all firms, schools, and associations providing equipment or services for the hearing impaired.

Incorporating years of experience and success at the National Technical Institute for the Deaf (NTID) in preparing hearing impaired students for employment, the book includes these special features:

- A solid orientation on deafness and its impact on hearing impaired employees
- Down-to-earth supervising techniques to use with hearing impaired employees
- Practical suggestions about training and workplace accomodations for hearing impaired employees
- Valuable resources to help accomodate hearing impaired employees, including interpreting services, notetaking services, tutoring, media resources (including captioning), and TDD and other equipment information resources.

### CONTENTS

1. Hearing Impairment: Its potential Impact on the Individual. 2. Hearing-Impaired Job Candidates: Recruiting Them. 3. On the Job: Integrating the Hearing-Impaired Employee. 4. Support Services: Improving Job Performance. 5. Aids for the Hearing-Impaired Employee: Special Products and Equipment. 6. The Hearing-Impaired Employee: A Recognized Asset. *Appendices. Acknowledgments. Index.*

1985, 140 pages, large format. Softcover, #0-316-29367-9, $21.00.

# ORDER INFORMATION:

✂

**YES!** I would like to order the books specified below. I understand that I may return any book I don't wish to keep within 30 days for a full refund.

Name_____ Phone (_____)_____

Street Address_____City_____State_____ Zip_____

**PAYMENT:**    ___ Please CHARGE my: Visa  AmX  MC  #_____ Exp_____

Signature (required) _____

___ My CHECK is enclosed. (*Publisher pays Shipping & Handling for check and credit card orders.*)

___ Please BILL me. (*Shipping charges apply, 50¢ per book up to a maximum of $2.50 per order.*)

| Author | Title | ISBN# | Cost | Qty | TOTAL |
|---|---|---|---|---|---|
| Muklewicz | Competitive Job-Finding Guide | 589233 | $ 29.50 X | ____ | =$_____ |
| Muklewicz | Job-Finder's Workbook (set of 10) | 589144 | $ 35.00 X | ____ | =$_____ |
| Hursh/Kerns | Vocational Evaluation in Special Education | 383317 | $ 24.50 X | ____ | =$_____ |
| Fritz/Smith | The Hearing-Impaired Employee | 293679 | $ 21.00 X | ____ | =$_____ |

**Mail orders to:**
**Or CALL ☎**
***1-800-343-9204***
**to ORDER NOW!**

**COLLEGE-HILL PRESS** / Little, Brown & Co.
✉ Order Department
200 West Street
Waltham, MA 02254-9931

SUBTOTAL    =$_____
Shipping ($2.50 max.)    =$_____
TOTAL COST    =$_____

---

**YES!** I would like to order the books specified below. I understand that I may return any book I don't wish to keep within 30 days for a full refund.

Name_____ Phone (_____)_____

Street Address_____City_____State_____ Zip_____

**PAYMENT:**    ___ Please CHARGE my: Visa  AmX  MC  #_____ Exp_____

Signature (required) _____

___ My CHECK is enclosed. (*Publisher pays Shipping & Handling for check and credit card orders.*)

___ Please BILL me. (*Shipping charges apply, 50¢ per book up to a maximum of $2.50 per order.*)

| Author | Title | ISBN# | Cost | Qty | TOTAL |
|---|---|---|---|---|---|
| Muklewicz | Competitive Job-Finding Guide | 589233 | $ 29.50 X | ____ | =$_____ |
| Muklewicz | Job-Finder's Workbook (set of 10) | 589144 | $ 35.00 X | ____ | =$_____ |
| Hursh/Kerns | Vocational Evaluation in Special Education | 383317 | $ 24.50 X | ____ | =$_____ |
| Fritz/Smith | The Hearing-Impaired Employee | 293679 | $ 21.00 X | ____ | =$_____ |

**Mail orders to:**
**Or CALL ☎**
***1-800-343-9204***
**to ORDER NOW!**

**COLLEGE-HILL PRESS** / Little, Brown & Co.
✉ Order Department
200 West Street
Waltham, MA 02254-9931

SUBTOTAL    =$_____
Shipping ($2.50 max.)    =$_____
TOTAL COST    =$_____

*See order information and forms on reverse!*